Unite, Proletarian Brothers!

Radicalism and Revolution in the Spanish Second Republic, 1931–6

New Historical PERSPECTIVES

New Historical Perspectives is a book series for early career scholars within the UK and the Republic of Ireland. Books in the series are overseen by an expert editorial board to ensure the highest standards of peer-reviewed scholarship. Commissioning and editing is undertaken by the Royal Historical Society, and the series is published under the imprint of the Institute of Historical Research by the University of London Press.

The series is supported by the Economic History Society and the Past and Present Society.

Unite, Proletarian Brothers!

Radicalism and Revolution in the Spanish Second Republic, 1931–6

Matthew Kerry

LONDON
ROYAL HISTORICAL SOCIETY
INSTITUTE OF HISTORICAL RESEARCH
UNIVERSITY OF LONDON PRESS

Published by

UNIVERSITY OF LONDON PRESS
SCHOOL OF ADVANCED STUDY
INSTITUTE OF HISTORICAL RESEARCH
Senate House, Malet Street, London WC1E 7HU

Available to download free or to purchase the hard copy edition at https://www.sas.ac.uk/publications.

ISBNs
978-1-912702-49-7 (hardback edition)
978-1-912702-50-3 (paperback edition)
978-1-912702-53-4 (PDF edition)
978-1-912702-51-0 (ePub edition)
978-1-912702-52-7(.mobi edition)

DOI 10.14296/920.9781912702534

New Historical
PERSPECTIVES

Cover image: adapted from 'Aprieta fuerte, compañero! [Squeeze tightly, comrade!]' (1936) by Germán Horacio Robles for the Interprovincial Council of Asturias and León. Reproduced with the permission of the Muséu del Pueblu d'Asturies.

Contents

Abbreviations

Organizations

ACNP	National Catholic Association of Propagandists
AP	Popular Action
BOC	Workers' and Peasants' Bloc
CEDA	Confederation of Autonomous Right-Wing Groups
CNT	National Confederation of Labour
FAI	Iberian Anarchist Federation
FE	Falange Española
FE-JONS	Falange Española de las JONS
FJS	Federation of the Socialist Youth
FNTT	National Federation of Landworkers
FSA	Asturian Socialist Federation
IR	Republican Left
JAP	Popular Action Youth
JC	Communist Youth
JS	Socialist Youth
MAOC	Antifascist Workers' and Peasants' Militias
PCE	Communist Party of Spain
POUM	Workers' Party of Marxist Unification
PSOE	Spanish Socialist Workers' Party
PRLD	Liberal-Democratic Republican Party
SCOM	Catholic Mineworkers' Union
SHE	Sociedad Hullera Española
SOMA	Mineworkers' Union of Asturias
SRI	International Red Aid
SUM	Mineworkers' Single Union

UGT	General Workers' Union
UR	Republican Union

Archives

AA	Archivo de Aller
AHPA	Archivo Histórico Provincial de Asturias
AL	Archivo de Langreo
AM	Archivo de Mieres
AO	Archivo de Oviedo
CDMH	Centro Documental de la Memoria Histórica

Acknowledgements

The origins of this book lie in a doctoral thesis defended at the University of Sheffield, later revised at York University, Durham University and the University of Leeds, and prepared for publication at the University of Stirling. The original research would not have been possible without a Hossein Farmy scholarship from the University of Sheffield and I am also grateful for further funding provided by the Royal Historical Society, a Scouloudi award from the Institute of Historical Research and a postdoctoral fellowship at York University. The Division of History, Heritage and Politics at the University of Stirling kindly funded the two maps produced by Cox Cartographic.

Staff at archives and libraries in Asturias, Madrid, Salamanca and Toronto were patient and helpful, even when faced with nebulous descriptions of what I was trying to do. A special mention is due to Councillor Ramón Francisco Velasco Fernández for entrusting me with the key to the municipal archive in Aller and allowing me to peruse documents in the elegant surroundings of the council chambers. The PhD thesis could not have been completed without the generous support of the Lavilla Cañedo family, who provided a welcoming and supportive environment for research and absorbing Asturian culture. Ángela shared the challenges of the doctoral journey, discussed ideas and commented on innumerable drafts.

Many colleagues and friends at Sheffield, York, Durham and Leeds have been a source of encouragement. The postgraduate community at Sheffield provided an excellent environment for testing ideas and sharing the tribulations of postgraduate studies. Colleagues at York were very welcoming of a scholar of Spain from across the pond and Bill Callahan regaled me with fine tales of researching in Spain and Latin America in the 1960s. Participants in the Modern European History seminar at Durham provided detailed and insightful critical comments on a draft chapter as I grappled with reshaping the thesis into a book. Richard Cleminson kindly supported an application for a visiting position at the University of Leeds as the threat loomed of sliding off the greasy pole of academia. Colleagues and friends further afield have also offered support and advice over the years, whether relating to research pertaining to the book or academic life more generally. Thanks in this regard are due to David Ruiz, Julio de la Cueva, Miguel Ángel del Arco Blanco, Hugo García and Stefan Berger.

Two friends in particular have been hugely important not only in the process of writing the book, but also as sources of mutual support as we share the trials and tribulations of forging a career in academia as early career scholars. James Yeoman and I began our doctoral studies on modern Spain at the same time. Our Friday night discussions in the pub were always rich and invigorating and many ideas developed in this book owe much to our debates then and since. Alex Paulin-Booth and I joined Durham as teaching fellows at the same time and she has been a source of support and insight as we share thoughts on the academic world and drafts of work.

Adrian Shubert examined the PhD thesis and has endured not only the burden of writing references for dozens of job and grant applications, but also the spectacle of someone rewriting his own thesis with patience and kindness. Mary Vincent has provided unstinting support from the beginning of my intellectual journey in Spanish history as an undergraduate in her special subject class in 2009. She read my lengthy, ranging texts with a judicious eye and provided insightful comments with a clearer sense of my direction of travel than I ever had myself. She has been a constant source of support since, whether reading drafts of work or providing references and advice on life after the PhD.

For the Royal Historical Society, Penny Summerfield, Heather Shore and Jane Winters patiently stewarded the manuscript towards publication and the staff at the IHR and University of London Press – Emily Morrell and Kerry Whitston in particular – were always efficient in responding to numerous questions on practical matters. I am also grateful to Federico Romero Salvadó and Peter Anderson for taking the time to not only review the manuscript, but to travel to London in order to discuss it with me. Thanks also to Klaus Weinhauer, who kindly commented on the manuscript in its final stages. Rubén Vega provided valuable aid in obtaining the cover image, which has been ceded by the Muséu del Pueblu d'Asturies.

My parents and family have always been supportive – from providing the most mundane and material assistance to moral and emotional support – of their son's drive to understand the political dynamics of coalfield communities in northern Spain. I blame them for fostering my intellectual curiosity and a love of languages through summer holidays in Europe.

Finally, a special thanks is due to Jane, for her love, encouragement and support as I wrestled the manuscript towards submission. When we met you asked me what a historian actually *does*. This book is my attempt to answer that question.

Map 1. The provincial division of Spain (map drawn by Cox Cartographic Ltd).

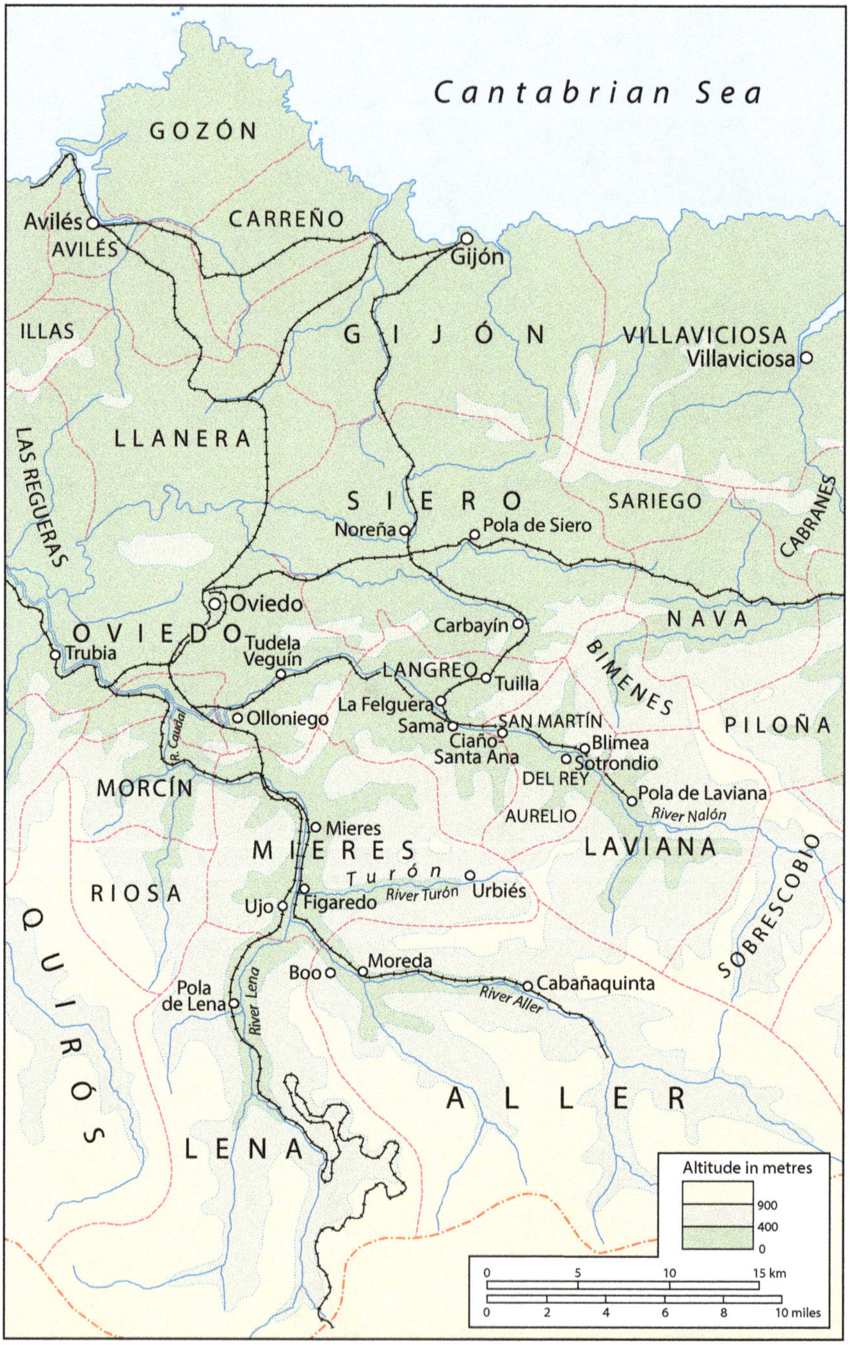

Map 2. Central Asturias, showing municipalities, relevant settlements and major rivers and railways (map drawn by Cox Cartographic Ltd).

Introduction

'UHP. Swear on these letters, brothers, death before tyranny' read the words daubed in white paint on the side of a railway carriage departing from Barcelona for the Republican front during the early days of the Spanish Civil War. Above the slogan, smiling men leaned out of the windows and raised their clenched fists in an antifascist salute towards Robert Capa, the Hungarian photographer who captured the moment in an iconic image.[1] During the months prior to the war, 'UHP' was often seen scrawled across walls, on the labels of cognac bottles and as a decorative motif on pottery.[2] The letters – shorthand for 'unite, proletarian brothers' (Uníos, hermanos proletarios!) – had been coined two years previously during a two-week revolutionary insurrection in the northern region of Asturias. In October 1934, the Spanish socialist movement triggered plans for a hazily defined and poorly prepared 'revolutionary movement' in response to the ascent to government of a right-wing party that professed little respect for the young Second Republic (1931–6). Envisaged as a nationwide revolt, only in Asturias did the October rebellion take the form of a prolonged assault on state power and an experiment in revolution.

While the Asturian capital, Oviedo, reverberated with the sound of gunfire and exploding dynamite as government forces and left-wing militias fought for control of the streets, revolutionary patrols performed the clenched fist salute and demanded the password of 'UHP' in the coalfields that constituted the heartland of the insurrection. The towns and villages of the narrow, steep-sided coal valleys lay in the hands of revolutionary committees staffed by local politicians and trade unionists drawn from the ranks of the socialists, anarchists and communists. The committees undertook a range of self-consciously revolutionary acts, from banning money to centralizing the distribution of requisitioned goods and foodstuffs, while also reconfiguring the local economy for the needs of a rudimentary war effort, including

[1] See <https://pro.magnumphotos.com/image/PAR75398.html> [accessed 2 Aug. 2019]. Both Capa, who was born André Friedmann, and his partner Gerda Taro published photographs under the name of Robert Capa, but their images from the beginning of the Civil War can be distinguished thanks to their use of different equipment.

[2] J. Langdon-Davies, *Behind the Spanish Barricades* (New York, 1936), pp. 4, 23; *Avance*, 11 July 1936.

'Introduction', in M. Kerry, *Unite, Proletarian Brothers! Radicalism and Revolution in the Spanish Second Republic, 1931–6* (London, 2020), pp. 1–17.

retooling steel plants to armour-plate vehicles. Patrols detained alleged enemies of the revolution, including rightists, employers and, in particular, members of the Catholic Church, who accounted for nearly two-thirds of the approximately fifty victims of the revolutionary 'furies' who were either murdered or died in unclear circumstances during the insurrection.[3] After two weeks, the movement was defeated by the Spanish army. The total number of dead approached 1,500, which translated into more than half of the deaths caused by political violence during the Second Republic.[4]

The revolutionary insurrection was not the only episode of mass left-wing mobilization in Europe in 1934. Austrian socialists rebelled when Chancellor Dollfuss strengthened his authoritarian grip on the developing Catholic, corporatist state while almost simultaneously rank-and-file French socialists and communists united in a massive protest against the threat posed by extreme right-wing leagues to the French Third Republic.[5] The episodes were rooted in the particular period of crisis between 1933 and 1935 as the left grappled with the continued growth of fascism and the authoritarian right, and the effects of the Great Depression.[6] But these defensive reactions did not match the scale and revolutionary pretensions of the Asturian insurrection. Not only was this the most important episode of revolutionary upheaval in Europe between the early 1920s and the Spanish Civil War, it was also the last attempt at the seizure of state power via a mass armed insurrection by the working class in Europe.[7]

How and why thousands of inhabitants of the coalfields became willing to take up arms against the government and participate in the revolt are the questions at the heart of this study, which examines the origins, unfolding and ramifications of the Asturian October within the context of the Second

[3] For a comparative study of the 'furies' in the French and Russian Revolutions, see A. J. Mayer, *The Furies: Violence and Terror in the French and Russian Revolutions* (Princeton, N.J., 2000).

[4] For a discussion of the figures, see E. González Calleja, *Cifras cruentas: las víctimas mortales de la violencia sociopolítica en la Segunda República española (1931–1936)* (Granada, 2015), pp. 11, 175–6. Further discussion in ch. 5 of this volume. This book went to press before the publication of Pablo Gil Vico, *Verdugos de Asturias. La violencia y sus relatos en la revolución de Asturias de 1934* (Gijón, 2019).

[5] See A. Rabinbach, *The Crisis of Austrian Socialism: from Red Vienna to Civil War, 1927–1934* (Chicago, Ill., 1983) and B. Jenkins and C. Millington, *France and Fascism: February 1934 and the Dynamics of Political Crisis* (Abingdon, 2015).

[6] See G.-R. Horn, *European Socialists Respond to Fascism: Ideology, Activism and Contingency in the 1930s* (New York, 1996) and G. Eley, *Forging Democracy: the History of the Left in Europe, 1850–2000* (Oxford, 2002), ch. 17.

[7] As highlighted by D. Ruiz, *Octubre de 1934: revolución en la República española* (Madrid, 2008).

Republic. On a superficial level, the insurrection was sparked by an order from the socialist leadership, yet socialist conspiring does not explain the force of the revolt in Asturias. Nor do existing explanations of the 'radicalization' process – which is central to histories of the Republic – capture the breadth, nature and dynamism of conflict and militancy in the coalfields during the 1930s. This book re-evaluates radicalism as a confrontational mode of politics – as defined in more detail below – that emerged from cleavages and conflicts at the local level and the lived experience of politics. It frees radicalization from the strictures of union and party politics and the conventional timeframe of 1933–4 by examining how inhabitants of the coalfields claimed to speak for and 'police' the community. The ideas and actions of these activists were moulded by social relations and the experience of politics and state power at the local level, yet imagined and understood in relation to a wider national and international context.[8]

Radicalization is a touchstone in histories of the Second Republic. It is central to the long-running debate as to who was responsible for delivering Spain to the threshold of civil war five years after the proclamation of the Republic promised its supporters a new beginning of democracy, freedom, secularism and social justice.[9] Historians have either emphasized the unwillingness of sectors of the right, Church, landowners and businesses to accept the reforming intentions of Republican-socialist governments, which radicalized supporters of the government, or else accused the left of 'excluding' the right and adopting a possessive attitude towards the Republic.[10] Accordingly, the Asturian October was either a gesture aimed at stemming the rise of a radicalizing right or confirmation of the left's undemocratic values and methods. Such visions neglect the view from the coalfields and the revolutionary pretensions of Asturian militants and reify a particular idea of the Republic that overlooks the shifting, disputed understandings of the regime between 1931 and 1936.

[8] I am influenced by narrative approaches to collective action. For an overview, see F. Polletta and B. G. Gardner, 'Narrative and social movements', in *The Oxford Handbook of Social Movements*, ed. D. Della Porta and M. Diani (Oxford, 2015), pp. 534–48. See also M. R. Somers, 'Narrativity, narrative identity, and social action: rethinking English working-class formation', *Social Science History*, xvi (1992), 591–629.

[9] For an extended discussion on the promise of the Republic, see R. Cruz, *Una revolución elegante: España 1931* (Madrid, 2014), pp. 203–53.

[10] The classic work on reform and reaction is P. Preston, *The Coming of the Spanish Civil War: Reform, Reaction and Revolution in the Second Republic* (London, 1978). For alleged socialist 'intransigence' and exclusion, see, e.g., S. Payne, *The Collapse of the Spanish Republic, 1933–1936: the Origins of the Civil War* (New Haven, Conn., 2006). See also *Palabras como puños: la intransigencia política en la Segunda República*, ed. F. del Rey (Madrid, 2011).

Seeking answers to the alleged failure of democratic politics in the interwar period was a principal concern for historians during the 1970s and 1980s, as was writing the history of the revolutions and politics of the European working class left between the wars.[11] The latter largely fell out of fashion at the end of the Cold War.[12] More recent histories of political cultures during the interwar period have eroded the previous tendency to make stark distinctions between left and right in favour of uncovering crossovers, interaction and mimicry. For example, Timothy Brown examined why some left-wing radicals in the late Weimar period switched to the Nazi Party, something he attributed to their holding common assumptions regarding a radical approach to politics.[13] Nadine Rossol and Joan Tumblety questioned the existence of a distinctive fascist aesthetic by revealing an emphasis on mass spectacle and aesthetics across the political spectrum, while Jessica Wardhaugh showed that shared symbols and language constituted a key political battleground between different groups as France underwent a crisis of representation of the 'people' between 1934 and 1938.[14] An emphasis on how politics is waged in an interactional, relational way at the level of the community is central to this book, which examines how political differences were understood and negotiated in the context of a local social order dominated by the left. As Joachim Häberlen recently highlighted regarding Weimar Germany, a focus on the interplay between the understanding of politics and political action may provide a way of writing a new social and cultural history of radical politics.[15] Such an approach could be applied

[11] A landmark essay questioning the alleged failure of the Weimar Republic is P. Fritzsche, 'Did Weimar fail?', *Journal of Modern History*, lxviii (1996), 629–56.

[12] As ever, there are exceptions, e.g., Horn, *European Socialists* and P. Swett, *Neighbors and Enemies: the Culture of Radicalism in Berlin, 1929–1933* (Cambridge, 2004). One of the first of a new wave of studies of the German revolution of 1918–19 is *Germany 1916–23: a Revolution in Context*, ed. K. Weinhauer, A. McElligott and K. Heinsohn (Bielefeld, 2015). Classic earlier studies include F. L. Carsten, *Revolution in Eastern Europe* (London, 1972) and Rabinbach, *Crisis*. In contrast, debates on the right have remained rich, e.g., J. Wasserman's study of interwar Austrian 'radical' politics: *Black Vienna: the Radical Right in the Red City, 1918–1938* (Ithaca, N.Y., 2014).

[13] T. S. Brown, *Weimar Radicals: Nazis and Communists between Authenticity and Performance* (New York, 2009).

[14] N. Rossol, *Performing the Nation: Sport, Spectacle and Political Symbolism, 1926–1936* (Basingstoke, 2010); J. Tumblety, 'Rethinking the fascist aesthetic: mass gymnastics, political spectacle and the stadium in 1930s France', *European History Quarterly*, xliii (2013), 707–30; J. Wardhaugh, *In Pursuit of the People: Political Culture in France, 1934–1939* (Basingstoke, 2009).

[15] J. Häberlen, 'Scope for agency and political options: the German working-class movement and the rise of Nazism', *Politics, Religion and Ideology*, xiv (2013), 377–94.

more widely, and this book seeks to provide an example of how this may be achieved in the context of Spain.

Radicalism in Europe and Spain

The European interwar period is often depicted as a 'radical era'.[16] This radicalism can refer to the construction of the world's first socialist state in Russia, the waves of strike action in the aftermath of the First World War, the acuteness of social and political conflict, or the emergence of the new ideologies of fascism and Communism or new ways of waging politics, particularly street-fighting between paramilitary groups.

One way of approaching left-wing radicalism is to focus on 'red cities' or 'little Moscows': localities or neighbourhoods with distinctive left-wing traditions, which pursued projects of 'municipal socialism' or were particular hotbeds of activism.[17] Vienna is the iconic example.[18] Examinations of conflict and radicalism in these areas have often paid close attention to the degree of political and social homogeneity of the locality or district in question, although fragmentation and rivalry have also been used to explain radicalism. In the context of provincial Austria, for example, socialist strongholds were isolated and surrounded by antagonistic political forces, and their sense of weakness was channelled into a militant hostility to Catholic conservatism.[19] Other cases similarly argue for the importance of local rivalries and disputed territory in the development of radical politics. The 'radical' districts of Neukölln and Kreuzberg in Weimar Berlin harboured important levels of support for both Communism and

[16] D. Priestland, 'The left and revolutions', in *The Oxford Handbook of European history, 1914–1945*, ed. N. Doumanis (Oxford, 2016), p. 78.

[17] The literature on these areas is extensive, e.g., J. Merriman, *The Red City: Limoges and the French Nineteenth Century* (New York, 1985); *Red Barcelona: Social Protest and Labour Mobilization in the Twentieth Century*, ed. A. Smith (London, 2002); T. Kaplan, *Red City, Blue Period: Social Movements in Picasso's Barcelona* (Berkeley, Calif., 1992); T. Stovall, *The Rise of the Parisian Red Belt* (Berkeley, Calif., 1990); D. H. Bell, *Sesto San Giovanni: Workers, Culture and Politics in an Italian Town, 1880–1922* (New Brunswick, N.J., 1986); S. Macintyre, *Little Moscows: Communism and Working Class Militancy in Interwar Britain* (London, 1980); L. Boswell, *Rural Communism in France, 1920–1939* (Ithaca, N.Y., 1998). See also A. Knotter, '"Little Moscows" in western Europe: the ecology of small-place communism', *International Review of Social History*, lvi (2011), 475–510.

[18] E.g., H. Gruber, *Red Vienna: Experiment in Working Class Culture, 1919–1934* (New York, 1991).

[19] C. Jeffery, *Social Democracy in the Austrian Provinces, 1918–1934: Beyond Red Vienna* (London, 1995), pp. 62ff.

Nazism.[20] While not an area where municipal socialism operated, the Asturian coalfields have nevertheless long been identified as a red area that was underpinned by a number of political cultures, including socialism, anarchism and communism. These movements shared an idiom and certain political values, but were separated by rivalry and at times hatred. The right, although a minority force in the valleys, continued to attract support. The situation of left-wing hegemony – which was assumed by left-wing activists to mean a political monopoly – undercut by a significant right-wing presence is vital to understanding the conflict and resultant radicalism in the coalfields in the 1930s.

A different yet complimentary approach to interwar radicalism is evident in studies of the explosion of 'working-class unrest and revolutionary potential … unparalleled in the twentieth century' that followed the First World War.[21] The pressures of total war loom large in such interpretations of post-war radicalism. The disciplining of labour for the needs of total war, shortages of basic goods and price rises led to growing strikes towards the end of the conflict. The perceived opening of a new horizon of revolutionary possibility in the wake of the collapse of Tsarism and the Bolshevik seizure of power in Russia further stimulated militancy. Post-war radicalism manifested itself in a combination of strike waves across Europe, the council movement in Italy and the proclamation of 'soviets' in areas like Hungary and Munich, where radicalized sections of the left attempted to press beyond the replacement of the collapsed imperial order with new republics.[22] However, even as Europe appeared to be on the threshold of social revolution, workers' demands tended to centre on wage increases and improvements to working conditions rather than overturning the social order.[23] The Asturian insurrection of 1934 shared the pretensions of some of these post-war attempts at revolution, although the context of the 1930s was significantly different and Spain was not emerging from an international armed conflict. The insurrection was nevertheless shaped by the particular political dynamics of the 1930s and how international developments were interpreted at a local level.

[20] Swett, *Neighbors*, pp. 54–5.

[21] D. Sassoon, *One Hundred Years of Socialism: the West European Left in the Twentieth Century* (London, 1996), p. 32. See also Eley, *Forging*, pp. 131–8.

[22] See *Challenges of Labour: Central and Western Europe, 1917–1920*, ed. C. Wrigley (London, 1993).

[23] As argued in, e.g., R. Bessel, 'Revolution', in *The Cambridge History of the First World War*, ed. J. Winter (3 vols, Cambridge, 2014), ii. 126–44 and Priestland, 'The left'.

Spain did not participate in the First World War, yet was not immune to the effects of the conflict.[24] An economic boom fuelled rising inflation and widespread discontent, which added to the pressures on the corrupt, controlled parliamentary regime of the Restoration monarchy (1875–1923). In 1917, the government faced three interlocking crises: a conspiracy among army officers, a revolutionary strike and demands for greater autonomy for Catalonia. The government ceded to the pressures from sectors of the army while resisting the other challenges. The nationwide revolutionary strike in August, which lasted longest in the Asturian coal valleys, was not well prepared for, and easily suppressed by the army. As a revolutionary movement organized by socialists, it appears to show parallels with October 1934, yet it has differing characteristics. In contrast to the insurrectionary and revolutionary character of 1934, the 1917 movement was envisaged as an auxiliary action to support Republican-socialist demands for a new parliament that would construct a new regime.[25] Like the rest of Europe, Spain saw waves of strikes in industrial areas over the following years with the red city of Barcelona a particular hotspot, while peasants undertook land occupations in the south. Although termed the Spanish 'Bolshevik triennium', the degree to which the strikers desired revolutionary change is questionable.

In September 1923, Miguel Primo de Rivera, captain general of Barcelona, removed parliamentary rule via a military coup sanctioned by King Alfonso XIII. Primo de Rivera aimed to put an end to labour conflict, resolve the protracted crisis of the political system and restore Spain's honour after an embarrassing defeat at the hands of Moroccan forces in North Africa. His seven-year experiment in constructing an authoritarian, Catholic, corporatist regime combined massive investment in public works and a nationalizing project that cracked down on the anarchist movement and Catalan and Basque nationalism. While anarchists faced persecution, the socialist movement adopted a neutral position towards the dictatorship and participated in the corporatist mechanisms of the regime to protect its members and increase its influence. Towards the end of the 1920s, Primo de Rivera's project lost momentum, funding for public works disappeared after the Wall Street Crash and the socialists joined Republican parties in conspiring against the regime. Primo de Rivera resigned in January 1930 and municipal elections fifteen months

[24] For a discussion of Spain within a European context, see J. Casanova, 'Republic, civil war and dictatorship: the peculiarities of Spanish history', *Journal of Contemporary History*, lii (2017), 148–56.

[25] E.g., *The Agony of Spanish Liberalism: from Revolution to Dictatorship 1913–23*, ed. F. J. Romero Salvadó and A. Smith (Basingstoke, 2010).

later delivered a pro-Republican result that caused King Alfonso XIII to flee into exile.[26]

Spain's experience of authoritarian right-wing dictatorship under Primo de Rivera was far from distinctive in the context of interwar Europe, but the attempt to construct a democratic Republic after an experiment in dictatorship set Spain apart. The establishment of the Second Republic in April 1931 constituted the last breaker of the democratizing wave that had surged through Europe at the end of the First World War. The rollback of restrictions on democratic rule began in Hungary and Italy and gathered pace in central and Eastern Europe in the 1930s as European states battled the consequences of the Great Depression, including the linked problems of mass unemployment and disaffected voters, along with renewed radicalism and scenes of political violence on the streets. Even as the prevailing political winds shifted away from the advance of liberal democracy, in Spain a Republican-socialist coalition (1931–3) attempted to implement its vision of a secular, liberal, democratic state.

The bulwark of the new Republic was the socialist movement. The Spanish Socialist Workers' Party (PSOE) joined European counterparts in gaining its first experience of government office after the war in a situation 'unimaginable before 1914'.[27] The Spanish socialist movement formed the backbone of the new democracy insofar as it provided the mass membership that the Republican parties lacked.[28] The social and political influence of the socialist movement on a national level during the Republic – and as the principal political and trade union force in the Asturian coalfields – has ensured that no history of the Second Republic would be complete without the 'phenomenon known as the radicalization of the socialists'.[29]

'Radicalization' serves to describe the shift in the socialist movement from participating in government in 1931–3 to planning a revolutionary movement in 1933–4. The crucial turning point is usually held to be the summer of 1933, when socialist leader Francisco Largo Caballero responded to developing rank-and-file frustration by adopting a more radical rhetoric. This is the standard portrayal of radicalization, yet it has long

[26] On the dictatorship, see e.g., S. Ben-Ami, *Fascism from Above: the Dictatorship of Primo de Rivera in Spain, 1923–30* (Oxford, 1983); A. Quiroga, *Making Spaniards: Primo de Rivera and the Nationalization of the Masses, 1923–30* (Basingstoke, 2007).

[27] S. Berman, *The Social Democratic Moment: Ideas and Politics in the Making of Interwar Europe* (Boston, Mass., 1998), p. 2.

[28] P. Radcliff, 'The political "left" in the interwar period, 1924–1939', in *The Oxford handbook of European history, 1914–1945*, ed. N. Doumanis (Oxford, 2016), pp. 286–7.

[29] S. Juliá, *La izquierda del PSOE (1935–1936)* (Madrid, 1977), p. 1. See also Payne, *Collapse*, p. 52.

been bemoaned as underexplored and little understood.[30] There are also a number of problems with how the process is traditionally described. First, the lack of clarity as to the definition of radicalization and its usage means it lacks analytical purchase, for it has become shorthand for a period as much as a process.[31] Second, so closely linked is the term to the socialists that it is much less commonly used in the context of anarchism or the political right, even if the term does provide insight into these movements.[32] Third, the desire to explain October 1934 through radicalization encourages teleology at the expense of contingency and dynamism. Fourth, the measurement and description of socialist radicalization is often reduced to the figure of Largo Caballero, who laid the plans for the 'revolutionary movement' in 1934. His adoption of radical rhetoric and ascent to presiding over both the socialist trade union federation (UGT) and the PSOE are deployed as evidence for radicalization. This is founded on Largo Caballero's reputation as a bellwether of the rank-and-file mood. Even so, scholars have long noted that his radical rhetoric is subtler than simple appeals for revolution.[33] Finally, as regards the rank and file, strikes and unemployment figures have been the usual indicator of the mood of the working class and peasantry, although by 1982 José Manuel Macarro Vera had rightly questioned the use of strike figures.[34] As he pointed out, strikes were often 'moderate' and

[30] For criticism that radicalization is not explained adequately, see e.g., Preston, *Coming of the Spanish Civil War*, p. 2; J. M. Macarro Vera, 'Causas de la radicalización socialista en la II República', *Revista de historia contemporánea*, i (1982), 178–226, at p. 222; S. Souto Kustrín, 'Taking the street: workers' youth organizations and political conflict in the Spanish Second Republic', *European History Quarterly*, xxxiv (2004), 131–56, at pp.132, 134.

[31] Foundational accounts include A. de Blas Guerrero, *El socialismo radical en la II República* (Madrid, 1978) and M. Bizcarrondo, 'Democracia y revolución en la estrategia socialista de la Segunda República', *Estudios de Historia Social*, xvi–xvii (1981), 227–459.

[32] Exceptions are C. Ealham, *Class, Culture and Conflict in Barcelona, 1898–1937* (Abingdon, 2005); E. González Calleja, *Contrarrevolucionarios: radicalización violenta de las derechas durante la Segunda República, 1931–1936* (Madrid, 2011); S. Lowe, *Catholicism, War and the Foundation of Francoism* (Eastbourne, 2010). 'Fascistization' serves a similar purpose, e.g., I. Saz, *Fascismo y franquismo* (Valencia, 2004) and E. González Calleja, 'La violencia y sus discursos: los límites de la "fascistización" de la derecha española durante el régimen de la Segunda República', *Ayer*, lxxi (2008), 85–116.

[33] S. Juliá, 'Los socialistas y el escenario de la futura revolución', in *Octubre 1934: cincuenta años para la reflexión*, ed. G. Jackson et al. (Madrid, 1985), pp. 103–30. For Largo Caballero responding to the grassroots, see e.g., H. Graham, *Socialism and War: the Spanish Socialist Party in Power and Crisis, 1936–1939* (Cambridge, 1991), pp. 44–7 and J. Aróstegui, *Largo Caballero: el tesón y la quimera* (Barcelona, 2013), p. 297.

[34] Blas Guerrero, *El socialismo*, pp. 20–1.

aimed at defending the Republic and social legislation.[35] Conflict was not coterminous with radicalism.

More convincing explanations of radicalization have tended to combine economic and political factors. Marta Bizcarrondo argued that the radicalization resulted from the 'intensification of class struggle' due to the rightist 'counteroffensive against reformism', the economic context, the ascent of fascism and the 'rapid deterioration of the political situation' in early 1933.[36] Nevertheless, these arguments are inevitably anchored in the assumptions of 1970s and 1980s labour history, allowing little room for engagement with cultural approaches. Where the threat of fascism is recognized, it is a contextual, international factor rather than present in the thoughts, ideas and experiences of citizens in everyday life.

Explanations as to why the Asturian mineworkers rebelled have tended to mirror the broader narrative of socialist radicalization. David Ruiz's early interpretation emphasized the importance of unemployment, but the number of layoffs in the coal industry was small and cannot be easily mapped onto surges in militancy.[37] Ruiz later revised his argument to incorporate the influence of culture, highlighting that the revolutionaries' ideas were the result of their accumulated experiences, while still emphasizing socialist conspiring and the achievement of working class unity via the Asturian Workers' Alliance.[38] However, the much lauded and mythologized Workers' Alliance does not explain the origins of the insurrection.

Adrian Shubert's pre-history of the Asturian October consisted of an examination of the long-term formation of the Asturian mining working class. His reconstruction of the living conditions, work experience and conflicts that served to shape the local working class remains a valuable classic social history. Only one chapter is devoted to the Republic, in which he argued that working-class hopes were frustrated by the failure of Republican reform. This bred radicalism, which translated into a politicization of strikes hitherto focused on economic issues. Such an approach neglects the wider struggles within the coalfields beyond trade union politics and pays less attention to the language of frustration, fear and radicalism, which is understandable given that *The Road to Revolution* is rooted in the tradition of 1960s and 1970s social histories.[39] The politics

[35] Macarro Vera, 'Causas', pp. 183–6.

[36] Bizcarrondo, 'Democracia'.

[37] D. Ruiz, *Insurrección defensiva y revolución obrera: el octubre español de 1934* (Barcelona, 1988), especially p. 63.

[38] Ruiz, *Octubre*.

[39] A. Shubert, *The Road to Revolution in Spain: the Coal Miners of Asturias, 1860–1934* (Urbana, Ill., 1987).

of labour were a fundamental aspect of conflict in the coalfields, but the net needs to be cast wider to consider other points of friction and cleavages at the local level. From rent activism, to struggles over the role of Catholicism in Spanish society, to fears over the emergence of fascism, a wide range of factors combined to fuel militancy. Understanding them requires close attention to political language and imaginaries, and how social, political and cultural boundaries were policed at the local level.

The meaning of radicalism

Little attempt is made to define the concept of 'radicalism' or 'radicalization' in studies of Republican Spain. This could reflect a wider lack of interest in theorizing about radicalism, particularly compared to associated concepts like revolution. The meaning of radicalism is instead assumed to be self-evident. Scholars who have meditated on the concept of radicalism have tended to take an etymological approach, according to which radicalism has its origins in the Latin term *radicalis* (root).[40] Yet defining radicalism as seeking the root of a problem fails to shed much light on radicalism as a historical phenomenon and neither does it distinguish between radicalism and revolutionary politics.

It is more useful to reframe the history of radicalism in terms of shifting, myriad challenges as to what constituted the realm of politics.[41] This encompasses different historical moments in which individuals and groups have contested the place it occupies in private and public spheres, who is permitted to participate in political processes and how political struggle should be waged. Such an understanding of radicalism allows similarities, contrasts and continuities to be drawn between episodes like the struggles by nineteenth-century radicals to extend boundaries or citizenship; the 'politicization of aspects of daily life once considered outside the political realm' that Pamela Swett noted in Weimar Berlin; and attempts by 1970s radicals to embody a new way of being and feeling that challenged the capitalist order.[42] The character of radicalism thus changed in accordance

[40] E.g., P. McLaughlin, *Radicalism: a Philosophical Study* (Basingstoke, 2012).

[41] Accordingly, radicalism has tended to be associated with the left, even if scholars argue that the two are not coterminous. For an important critique, see C. Calhoun, *The Roots of Radicalism: Tradition, the Public Sphere and Early Nineteenth-Century Social Movements* (Chicago, Ill., 2012).

[42] E.g., Swett, *Neighbors*, quotation at p. 139; J. Häberlen, *The Emotional Politics of the Alternative Left: West Germany, 1968–1984* (Cambridge, 2018). For 19th-century radicals, see G. Claeys and C. Lattek, 'Radicalism, republicanism and revolutionism: from the principles of '89 to the origins of modern terrorism', in *The Cambridge History of Nineteenth-Century Political Thought*, ed. G. Claeys and G. Stedman Jones (Cambridge, 2011), pp. 200–54.

with the evolving nature of politics. This can also be applied to the use of radicalism as a term. Shifts in meaning could be abrupt. Zsuzsa Nagy's examination of the background to the Hungarian Soviet pinpoints a sudden change in the meaning of radicalism: whereas previously it designated bourgeois opposition to feudalism, in early 1919 the term was refashioned to signify support for Bolshevism and opposition to the young Hungarian Republic.[43]

Rooting the meaning of radicalism in its historical context is therefore important. This study employs radicalism to characterize a way of doing politics defined by a confrontational, militant style that corresponds with the interwar period. This mode of politics manifested itself in an assertive, even aggressive policing of political and geographical communities. By extension, 'radicalization' was the dynamic, unstable and contingent process by which this confrontational style of radicalism was adopted.[44] Radicalization signified growing militancy and confrontation rather than the pursuit or defence of a 'fixed' radical position. Radicalism often slid into revolutionary politics, yet did not simply equate to exhibiting Communist sympathies or a lurch to the left, as some have argued.[45] It was quite possible for Communist parties to be conservative in their mode of action. As a contingent way of doing politics, radicalism could be inflected with particular qualities, as the following chapters will show. For example, Spanish socialists unsuccessfully tried to harness the radical impulse among the rank and file and reorient it towards moderation in 1932, while four years later radicalism would be inflected with fragility as boycotts and political purges in the coalfields revealed a crisis of community in the wake of the insurrection and government repression. This book traces radicalism on a collective level by weaving together episodes of conflict, the experiences of individuals and the shifting nature of political language at the local level.

This book roots radicalism within the context of the interwar period, rather than defining it against the backdrop of mining. This marks a departure from the long-running debate in the literature regarding the alleged correlation between coalfields and radical politics. Since the Kerr-Siegel hypothesis predicated on mineworkers living in isolated, homogenous communities, scholars have proposed contrasting theories as to why this

[43] Z. Nagy, 'Budapest and the revolutions of 1918–19', in Wrigley, *Challenges*, p. 78.

[44] Some sociological perspectives have begun to move in a similar direction, e.g., E. Y. Alimi, L. Bosi and C. Demetriou, *The Dynamics of Radicalization: a Relational and Comparative Perspective* (Oxford, 2015).

[45] See Souto Kustrín, 'Taking', pp. 134–5 and J. Uría, 'Asturias 1920–1937, el espacio cultural comunista y la cultura de la izquierda: historia de un diálogo entre dos décadas', in *Los comunistas en Asturias (1920–1982)*, ed. F. Erice (Gijón, 1996), pp. 271–5.

group of workers was more likely to strike than any other. Recent scholarly attention paid to figures who do not fit the archetype of the combative miner and to mining areas lacking in militancy have revealed this debate to rest on shaky foundations.[46] The industrial environment of the Asturian coalfields was an important factor in conditioning the political dynamics and social and economic relationships in the Asturian coalfields, particularly because of its high levels of union membership and dense network of political and cultural institutions. However, radicalism needs to be seen as emerging from the interaction of this particular political and social order and the wider national and international context of the 1930s.

The trade unions were mass organizations that remained central to the dynamics of economic and political struggle in the coalfields, but society in the valleys cannot be reduced to the unions. Instead, a focus on 'community' provides an opportunity to capture a wider range of conflicts beyond strike action and avoids approaching local politics through the institutional lens of the union. The concept of community has long been criticized, often for its haziness and positive connotations, to the extent of appeals for it to be jettisoned completely as an analytical category.[47] However, the term 'community' encapsulates the meaning of the Spanish term '*pueblo*', which signifies both people and town or village. It blurs the distinction between geography and collective identity as well as resonating with affective power. This duality makes 'community' an evocative and productive concept for examining local politics in the 1930s. In the context of this study, community is an imagined collective group that overlays or is associated with a given geographical area. The group has no fixed boundaries, but is at once fluid, and subject to a constant process of delineation and contestation through informal and formal 'policing' by individuals and collective groups.[48]

During the interwar period, the governance of town, village or neighbourhood continued to be the space in which many people engaged with politics. It provided a reference point for understanding the wider political world and was a 'common source of grievance and a common

46 For the original theory, see C. Kerr and A. Siegel, 'The interindustry propensity to strike – an international comparison', in *Industrial Conflict*, ed. A. Kornhauser, R. Kubin and A. Ross (New York, 1954), pp. 189–212. For a skewering of the link between mining and radicalism, see D. Geary, 'The myth of the radical miner', in *Towards a Comparative History of Coalfield Societies*, ed. S. Berger, A. Croll and N. LaPorte (Aldershot, 2005), pp. 43–64.

47 E.g., Macfarlane, 'History, anthropology and the study of communities', cited in H. Barron, *The 1926 Miners' Lockout: Meanings of Community in the Durham Coalfield* (Oxford, 2009), p. 6.

48 My thinking on community is influenced by A. Cohen, *The Symbolic Construction of Community* (London, 1985). See also G. Delanty, *Community* (London, 2003).

medium of political expression', whether in Spain, interwar Berlin or the Durham coalfields.[49] In Spain, the locality has traditionally played a prominent role in identities and as a source for political action, whether in rural areas or industrial zones, although how ideas of the local community were projected and mobilized is not a common object of study, with the exception of the important work of Pamela Radcliff, Temma Kaplan and Chris Ealham.[50] Ideas of who and what constituted the local community, how the Republic was to be constructed at the local level, and claims to represent and embody the local community were all ways in which community was a fundamental component of political action and conflict, and fed into radicalism. It is therefore a mistake to label community-rooted protest as a decidedly less 'modern' form of collective action.[51]

The following chapters will show how the idea of community was disputed at a local level, from leftists identifying the working class with the community or rejecting Catholicism as a legitimate expression of local identity, to community-based defence against the alleged invasion of state police forces into 'their' communities.[52] The first two chapters introduce themes and provide a framework for understanding the mechanics of radicalism in the rest of the book. Chapter 1 surveys the industrial, social and political environment of the coalfields prior to 1931. An examination of politics and how conflict was waged in 1931 and 1932 follows in chapter 2, where the focus is on the construction of the Republic. The next two chapters reveal the development of radicalism between 1932 and 1934 through an analysis of a range of factors, from rivalries over anticlericalism and Catholicism to local imaginings of fascism. After chapter 5 examines

[49] E. Rosenhaft, *Beating the Fascists? The German Communist Party and Political Violence, 1929–1933* (Cambridge, 1983), p. 11. Similar arguments appear in e.g., Swett, *Neighbors*; Barron, *1926*, p. 271; Ealham, *Class*, p. 21.

[50] E.g. as noted by observers, including R. Ford, in *A Handbook for Travellers in Spain* (2 vols, Cambridge, 2011 [1845]), i. 2; G. Brenan, *The Spanish Labyrinth: an Account of the Social and Political Background of the Civil War* (London, 1966 [1943]), ix; and J. Pitt-Rivers, *The People of the Sierra* (London, 1954), e.g. pp. 28–30. Scholarly approaches are in P. Radcliff, *From Mobilization to Civil War: the Politics of Polarization in the Spanish City of Gijón, 1900–1937* (Cambridge, 1996); Kaplan, *Red City*; Ealham, *Class*. See also discussion in A. Shubert, *A Social History of Modern Spain* (London, 1990), pp. 190–2. Classic anthropological studies often made the community an object of study, but tended to focus on rural areas, e.g., C. Lisón Tolosana, *Belmonte de los Caballeros: Anthropology and History in an Aragonese Community* (Princeton, N.J., 1983); W. A. Christian, *Person and God in a Spanish Valley* (New York, 1972).

[51] E.g., R. Cruz, who builds on Tilly in *Protestar en España* (Madrid, 2015).

[52] Similar approaches are found in Rosenhaft, *Beating* and C. Millington, 'Street-fighting men: political violence in interwar France', *English Historical Review*, cxxix (2014), 606–38.

the revolution as a liminal moment in which revolutionaries were caught between reasserting control over their communities and re-founding the social order, chapters 6 and 7 explore the effects of the insurrection and the repression. In 1936, these last led to a crisis of community that was particularly evident in boycotts and purges. These mechanisms were an attempt to remake community even as they simultaneously fuelled a fragile radicalism that underpinned the identities of those who would set out to resist the military coup of July 1936 that plunged Spain into a three-year civil war.

Sources

In order to reconstruct the lived experience of politics in the Asturian coalfields during the 1930s, this study rests principally on three complimentary source bases, which provide a kaleidoscopic lens through which to observe the period: the press, municipal records and court files. All three are incomplete due to the loss of documentation during the 1934 insurrection, Civil War and Francoist dictatorship.

The provincial press provides the best overarching vision of local politics and is often the only surviving source for what occurred in certain localities during the Republic. The titles that form the basis of this study are *Región*, *El Noroeste* and the Asturian socialist press, all surviving editions of which were consulted for the entire period between April 1931 and July 1936. In late 1931 the Asturian socialist daily *Avance* replaced the veteran weekly *La Aurora Social*. *Avance* enjoyed a wide readership under the editorship of Javier Bueno and reached a print run of 25,000 in 1934.[53] So important was the perceived role of *Avance* in inciting the revolutionary insurrection that police arrested Bueno when it began, and government troops destroyed the printing presses. Some limited socialist publications were permitted in 1935 (*La Tarde* and *Asturias*), but these were smaller operations which faced censorship and the threat of sequestration. Together, the pre-eminent right-wing daily *Región*, Gijón-based liberal Republican *El Noroeste* and the socialist press provide panoramic, contrasting visions of the coalfields and wider Asturias during the 1930s.

Región, *El Noroeste* and *Avance* were all efficient, modern press operations. They had sections dedicated to local news that relied on a network of correspondents in towns and villages and contributions by readers and political groups.[54] Each newspaper maintained its own editorial line, but

[53] Shubert, *Road*, p. 151.

[54] J. Uría, 'Cultura y comunicación de masas en Asturias (1931–1934): aproximación a su estudio', *Estudios de Historia Social*, xxxi (1984), 145–60, at p. 147.

the newspapers attempted to balance the editor's position with providing a voice to the towns and villages, lending them a choral character. Different and even contradictory reports could be published in the same newspaper. *El Noroeste*'s liberal principles – and animosity towards the socialists – ensured that it provided a space for anarchist and Communist writers to announce meetings and publish reports. Even as different political groups maintained their own mouthpieces, rival newspapers were not always taboo for readers; the socialist press was a source of news and opinion for the wider left, particularly from 1934. The effect of the local news pages was to create a public sphere within the pages themselves and between newspapers. Local news sections thus constituted a voice of the local community, even if this did not represent the majority of the town or village in question, and was refracted through the opinions of the author.

Documents from local and provincial Asturian archives enrich the vision of the 1930s further. The minutes of municipal council meetings [*actas municipales*] have been underused by historians but show a different facet of local politics beyond the trade unions, particularly in terms of how councillors envisaged the Republic and attempted to balance the demands of administrating local affairs and pursuing a political agenda. The archive of the provincial authority in charge of public order, the office of the civil governor, has not survived, but court records from district and provincial tribunals allow for analysis of episodes of crime, in this case violence. The loss of records means that a comprehensive study is impossible, but individual cases – and particularly witness statements therein – allow an examination of how politics and community were imagined and policed in violent encounters, and offer a voice to those absent from other sources. Letters housed in the Centro Documental de la Memoria Histórica (CDMH) in Salamanca denouncing neighbours to military officials in the wake of the insurrection provide similar insight into how the local social and political order was imagined, as well as the effects of the repression on the coalfield communities.

Newspaper production ceased during the revolutionary insurrection. The committees that managed the revolutionary process produced a number of proclamations [*bandos*] that historians have disregarded for their fervour and falsehoods, yet used with care, they allow a glimpse into revolutionary dreams and ideas as the insurrection unfolded. The flood of reports published in the wake of October 1934 that related the terror wreaked by the revolutionary hordes, or else the deeds of the heroic revolutionaries, is similarly problematic: they include personal testimony, eyewitness statements or even novelized accounts. These left-wing texts formed part of a nationwide struggle to control the narrative of the insurrection in the high-stakes political context of 1935–6.[55] They disseminated the lessons, names of the revolutionary martyrs and symbols of the insurrection, which cemented the place of 'unite, proletarian brothers!' as an antifascist slogan and battle cry for the Spanish left.[56]

Author's note

Place names are spelled according to current conventions. Andalucía is anglicized to Andalusia, as is Sevilla to Seville, but Zaragoza is preferred to Saragossa and Navarra to Navarre. Villages in the Asturian coalfields that do not appear on the map are followed by the municipality in brackets. According to convention and in the interest of brevity, newspaper articles are referenced by the title and date of the publication only. The names of individuals whose identity is secondary to the information conveyed about the social and political context by their crime have been cited in a shortened form that reduces surnames to initials (for example, 'Jaime C.'). The names of ideologies and parties are not capitalized, with the exception of Communism and Republicanism. Communism is capitalized to denote the 'official' Communist Party whereas communism in the lowercase refers to those estranged from Comintern orthodoxy. Republicanism, indicating support for the principles of the Second Republic, is capitalized. Anarchism is employed as an umbrella term to designate the broad, heterogeneous Spanish anarchist movement.

[55] See B. D. Bunk, *Ghosts of Passion: Martyrdom, Gender, and the origins of the Spanish Civil War* (Durham, N.C., 2007).

[56] UHP was even incorporated into book titles, e.g., M. Álvarez Suárez, *Sangre de octubre: U.H.P. Episodios de la revolución en Asturias* (Madrid, 1936); N. Molins i Fábrega, *UHP: la insurrección proletaria en Asturias* (Gijón, 1977 [1935]).

1. Rethinking the red valleys

Dark dust floated in the air, covering the lush, green hillsides. As the train snaked its way down the narrow valley in tandem with the rushing black waters of the river Candín, lines of straw-hatted men and women shovelling huge piles of coal could be observed from the carriage. The valley widened and opened onto the industrial expanse of La Felguera. On alighting, Roberto Arlt was struck by the landscape of Asturian industry, from the sight of 'armour-plated blast furnaces' and pitheads to 'chimneys spewing plumes of smoke sideways'. For the Argentine journalist, industry lent the Asturian coal valleys an air of 'severe, sombre dynamism'.[1] The region was the country's coal capital and, together with the Basque Country and Catalonia, one of the heartlands of Spanish industry, but the image of a smoke-belching powerhouse requires careful examination. This chapter explores the industrial, social and political development of the coalfields within a wider Spanish context from the vantage point of 1931, before ending with a look at the proclamation of the Second Republic in April 1931 and the political panorama at the national and local level.

The Asturian coalfields have long had a reputation as 'red valleys' with the mineworkers mythologized as the vanguard of the organized Spanish working class, as witnessed not only in the 1934 revolutionary insurrection but also in the 1962 'silent' strike against the Francoist dictatorship. As an area with strong, distinctive left-wing traditions and political activism, the coal valleys can be compared to similar areas in Europe and beyond, from 'little Moscows' like Halluin in northern France or 'red Clydeside' in Glasgow, to the 'red cities' of Vienna and Turin.[2] While the left – understood in broad terms – was hegemonic in the coalfields, society was neither monolithic nor monochrome. Scholars have often emphasized the rivalry between socialists, anarchists and Communists, yet it is also necessary to incorporate the presence of the right and Catholicism, and to complicate

[1] R. Arlt, *Aguafuertes (andaluzas, marroquíes, gallegas, asturianas, vascas y madrileñas)* (Paracuellos de Jarama, 2015), p. 276.

[2] E.g., L. Boswell, *Rural Communism in France, 1920–1939* (Ithaca, N.Y., 1998); T. Stovall, *The Rise of the Parisian Red Belt* (Berkeley, Calif., 1990); D. H. Bell, *Sesto San Giovanni: Workers, Culture and Politics in an Italian Town, 1880–1922* (New Brunswick, N.J., 1986); C. Ealham, *Class, Culture and Conflict in Barcelona, 1898–1937* (Abingdon, 2005).

the relationship between left-wing groups in order to provide a fuller picture of political dynamics in the coalfields.[3] The combination of small communities and overlapping networks of sociability, work and politics meant that male mineworkers of different beliefs coexisted in the village and in the workplace, ensuring interaction and friction, but also the possibility of understanding. Communities were thus multi-layered, which meant that multiple axes of identification and mobilization existed, including affiliations along the lines of politics, class, one's workplace, gender or place of residence. This was vital for the evolution of the struggles examined in the following chapters.[4] Radicalism emerged from a combination of the left's position of power and local rivalries and cleavages.

Environment and industry

Some 450km and an 11-hour train journey north of Madrid in the 1930s, Asturias – or the province of Oviedo as it was then officially known – comprises over 10,000km^2 nestled between the Cantabrian Sea and peaks of the cordillera that divide it from the central plains of the Spanish *Meseta*. The rolling hills along the coast and mountainous valleys traditionally supported a largely subsistence economy, based mainly on cattle rearing, fishing and smallholdings, but by the twentieth century, coal and iron production had emerged to form the backbone of the Asturian economy. The provincial capital was the regional seat of banking and commerce, but also accommodated two arms producers, two explosives factories and a cement plant within its municipal boundaries. The capital was rivalled by the port city of Gijón, which was both a 'summer resort and [an] industrial powerhouse', thanks to coal exporting, shipbuilding and metallurgy, as well as glass-making, ceramics, textiles, tobacco, fishing and construction.[5] The principal coal zones were the steep-sided, winding valleys of the Nalón, Caudal, Aller and Turón rivers to the south of Oviedo, towered over by peaks up to 1000m tall.[6] Outside the central area formed by Oviedo, Gijón

[3] On rivalry, see e.g., D. Ruiz, *Insurrección defensiva y revolución obrera: el octubre español de 1934* (Barcelona, 1988).

[4] For similar approaches, see e.g., H. Barron, *The 1926 Miners' Lockout: Meanings of Community in the Durham Coalfield* (Oxford, 2009); S. Ward, *Unemployment and the State in Britain: the Means Test and Protest in 1930s South Wales and North-East England* (Manchester, 2013).

[5] P. Radcliff, *From Mobilization to Civil War: the Politics of Polarization in the Spanish City of Gijón, 1900–1937* (Cambridge, 1996), pp. 19–20, 66.

[6] The Nalón valley accounted for 43% of coal production, the Caudal (including Turón) 28% and the Aller 18% in 1931 (*Estadística Minera y Metalúrgica de España* [1931] (2 vols, Madrid, 1931), ii. 281).

and the coalfields, the rest of the province's 800,000 inhabitants – of a national population of 23.5 million in 1931 – were widely dispersed.[7]

The mining of coal in Asturias began in the eighteenth century, but the industry developed slowly. Geology and geography posed significant obstacles. Asturian coal was soft and required washing. Extraction was difficult and the labour process resisted mechanization, for seams were usually narrow and sloped diagonally. The poor quality of the coal and costly transportation out of the valleys meant that Asturian coal was expensive and initially a product destined primarily for local consumption. From the mid nineteenth century onwards, an increase in demand, improvements in transport and infrastructure, the consolidation of larger mining companies, including Fábrica de Mieres (1879), Sociedad Hullera Española (1892) and Duro-Felguera (1900), and the introduction of a tariff on foreign coal, stimulated the development of the industry. Output, which had oscillated between 350,000 and 500,000 tons between 1870 and 1887, increased to over a million tons in 1895 and reached two million tons in 1907.[8] As a result, Asturian coal went from being a product for local consumption, to one for export to other provinces by train and ship, although its price ensured that it continued to struggle to compete with foreign imports on the domestic market.

Even as the capital of Spanish coal, the Asturian coalfields never rivalled areas like the Ruhr, northern England or south Wales, which were much larger in scale and production.[9] Nor could Asturias match the success and wealth of the other two heartlands of Spanish industry: the Basque Country and Catalonia, whose industrial foundations rested on iron ore extraction and textile production respectively. The Basques were favoured by large deposits of the phosphorous-free iron ore required by the Bessemer process and exported it to Britain; cheap coal flowed in the opposite direction to fuel the Basque Country's own steel production.[10] The interruption of this

[7] V. Rodríguez Infiesta, 'Asturias en los siglos xx y xxi', in *Historia de Asturias*, ed. A. Fernández Pérez and F. Friera Suárez (Oviedo, 2005), p. 702; A. Shubert, *A Social History of Modern Spain* (London, 1990), p. 24.

[8] G. Ojeda, *Asturias en la industrialización española, 1833–1907* (Madrid, 1985), pp. 335, 355, 363.

[9] The Ruhr coal basin yielded 123 million tons in 1929 before the onset of the Great Depression (J. Gillingham, *Industry and Politics in the Third Reich: Ruhr Coal, Hitler and Europe* (London, 1985), p. 58). The 'precarious' south Welsh coal industry produced 36 million tons in 1898 (C. Williams, *Capitalism, Community, and Conflict: the South Wales Coalfield, 1898–1947* (Cardiff, 1998), ch. 2, at p. 26).

[10] G. Tortella, *The Development of Modern Spain: an Economic History of the Nineteenth and Twentieth Centuries* (Cambridge, Mass., 2000), pp. 86–9. See also J. P. Fusi, *Política*

trade during the First World War sparked a boom in profits for Asturian coal companies. When British coal reappeared on the Spanish market after the war, the contraction was sharp. In an attempt to stay competitive, mining companies lowered wages while forcing mineworkers to cut increased amounts of Asturian coal. Production reached nearly five million tons in 1929 before further economic problems hit the industry during the Republic.[11]

The expansion of the coal industry during the First World War had created thousands of jobs, which later disappeared in the post-war slump. Dismissals helped the companies maintain the pressure on wages during the 1920s. The mining workforce had peaked at 39,000 in 1920 – which translated into a three-fold increase since 1900 – and had largely been fuelled by an influx of migrants from Portugal and other areas of Spain. The post-war difficulties in the industry meant that between 1922 and 1934 the number of mineworkers fluctuated between 25,000 and 30,000.[12] The iron and steel industry in the valleys was much smaller, employing approximately 2,100 and 1,300 workers in La Felguera and Ablaña (Mieres) respectively. (A further plant in Gijón employed another 1,300 workers.)[13]

Coalmining was almost entirely a male occupation thanks to a legal prohibition on women labouring in the pit galleries. Women were employed in the coal-washing facilities, but their number was in long-term decline and by 1934, they summed only 700 workers.[14] In contrast, women outnumbered male workers in the explosives factories that supplied the mines.[15] According to official figures, much of women's employment in the province was concentrated in agriculture, domestic service and tailoring, which reflected national patterns, although such sources neglect less formalized activities and unpaid labour.[16] Fragments from contemporary accounts, the press or court records show that women worked in bars and shops, ran lodging houses and market stalls, and engaged in informal activities to supplement the family income, such as coal picking.[17] Even

obrera en el País Vasco, 1880–1923 (Madrid, 1975), p. 19.

[11] A. Shubert, *The Road to Revolution in Spain: the Coal Miners of Asturias, 1860–1934* (Urbana, Ill., 1987), pp. 27–30.

[12] Shubert, *Road*, pp. 29, 38–40.

[13] *Estadística Minera y Metalúrgica de España* [1931], ii. 306–7.

[14] *Estadística Minera y Metalúrgica de España* [1934], 477.

[15] *Estadística Minera y Metalúrgica de España* [1931], i. 94.

[16] Ministerio del Trabajo, *Censo de la población de España* [1930] … *regiones de Asturias y León. Cuadernos III y X* (Madrid, 1942), pp. 40–1, 44–5; Shubert, *Social History*, p. 38.

[17] For lodging houses, see e.g., cases in Archivo Histórico Provincial de Asturias (AHPA),

so, paid employment among young women was high enough in the 1920s for Dr Jove y Canella to lament that young women in San Martín del Rey Aurelio were not prepared for homemaking, as they spent their youth working rather than learning their domestic duties.[18] Jove y Canella published several 'medical topographies' of coalfield districts in the 1920s and 1930s, in which he surveyed the factors that impacted on the health of residents, from living conditions and lifestyles to nutrition and disease.

For the men who worked in coal extraction, mine work varied greatly from pit to pit. Companies sank the first shafts in 1916 and thereafter hundreds of workers queued every day for the cages that plummeted to the galleries in the deeper pits, like Sotón, Fondón or the Lláscares mine visited by Roberto Arlt.[19] In Aller, in contrast, drift mines peppered the valley sides and the first shaft did not enter into operation until 1942. Drift mines employed much smaller workforces and groups of workers trekked, 'staff in […] hand', up the mountainsides.[20] The level of mechanization inside the mines varied significantly between different pits, and workforces were highly stratified according to their role and wage. Subcontracting had become increasingly prevalent and served as a further potential dividing factor within the workforce.[21] Stratification and different workplace experiences posed potential obstacles to solidarity and co-operation.

While the image of a highly industrialized area and the identity of the 'mineworker' loomed large and proudly in the collective imagination, the reality was inevitably more complicated. That mineworkers sought other ways of earning a living, from running bars to book-selling, is unsurprising given the precarious nature of employment in the coal industry, and can be illustrated by the cases of two young socialists. Herminio Vallina appears in the archival record as a mineworker, correspondent for the socialist newspaper, *Avance*, and shop assistant in a pharmacy, while Silverio

---

Audiencia Provincial (AP), box 78436. A woman in a police investigation defined as a homemaker actually ran a bar, see AHPA, AP, box 79435, file 251 (1934). For coal picking, see *Región*, 28 Oct. 1931. For lodging houses in Bilbao, see P. Pérez-Fuentes Hernández, *"Ganadores de pan" y "amas de casa": otras miradas sobre la industrialización vasca* (Bilbao, 2003), pp. 46–8.

[18] J. M. Jove y Canella, *Topografía médica del concejo de San Martín del Rey Aurelio* (Madrid, 1923), pp. 64, 84–5.

[19] Arlt, *Aguafuertes*, pp. 278–84.

[20] S. Nevares, *El patrono ejemplar: una obra maestra de Acción Social* (Madrid, 1936), pp. 16–17.

[21] Shubert, *Road*, pp. 47, 58–9. It was also present in Britain 'well into the twentieth century' (R. Church and Q. Outram, *Strikes and Solidarity: Coalfield Conflict in Britain, 1889–1966* (Cambridge, 1998), pp. 27–9).

Castañón described working in construction and selling newspapers and novels after he was sacked for striking.[22] Many mineworkers continued to be connected to the rural environment, both in terms of labour and sociability. Historians have suggested that 'mixed workers', who combined mining and agricultural labour, predominated prior to 1914, but mineworkers returned to agriculture amid the crisis in the coal industry at the end of the First World War.[23] As women worked the land more than men, reframing the unit of economic analysis on the family also highlights that mining families continued to be entangled in some of the rhythms and practices of rural society. Police investigations from the 1930s also reveal quarrels between mineworkers over the demarcation of plots of land belonging to family members and brawling at an *esfoyaza*, a traditional communal gathering to strip leaves from maize.[24]

If the reality was more nuanced than Arlt's vision of the coalfields, the valleys were still starkly different from much of Spain, which continued to be predominantly agricultural. The percentage of Spain's population working in agriculture – over 50 per cent – was aligned with Mediterranean Europe (Italy and Greece) and halfway between the agrarian east of the continent and more industrialized western and northern Europe.[25] As travellers and observers have long remarked, Spain exhibits great geographical and climatological variation from the rainy, fertile valleys of the north to the arid plains of the interior. The different conditions shaped the selection of crops, farming methods and property structures. Market gardening and livestock husbandry tended to characterize the smallholdings of the north. Cereals and legumes were concentrated on the north-central plains – although they were cultivated all over Spain where the topography allowed – and olive trees, vines and fruit trees were mainly grown in Andalusia and on the Mediterranean coast. While large agricultural estates [*latifundia*] are associated with the southern regions of Extremadura, La Mancha and

[22] *La Libertad*, 7 Aug. 1930; *Avance*, 14 Apr. 1932; AHPA, AP, box 97435, file 280 (1934); *Mundo Gráfico*, 1 Sept. 1937. See also R. García Montes' recollections of his father in *Ángeles rojos sin alas para volar* (Siero, 2009), pp. 19–20.

[23] Shubert, *Road*, p. 42; Jove y Canella, *Topografía médica del concejo de San Martín del Rey Aurelio*, p. 142.

[24] J. M. Jove y Canella, *Topografía médica del concejo de Laviana* (Madrid, 1927) p. 63; AHPA, AP, box 78437, file 335 (1934) and box 79435, file 319 (1934). For a description of an *esfoyaza*, see Jove y Canella, *Topografía médica del concejo de San Martín del Rey Aurelio*, p. 65.

[25] L. Boswell, 'Rural society in crisis', in *The Oxford Handbook of European history, 1914–1945*, ed. N. Doumanis (Oxford, 2016), p. 245.

Andalusia, even in these areas the size of farms varied greatly.[26] Although less than one per cent of the landowners possessed nearly half of the agricultural land of Jaén province, the presence of small tenants and sharecroppers should not be overlooked.[27] Likewise, small farms [*minifundia*] populated the valleys and rolling hills of the northern coast, but there were also important differences between regions like Galicia and the Basque Country. Whereas family farms were indivisible and passed to the eldest son in the latter, Galician smallholdings were 'minute' and subject to 'fragmented ownership'. The subdivision of plots stimulated emigration abroad to escape poverty.[28]

The dependence on agriculture traditionally resulted in a portrait of Spain as economically backward and stagnant, but recent research has depicted instead a country experiencing uneven development and highlighted the evolving nature of the agricultural sector. Mechanization and the use of artificial fertilizers were underdeveloped, but expanded during the early twentieth century, while at the same time agriculture became increasingly oriented towards a capitalist market economy.[29] Land dedicated to agriculture increased by nearly a third between 1900 and 1939, and market demands stimulated a gradual shift towards cultivating more profitable products, which in Asturias translated into an increase in cattle production as peasants slowly became integrated into capitalist market dynamics.[30] The number of landless agricultural labourers who worked the large estates in the south was in long-term decline, even if their underemployment, poverty and thirst for land posed an important problem for the governments of the Second Republic. The Spanish economy thus followed a 'Mediterranean path' of development, characterized by sluggish but consistent growth

[26] As noted early on by E. Malefakis in *Agrarian Reform and Peasant Revolution in Spain: Origins of the Spanish Civil War* (New Haven, Conn., 1970), pp. 35–6, and frequently emphasized since.

[27] F. Cobo Romero, *De campesinos a electores: modernización agraria en Andalucía, politización campesina y derechización de los pequeños propietarios y arrendatarios: el caso de la provincia de Jaén, 1931–1936* (Madrid, 2003), p. 133.

[28] This summary is based on J. Simpson, *Spanish Agriculture: the Long Siesta, 1765–1965* (Cambridge, 1995), ch. 2. For more detail on Ourense, see J. Prada Rodríguez, *De la agitación republicana a la represión franquista (Ourense 1934–1939)* (Barcelona, 2006), pp. 12–13.

[29] Simpson, *Spanish Agriculture*, chs 5 and 7.

[30] F. Sánchez Marroyo, *La España del siglo XX: economía, demografía y sociedad* (Madrid, 2003), p. 41. For the shift from cereals to wine in La Mancha, see F. Rey, *Paisanos en lucha: exclusión política y violencia en la Segunda República española* (Madrid, 2008), p. 31 and for the preference for almonds in Andalusia, see Cobo Romero, *De campesinos*, pp. 89–90. See also Shubert, *Social History*, p. 13. On Asturias, see J. Uría, 'Asturias, 1898–1914: el fin de un campesinado amable', *Hispania*, lxii (2002), 1059–98.

compared to its northern European neighbours. Rapid transformation of the agrarian sector would only occur during the 1950s and 1960s.[31]

As the economy evolved during the first third of the twentieth century, Spain underwent an important demographic transformation. Between 1900 and 1931, the population increased from 18.5 million to 23.5 million, facilitated by a decrease in the death rate. Cities across the country expanded.[32] Madrid nearly doubled in size, rising from 540,000 to almost one million inhabitants, alongside provincial capitals like Zaragoza and Córdoba, which swelled from 99,000 and 58,000 to 173,000 and 103,000 inhabitants respectively. Barcelona's industrial complexes attracted labour from southern Spain in search of job opportunities, with the result that a third of the city's residents were not Catalan by birth in 1930.[33] The Asturian coalfields mirrored these wider demographic trends. During the first third of the century, the number of inhabitants of Mieres, San Martín del Rey Aurelio and Langreo more than doubled; in the latter, the population increased from 19,000 to over 39,000. By 1930 the principal coalfield municipalities totalled over 140,000 residents, while 75,000 lived in the municipal district of Oviedo – 42,000 in the capital itself.[34]

The swelling population posed a significant challenge for housing and infrastructure in the coalfields. Some of the mining companies had financed housing, schools, medical services, company shops, churches, water supplies, washing facilities, and even posts for the national police force, the Civil Guard.[35] However, provision was uneven. Not all areas bore the same imprint of paternalism as Turón, where every 'manifestation of cultural or mechanical labour' in the valley allegedly had the 'constant and determined support' of the mining company Hulleras del Turón.[36] Some historians have tended to understand these paternalistic practices reductively as an attempt to inhibit the growth of socialist politics, but this fails to account for why paternalism shrank from the First World War onwards just as the socialist

[31] See Tortella, *Development*; Sánchez Marroyo, *España*, p. 26.

[32] Shubert, *Social History*, p. 23.

[33] Ealham, *Class*, p. 4.

[34] 'Alteraciones de los municipios en los censos de población desde 1842' <http://www.ine.es/intercensal/> [accessed 5 May 2017].

[35] For a contemporary description of Aller, see Nevares, *El patrono*, pp. 42–4. For a recent analysis, see J. Muñiz Sánchez, *Del pozo a casa: genealogías del paternalismo minero contemporáneo en Asturias* (Gijón, 2007). On housing, see e.g., J. Sierra Álvarez, 'Política de vivienda y políticas industriales paternalistas', *Ería*, viii (1985), 61–71. On education, see e.g., M. V. Álvarez Fernández, *La escuela del paternalismo industrial asturiano (1880–1937)* (Gijón, 2006).

[36] *Región*, 24 June 1931.

mining union expanded and sought recognition.[37] More convincingly, paternalism was a form of 'social engineering' designed to attract and 'fix' an agricultural society to industrial discipline, and the paternalist drive was considered less necessary during the boom of immigrant labour during the First World War.[38] By the 1930s, paternalism was limited to the building of schools, company shops and housing, although provision of the latter continued to be uneven, piecemeal and never sufficient for the needs of the local population.

Company decisions on industrial development shaped patterns of urbanization in the coalfields. As coal pits were sunk, urban density increased on the valley floors, although the lack of overall investment in housing meant that many mineworkers continued to live in the villages clinging to the steep valley-sides. The peculiar case of Aller demonstrates how company decisions on industrial development determined settlement patterns. In the Aller valley, Sociedad Hullera Española (SHE) had resisted the construction of a railway to prevent the emergence of larger conurbations and what the company perceived to be associated vices, including socialism.[39] This resistance, combined with the lack of pits, meant that urban settlements in Aller did not reach the size of their counterparts in Mieres and Langreo.

Yet even the more densely populated areas in the coalfields did not see the emergence of large urban centres. Residential patterns resembled the valleys of south Wales rather than the large conurbations of the Ruhr or the self-contained coal villages in north-east England.[40] A large proportion of the Asturian coalfield population continued to live in villages and hamlets, as Jove y Canella observed in the early 1920s. He calculated that in San Martín del Rey Aurelio a quarter of the 16,000 inhabitants lived in the main urban centres and the rest were distributed among 124 villages and hamlets.[41] San Martín del Rey Aurelio was somewhat exceptional. Forty-seven per cent of the municipality's population lived in settlements of fewer than 100 inhabitants in 1930, which was higher than in Langreo (18 per cent), Mieres (25 per cent) and Laviana (39 per cent). Even so, the largest conurbations in the coalfields in Langreo and Laviana only accommodated

[37] See Shubert, *Road*, ch. 4.

[38] J. Sierra Álvarez, *El obrero soñado: ensayo sobre el paternalismo industrial (Asturias, 1860–1917)* (Madrid, 1990).

[39] Muñiz Sánchez, *Del pozo*, pp. 181, 190.

[40] L. James, *The Politics of Identity and Civil Society in Britain and Germany: the Miners in the Ruhr and South Wales, 1890–1926* (Manchester, 2008), p. 31; Ward, *Unemployment*, p. 9.

[41] Jove y Canella, *Topografía médica del concejo de San Martín del Rey Aurelio*, pp. 49, 50–1, 99.

between 2,000 and 5,000 residents, and represented approximately a third of the municipal population, while in Mieres only 15 per cent resided in the capital.[42] The contrast with the south of Spain is striking. The population of the coalfields was less urbanized than in certain parts of the agricultural south, where day labourers who worked on the large estates often resided in large agro-towns. Three quarters of the population of Jaén province lived in towns of more than 5,000 people, including 70 per cent of the province's day labourers.[43]

The consequences of these settlement patterns in the coalfields were two-fold. First, the coalfield villages were not isolated, self-contained units. It was common for mineworkers to live in one settlement and work in another.[44] Neighbours and local kinship networks did not necessarily overlap with their network of workmates in the pit. Both the place of residence and the workplace were sites of sociability and identification that could form the basis for collective action. Second, the Asturian coalfields were largely formed of small communities in which residents were known to one another. This proximity was a double-edged sword. It could serve to forge solidarity rooted in identification with the community or engender bitter disputes and cleavages. Social pressures and gossip in these small communities could contribute to radicalism.

Social life and politics

In 1931, eleven years after construction had begun, the Casa del Pueblo opened in La Oscura (San Martín del Rey Aurelio). Measuring 1,526m^2, the building was another jewel in the crown of the Asturian socialist movement. The network of Asturian socialist 'Houses of the People' had developed from the first planned Casa del Pueblo in Mieres in 1900 to number sixty-six in the 1930s. Although the size and facilities varied, the Casas del Pueblo, in addition to housing local socialist union and party sections, could offer assembly halls, theatres, co-operatives, libraries, cinemas, schools, sports clubs, choirs and friendly societies to their male and female members.[45]

[42] Shubert, *Road*, p. 66.

[43] Cobo Romero, *De campesinos*, p. 129.

[44] Shubert, *Road*, pp. 66–7.

[45] L. Arias González and M. J. Álvarez García, *Los palacios obreros: Casas del Pueblo socialistas en Asturias, 1902–1937* (Oviedo, 2010), pp. 83–111, 187, 190–3, 196; L. Arias González and F. de Luis Martín, 'Las Casas del Pueblo y sus implicaciones geograficas', *Biblio 3W: Revista bibliográfica de geografía y ciencias sociales*, xv (2010), available at <http://www.ub.edu/geocrit/b3w-884.htm> [accessed 12 Sept. 2018]. For a contemporary overview, see *Boletín de la Unión General de Trabajadores de España*, liii, May 1933.

The Casas del Pueblo were not solely an Asturian phenomenon, although the coalfields possessed a particularly dense, active and well-resourced network of such institutions. They existed across the country and in other parts of Europe, where they had first emerged as meeting rooms for socialist organizations towards the end of the nineteenth century. Often financed by co-operatives or mutual aid societies, they responded to a need for spaces in which to educate, socialize, or organize campaigns.[46] The network of socialist institutions in 'red Vienna' was particularly well developed. By 1931–2, the party had established forty cultural organizations, published 127 newspapers and provided a range of sporting activities for its followers. The objective was to provide cultural education for the working masses in order to forge fit, educated citizens for the Republic and work towards the future establishment of socialism.[47]

The development of the Casas del Pueblo in Asturias came after the consolidation of an embryonic socialist movement at the turn of the century. An Asturian socialist newspaper – *La Aurora Social* – was founded in 1896 and there were over 4,200 Asturian members of the socialist trade union federation, the UGT, by the time the Asturian Socialist Federation (FSA) was established five years later.[48] Mineworkers continued to organize in pit-based unions until the creation of the socialist Mineworkers' Union of Asturias (SOMA) in 1910, which quickly became a powerful voice for the coal miners. The key figure behind the establishment of the SOMA was Manuel Llaneza. His experience in self-imposed exile in northern France after being sacked for striking in Mieres in 1906 convinced him of the need for sector-wide trade unions along the lines of the reformist, centralized Vieux Syndicat. Llaneza was also a prominent advocate of the construction of Casas del Pueblo, for he believed they would draw workers into the socialist sphere, away from both company paternalism and the vices of alcohol and sport.[49]

The SOMA's first decade was successful. It attracted members and achieved improved wages and working conditions. The union initially adopted a combative stance in labour relations, which led to rapid expansion – 10,000 members within two years – and forced the mining companies to recognize

[46] M. Kohn, *Radical Space: Building the House of the People* (Ithaca, N.Y., 2003), pp. 95ff.

[47] Gruber is nevertheless skeptical as to the achievements of these organizations, see H. Gruber, *Red Vienna: Experiment in Working Class Culture, 1919–1934* (New York, 1991), ch. 4.

[48] Shubert, *Road*, p. 108.

[49] J. Muñiz Sánchez, 'Encontrando el Norte: Manuel Llaneza y la influencia francesa en el sindicalismo español de principios del siglo XX', *Hispania: Revista española de historia*, lxix (2009), 793–820. For the early history of the SOMA, see also E. Moradiellos, *El Sindicato de los Obreros Mineros de Asturias, 1910–1930* (Oviedo, 1986).

the union as the legitimate representative of the workforce. The SOMA then assumed a more moderate and reformist approach in accordance with the strategy of the UGT and the philosophy of Spanish socialism as a whole. By 1919, it boasted 29,000 members out of a mining workforce of 35,000, for whom it had managed to secure the historic achievement of a seven-hour working day in the mines.[50] The union's growth aided the consolidation of socialism in the coalfields. In elections held in 1918, the PSOE had obtained 40 per cent of the vote in Mieres and San Martín del Rey Aurelio.[51]

Yet political and economic circumstances conspired to throw the SOMA into crisis during the next decade. The post-war contraction in the coal industry led companies to dismiss thousands of mineworkers and repeatedly cut wages, while the Communist call for the left to join the Third International caused a traumatic split in the Spanish socialist movement. The SOMA hierarchy struggled to respond to these challenges, which produced wildcat strikes and infighting for control of the union between 1920 and 1922. The expulsion of twenty-one SOMA sections did not resolve the union's woes and membership continued to slide. It had collapsed from nearly 30,000 in 1919 to 7,000 in 1922, before recovering to 12,000 two years later and then slipping again to 8,000 in 1926.[52]

Llaneza met with Primo de Rivera soon after he seized power in 1923, but socialist co-operation with the regime, including participation in the corporatist mechanisms of the dictatorship, did not improve the fortunes of the SOMA. Socialists defended co-operation with the dictatorship on the basis of defending workers and protecting their organizations. While the UGT maintained a similar level of membership in 1928 compared to 1922, such a situation was not reflected in Asturias, where the SOMA was incapable of defending mineworkers from short-time working, closures and layoffs.[53] Primo de Rivera's decision in 1927 to withdraw the seven-hour day tested SOMA's moderation further. The union executive finally decided to organize a strike, but only thanks to rank-and-file pressure.[54]

The SOMA's fortunes changed at the end of the decade, thanks to the socialist movement shifting to oppose the dictatorship, although the

[50] Shubert, *Road*, p. 112.

[51] A. R. Felgueroso Durán and A. Fernández García, 'La gestión de los socialistas en el Ayuntamiento de Langreo entre 1909 y 1936', in *Historia del socialismo en Langreo 1897–1997*, ed. A. Fernández García and J. Girón (Gijón, 1997), pp. 153–4.

[52] Shubert, *Road*, p. 133.

[53] J. L. Martín Ramos, *Historia de la UGT*, ii: *Entre la revolución y el reformismo, 1914–1931* (6 vols, Madrid, 2008), p. 157.

[54] Shubert, *Road*, ch. 6.

SOMA continued to advocate moderation. The union's membership doubled between 1930 and 1932, by which time it claimed 21,000 members and 69 per cent of the workforce, cementing its position as the primary trade union force in the coalfields.[55] The spectacular recovery in the SOMA appeared to be the result of returning former members. Growth in the wider UGT, which reached over one million members in June 1932, came from newcomers to the union, particularly in rural areas via the National Federation of Landworkers (FNTT).[56]

The main rival to the socialist unions both in Asturias and at a national level was the anarchist movement, whose presence in Spain stretched back to the 1870s. United by a desire to emancipate citizens through abolishing capitalism and authority – identified with the state and the Church – and establishing libertarian communism, anarchism nevertheless remained a heterogeneous movement. In 1910, syndicalists founded Spanish anarchism's most prominent organization – the National Confederation of Labour (CNT) – which sought to use direct action to gain material improvements for workers and further the anarchist cause. The CNT swelled to over 700,000 members at the end of the decade, before entering a spiralling crisis of radicalization and repression in the early 1920s. The Primo de Rivera dictatorship forced the union underground. After legalization in 1930, the CNT again grew rapidly to boast 800,000 members by the end of 1931.[57]

Anarchism had two particular strongholds in Asturias, whose differences reflected an important division within the overall movement. The port city of Gijón had long been the centre for a moderate syndicalism that was open to collaborating with socialists and in 1919 a prominent local anarchist and educator, Eleuterio Quintanilla, had proposed unification with the socialist movement. This is important, for the impulse behind the Asturian Workers' Alliance signed in spring 1934 originated in the Gijonese anarchist movement. In contrast, the anarchists of the iron and steel town of La Felguera were associated with the more radical, voluntarist and doctrinaire FAI (Iberian Anarchist Federation) – a clandestine organization of small affinity groups formed in 1927.[58] Anarchism had a greater hegemony over the steelworkers in La Felguera than over the mineworkers. The CNT-affiliated

[55] Shubert, *Road*, pp. 135, 142.

[56] M. Bizcarrondo, *Historia de la UGT*, iii. *Entre la democracia y la revolución, 1931–1936* (6 vols, Madrid, 2008), p. 18.

[57] J. Casanova, *Anarchism, the Republic and Civil War in Spain (1931–1939)* (Abingdon, 2004), p. 51.

[58] For anarchism in Asturias, see Á. Barrio Alonso, *Anarquismo y anarcosindicalismo en Asturias (1890–1936)* (Madrid, 1988).

mining union – the Mineworkers' Single Union (SUM) – vied with the SOMA for mineworkers' support but had much fewer members. While most rank-and-file SUM members were anarchists, in reality the union had been a coalition of anarchists and Communists since its creation in 1922 from the twenty-one sections expelled from the SOMA. Membership of the SUM swelled to 9,000 in June 1931 – just over a year after it was authorized to operate – yet this also coincided with the eruption during a strike of underlying tensions within the union due to an unstable combination of a largely anarchist rank and file and a Communist leadership.[59]

Even though the coalfields were an area of relative strength for the official Communist Party of Spain (PCE), the movement was small both in Asturias and in Spain as a whole. Throughout the 1920s, Asturian Communists struggled in the face of harassment by the state, frictions with the socialists and internal disagreement, which continued through the beginning of the Republic. There were less than a thousand members of the PCE in Asturias in 1932 and just over a thousand in the Communist Youth (JC).[60] The weakness of the PCE was also evident in its lack of bricks-and-mortar institutions when compared to the socialist Casas del Pueblo. Communists organized meetings and rallies in cinemas, theatres and bars, as did anarchists outside their stronghold of La Felguera, where 'La Justicia' was the hub for anarchist activity and was frequently raided by the police.

There was a third mineworkers' union beyond the SOMA and the SUM: the Catholic Mineworkers' Union (SCOM). The SCOM had been created in response to SOMA's attempts to organize mineworkers employed by Sociedad Hullera Española in Aller. SHE rejected proposals for an independent Catholic organization from one Spain's leading social Catholic voices, Maximiliano Arboleya, in favour of a yellow union that was amenable to the employers. The struggle between the SOMA and the SCOM in Aller culminated in a shootout in Moreda in 1920, by which time the SCOM had already reached its peak level of influence. Thereafter the SCOM's membership declined despite the favourable Catholic corporatist climate of the Primo de Rivera dictatorship. By 1932, it could only muster half of the 2,300 members it had claimed in 1919.[61] During the 1930s, the SCOM maintained a union centre in Moreda, but the main trace of its

[59] For the SUM, see C. Álvarez, *El Sindicato Único de Mineros de Asturias* (Oviedo, 2004).

[60] See F. Erice, 'El PCE en Asturias, de los orígenes a la guerra civil', in *Los comunistas en Asturias (1920–1982)*, ed. F. Erice (Gijón, 1996), pp. 41–84.

[61] A. Shubert, 'Entre Arboleya y Comillas: el fracaso del sindicalismo católico en Asturias', in *Octubre 1934: cincuenta años para la reflexión*, ed. G. Jackson et al. (Madrid, 1985), pp. 243–52. See also D. Benavides, *El fracaso social del catolicismo español: Arboleya Martínez, 1870–1951* (Barcelona, 1973).

public life was through opinion pieces published in *Región* penned by Vicente Madera Peña, SCOM leader and cousin of Ramón González Peña, a SOMA leader and so-called *generalísimo* of the Asturian October.

The centres operated by the trade unions constituted one hub of associational life and political and cultural education in the coalfields. Their main rival was the *ateneo*, which was a liberal, interclass cultural centre that tended to propagate Republican ideals and had its roots in the nineteenth century. The *ateneos* formed part of a constellation of initiatives including lending libraries and cultural associations that focused on enlightening citizens through education and culture, and which mushroomed during the 1930s. *Ateneos* appeared in neighbourhoods like working-class La Argañosa in Oviedo and settlements like La Canga in Langreo, where the Ateneo Popular and library newly inaugurated in 1932 boasted a membership of twenty-eight in a hamlet of only twenty-six inhabitants.[62] Membership levels were high, but overwhelmingly male. The *ateneos* in Mieres and Turón claimed 1,000 and 800 members respectively in 1932, and in Trubia the Casino-Theatre boasted 2,000. The Ateneo Popular in Mieres controversially voted to admit women members in autumn 1932, although they were only permitted to attend talks – and indeed, there were lectures on topics including women's health and rights.[63] Young women nevertheless were often an integral part of initiatives like theatre groups (*cuadros artísticos*).[64]

The *ateneos* were founded on a desire for collective self-improvement shared across Republicanism and the left. As one 'son of Langreo' declared, the 'weapon' of the time was the 'book, the newspaper'.[65] *Ateneos* organized a range of activities, including lectures, music and theatre, and frequently housed a reading room or library and often a radio.[66] Theatrical performances helped to mould and cement left-wing political values through social and political criticism, including the propagation of anticlerical ideas.[67] As in

[62] *El Noroeste*, 19 Oct. 1932.

[63] Á. Mato Díaz, *La Atenas del norte: ateneos, sociedades culturales y bibliotecas populares en Asturias (1876–1937)* (Oviedo, 2008), p. 96; *El Noroeste*, 20 Jan. 1932. For lectures on women's issues, see e.g., *El Noroeste*, 27 Aug. 1931, 18, 26 Feb. 1932.

[64] For a Communist *cuadro*, see e.g., *El Noroeste*, 10 June 1932.

[65] *El Noroeste*, 5 May 1931. For a similar focus in the Austrian socialist movement, see Gruber, *Red Vienna*, p. 87.

[66] For the installation of radios in *ateneos* in Trubia and Mieres, see *El Noroeste*, 9 Sept. 1931 and *Región*, 4 May 1932.

[67] See Uría, 'Traditional popular culture and industrial work discipline', in *A Social History of Spanish Labour: New Perspectives on Class, Politics and Gender*, ed. J. A. Piqueras and V. Sanz Rozalén (New York, 2007), pp. 166–7.

Vienna, where over 80 per cent of books loaned from socialist libraries were novels and poetry, there was a strong preference for literature over politics and economics. Popular authors included Vicente Blasco Ibáñez and Benito Pérez Galdós, whose works had a decidedly anticlerical flavour.[68] *Ateneos* emphasized their eschewal of formal politics, yet political debate was difficult to avoid in the 1930s, not least given that the membership of *ateneos* overlapped with that of parties and unions. The Ateneo Popular in Oviedo elected Javier Bueno as its president in 1934. Bueno was the editor of the socialist newspaper *Avance* and renowned for his radical views.[69]

Outside the workplace, *ateneos* and Casas del Pueblo vied with the football pitch, brothel and tavern as spaces of masculine leisure and sociability.[70] Bars were ubiquitous – Dr Jove y Canella claimed that there were no hamlets without a bar in San Martín del Rey Aurelio – and central to male working-class sociability. Bars were sites of leisure, but also places to find work and of political education, even if unions and political parties disapproved of bars as a vice-ridden distraction from politics.[71] Women's spaces of sociability are often hidden from view in the sources. Women would have come into contact through daily chores and errands imposed by running the household and caring for family members.[72] The riverbank or public washhouses were particularly important as sites where women gathered to talk as they laundered clothes.[73] Trade unions for women were formed in 1931, including that for seamstresses in the Nalón valley. Female socialist militancy continued to grow throughout 1932. Politically active women had to struggle against misogyny. Women in Laviana created their own socialist section after complaining that the local socialist group would not let them join.[74]

[68] Gruber, *Red Vienna*, p. 95; Uría, 'Cultura', p. 156.

[69] See the encyclopaedic Mato Díaz, *La Atenas*.

[70] For football, see Ruiz, *Octubre*, pp. 222–5. For prostitution and male sociability, see J-L. Guereña, 'El burdel como espacio de sociabilidad', *Hispania*, lxiii (2003), 551–69. Anecdotally, see criticism of the distractions of football and sex from Vegadotos (Mieres) in *La Aurora Social*, 24 May 1929.

[71] Jove y Canella, *Topografía médica del concejo de San Martín del Rey Aurelio*, p. 59; Uría, 'Asturias 1920–1937', p. 272 and his 'La taberna en Asturias a principios del siglo XX: notas para su estudio', *Historia contemporánea*, v (1991), pp. 64–7. For southern Spain, see J. Sierra Álvarez, '"Rough characters": miners, alcohol and violence in Linares at the end of the nineteenth century', in Piqueras and Sanz Rozalén, *Social History*, pp. 176–96.

[72] As in Gijón, see Radcliff, *Mobilization*, p. 98.

[73] Women also petitioned for improved washing facilities (*El Noroeste*, 27 March, 6 Apr. 1932).

[74] M. A. Mateos, *¡Salud, compañeras! Mujeres socialistas en Asturias (1900–1937)* (Oviedo, 2007), pp. 108–10, 129–30; *Avance*, 8 May, 15 June 1932.

Ateneos and bars attracted more heterogeneous crowds than the Casas del Pueblo, although the socialists did not limit themselves solely to the latter – the 'Red Bar' in Sama was a meeting place for Communists and the left in general.[75] Due to patterns of urban settlement and the organization of mining trade unions, there was no stark separation of individuals of different political affiliation in such spaces of sociability, at the workplace or at the level of the locality. Mining trade union sections were small and organized at the level of the locality. Whereas the CNT metalworkers' union in La Felguera claimed 3,000 members, the CNT-affiliated SUM in Ciaño-Santa-Ana had only twenty-five.[76] In the municipal district of San Martín del Rey Aurelio, there were nineteen SOMA sections for a population of less than 17,000.[77] Even as certain localities are associated with the predominance of a particular political culture, such as anarchism in La Felguera and Communism in Turón, pockets of Communism and anarchism coexisted with socialism throughout the valleys. The resultant image of the coalfields is one in which small communities predominated and where ideological rivals coexisted in villages and at the workplace. Such a picture is different to how scholars have sketched the relationship between social groups and political positions in the German-speaking lands and the Low Countries. Through 'pillarization' and 'milieu' they have argued for the close correlation of politics with the life-world of particular groups: each had its own values, spaces of sociability, institutions and representatives and was segregated from others.[78]

The effect of the patterns of residence, sociability and political and union affiliation in the coal valleys was that rivals tended to know one another intimately. In the slurs and attacks printed in the provincial press, they revealed a familiarity with the background and trajectories of their neighbours and political rivals.[79] Sabino Menéndez, a PCE member, used one such intimate encounter to challenge socialists to an open debate. He alleged that he was 'calmly' discussing politics at the annual La Laguna fiesta in Ciaño-Santa Ana when a group of drunken socialists approached him. Menéndez touched one of them on the arm in a sign of friendship,

[75] Erice, 'El PCE', p. 77.

[76] M. Villar, *El anarquismo en la insurrección de Asturias: la CNT y la FAI en octubre de 1934* (Madrid, 1994 [1935]), p. 68; *El Noroeste*, 2 March 1932.

[77] *La Aurora Social*, 16 Oct. 1931.

[78] The idea of pillarization has been the subject of some debate. For a critique, see J. C. H. Blom, 'Pillarisation in perspective', *West European Politics*, xxiii (2000), pp. 153–164. For a comparative discussion of milieux in the Ruhr and South Wales, see James, *Politics*, pp. 4–6.

[79] E.g. criticism of Benjamín Escobar, *Avance*, 25 June 1932.

but was brushed off with the comment, 'do not touch me; you'll defile me'.[80] The details were doubtless exaggerated, but encounters with rivals were nevertheless a quotidian occurrence, as a Communist warned rival anarchists: 'they forget … that we communists do not live on the moon, that we go to the workshop, mine and factory to work alongside our exploited companions, and it is there that we think of ways of mitigating our state of slavery'.[81]

Rivalry and conflict did not correlate with separation or estrangement, which is important for comprehending the dynamics of radicalism in the coalfields during the Republic. On the one hand, familiarity with a neighbour's background could provide fuel for impugning his anticlerical credentials and lead to radicalism, as chapter 3 will examine. On the other, familiarity with a rival who was more than a faceless socialist, anarchist or Communist could lay the foundations for solidarity and collaboration, which would emerge at the level of the workplace in 1933 and 1934. In the coalfields, the face-to-face communities and intersecting networks, combined with certain shared practices and values, explain the bitterness of the disputes, even though engagement could also open the door to mutual understanding. This is suggestive of the 'volatile intimacy' Radcliff used to describe the violent encounters between political opponents in Gijón. The blows exchanged suggested the 'existence of community ties, not their disintegration'.[82]

Later alliances between union rivals built on not only on the inhabitation of the same social spaces, but also shared values and practices across the left. This left-wing culture provided a common idiom through which different groups communicated and bitterly disagreed with one another. Rivals engaged with one another at the local level in a fractious and unstable form of grassroots 'democracy', characterized by a combination of dialogue and confrontation. During strikes, mineworkers from different unions participated in workplace assemblies to debate, and elect representatives to negotiate on their behalf.[83] More confrontational were the *controversias* – a form of verbal sparring in which local union or political figures debated formally and struggled to influence an expectant and critical audience. At times activists disrupted rival union meetings by shouting slogans and

[80] *El Noroeste*, 15 July 1932.

[81] *El Noroeste*, 21 Aug. 1932.

[82] Radcliff, *Mobilization*, p. 98.

[83] E.g. at Carbones La Nueva in 1933 the SOMA was chosen to represent the whole workforce, as it it represented 90% of mineworkers (*Avance*, 17 Aug. 1933).

demands for a platform for debate in an improvised *controversia*.[84] The ritualized rhetorical boxing of a *controversia* frequently descended into bitter conflict, as revealed in an observer's surprise at the good-natured atmosphere during an impromptu debate at a CNT rally in Barros (Langreo), at which all three speakers shook hands: 'a wonderful example of magnanimity … if only it was always thus!'[85]

Together the *controversias* and workplace assemblies provided the structures of a grassroots democratic culture, based not on consensus, but on dialogue and confrontation. Yet there was an interest in engaging with opposing ideas and sufficient openness and respect for two cathedral canons to be invited to the Communist stronghold of Turón to speak at the Ateneo on separate occasions. They both commented on how respectfully they were treated.[86] Two years later the most violent episode of anticlerical bloodletting during the revolutionary insurrection occurred in this same valley.[87]

There were significant frictions between the socialist, anarchist and Communist movements, but the differences between them at the local level could be difficult to identify. Boundaries were often more blurred than neat political labels imply, even if rivalries were very real. A more nebulous reality is unsurprising given that working-class movements across Europe were 'eclectic' and 'autodidactic' at the grassroots.[88] As Jorge Uría acknowledged, it is difficult to disentangle a specific Communist culture from a wider 'radical culture' in the coalfields.[89] PCE distinctiveness came in part through performing the self-image of the PCE member as a disciplined, austere and self-sacrificing activistas opposed to possessing a thorough knowledge of Communist doctrine, not least because key concepts like 'soviet' were not always well understood by the rank and file.[90]

An interest in the Soviet experiment was far from the exclusive domain of the Communists. In early 1932, Florentino Moral and Antonio Seoane gave a series of talks in the theatres and union centres of the coalfields on their impressions of their two-month visit to Russia (paid for by the International

[84] E.g. Communist disruption of a socialist meeting in Blimea (*El Noroeste*, 12 May 1932).

[85] *El Noroeste*, 14 May 1932.

[86] *Región*, 2, 30 Apr. 1932.

[87] For Arboleya's later reflections, see D. Benavides, 'Arboleya y su interpretación de la Revolución de Octubre', in Jackson, *Octubre*, pp. 259–60.

[88] G. Eley, *Forging Democracy: the History of the Left in Europe, 1850–2000* (Oxford, 2002), p. 46.

[89] See Uría, 'Asturias 1920–1937', pp. 250–9.

[90] For Communist culture, see R. Cruz, *El Partido Comunista de España en la Segunda República* (Madrid, 1987), pp. 77–9, 86.

Association of Friends of the Soviet Union). The talks were well attended by interested workers from across the left. The travellers' political affiliations were important. They had been elected at public assemblies to visit the USSR as objective – even critical – observers and 'authentic workers' in order to cut through polarized reports of the realities of the Soviet experiment.[91] The SOMA in Laviana ceded space for Moral to speak 'because he [was] not a Communist activist'.[92] Stressing this alleged neutrality was common. Most loquacious was PCE member Olegario Vega: 'The workers of Ciaño-Santa Ana said that no one could provide an account as impartial as Florentino, as he is an authentic worker, a metalworker and free of all prejudices that produce passion for one side or the other'.[93] It is possible that Moral was secretly a Communist, but the emphasis on authenticity and independence is nevertheless revealing of the interplay between the desire for objective knowledge of the USSR and anxieties over Communist proselytizing.

Beyond an interest in the Soviet Union, which ranged from critical and reserved curiosity to whole-hearted enthusiasm, there were shared reference points and practices across the left. At the most fundamental level all three movements promoted class-based solidarity, which was a matter of collective and personal pride. Newspapers published lists of contributors to strike funds and one worker even wrote to *El Noroeste* to correct the appearance of his name next to a 0.25-peseta donation. He had actually handed over a peseta and the confusion originated in two workers sharing the same name.[94] In 1933, a collective barbershop opened in Mieres offering free haircuts to the unemployed while municipal workers in Sama decided to donate a percentage of their wages to those out of work.[95] A commitment to anti-militarism meant that anti-war committees included delegates from a variety of groups, as in Mieres, where it represented Radical Socialists, Communists, socialists, cultural institutions, trade unions and local choirs.[96] Processions, banners and speeches honouring the working class on 1 May were an established tradition, although unions tended to organize separate celebrations.

One of the cornerstones of Spanish left-wing political culture was a commitment to secular or even anticlerical values. Activists expressed their values in ceremonies marking milestones in their own lives, facilitated by

[91] *El Noroeste*, 6, 10 Jan. 1932. Moral was even interviewed in *Región*, 16 Feb. 1932.

[92] *El Noroeste*, 12 March 1932. See also in Turón, *El Noroeste*, 6 Apr. 1932.

[93] *El Noroeste*, 17 Feb. 1932.

[94] *El Noroeste*, 23 Apr. 1932.

[95] *Avance*, 1 Feb., 22, 28 June 1933.

[96] *Avance*, 18 Oct. 1933.

the Republic's establishment of civil marriage as the default option. There are few details of these rites of passage in the press, but the description of the wedding of Gloria Orviz and José González provides a glimpse of what they could be like. The celebration included an 'intimate meal' in the 'Red Bar' – the local Communist haunt – attended by 200 guests. Two 'enormous portraits' of Lenin and Stalin against a red cloth presided over the meal and the well-wishing speech was followed by a collective intonation of *The Internationale* accompanied by the gramophone and dancing.[97] Such practices served to integrate individuals into particular political communities and cement left-wing identities.

This image of a left-wing working-class community that marched behind banners on 1 May, assiduously attended talks on international politics at the local *ateneo* and thumbed novels penned by Zola and Dumas does not tell the whole story of the coalfields. Left-wing culture predominated sufficiently for activists to project it onto their understanding of the community, yet hegemony did not signify a monopoly. The political right and Catholicism offered different world-views and visions of the community and both existed in the coalfields, although historians have hitherto neglected their presence. Catholic activists claimed to have obtained 2,000 and 3,300 signatures protesting against the secularizing intentions of the Republic in Ciaño-Santa Ana and Moreda respectively, both of which were areas of important socialist influence.[98]

To a certain extent, the Catholic community appeared separated from those exhibiting secular or anticlerical values. Catholic organizations and local elites maintained their own networks for charitable work and spaces for sociability, such as associations for the alumni of Catholic schools, or *casinos* – clubs for the middle and upper classes.[99] Overall, however, the working class far outnumbered middle-class residents of the coalfields and the Catholic community was less formally organized than the left. Catholic Youth circles were not created in coalfield towns until the end of 1931.[100] Catholicism continued to be woven into the physical fabric of the valleys and the lives of residents via the network of parish churches, shrines and the schools. The latter, owned by mining companies and staffed by religious orders and congregations, namely the Brothers of the Christian

[97] *El Noroeste*, 29 June 1932. For 'red baptisms' and 'red confirmations', see Cruz, *El Partido*, p. 88.

[98] *Región*, 14 June, 6 July 1931.

[99] The situation is complicated as some working class institutions also employed casino as a descriptor, like the Casino Obrero in Trubia.

[100] For the Catholic Youth, see *Región*, 24 Nov., 11 Dec. 1931.

Doctrine (de la Salle Brothers) and Dominicans, served over 5,000 children in the 1932–3 school year and inevitably catered for left-wing families.[101] Catholic schooling would become an important point of contention in 1932. Moreover, the liturgical calendar still had an imprint on social life in the valleys. Although many Holy Week processions disappeared from public space during the Republic, processions of children making their first communion or celebrating Corpus Christi were annual events – in 1931 300 and 400 children processed in Moreda and Ciaño respectively.[102] Catholicism maintained a public presence even in areas with a 'red' reputation. Grappling with the right and the Church would prove to be at the heart of radicalization between 1932 and 1934.

Catholicism did not suffuse local society in the coalfields as it did in other parts of Spain where 'the village and the parish were conterminous'.[103] In areas like the Basque town of Villava – a stronghold of the ultra-conservative, Catholic and monarchist Carlist movement – or the Andalusian village of Casas Viejas, where 'Catholic ritual and canon were interwoven into daily life', Catholic rituals could mark belonging to and the reproduction of a Catholic notion of community.[104] This did not necessarily mean regular attendance at mass, but rituals that marked the life course, like baptisms and funerals, or the practices of popular religiosity, such as leaving votive candles at local shrines.[105]

Comparing the Asturian coalfields with such areas throws the polarizing division over religion in the latter into sharp relief, which is clearer still when the valleys are contrasted with other mining regions. In Spain – and the coalfields in particular – the secular–religious divide mapped onto the left–right political cleavage in Spain with relative clarity, given Catholicism's close association with the monarchy and conservatism. In the Ruhr, religion was a divisive and fragmentary factor. Sectarianism was more important than a secular–religious divide. The Catholic–Protestant fracture existed both horizontally within the workforce and vertically, as pit owners were usually Protestant, while the workforce was further fragmented by ethnicity

[101] Á. Mato Díaz, *La escuela primaria en Asturias (1923–1937): los procesos de alfabetización y escolarización* (Oviedo, 1992), p. 205.

[102] *Región*, 3 June 1931.

[103] F. Lannon, *Privilege, Persecution and Prophecy: the Catholic Church in Spain, 1875–1975* (Oxford, 1987), p. 20. See also M. Vincent, *Catholicism in the Second Spanish Republic: Religion and Politics in Salamanca, 1930–1936* (Oxford, 1996).

[104] J. Mintz, *The Anarchists of Casas Viejas* (Bloomington, Ind., 1994 [1982]), p. 67; J. Balduz, *Segunda República y Guerra Civil en Villava (1931–1939)* (Villava, 2006).

[105] See Lannon, *Privilege*, p. 24. For popular religiosity and community in a later period, see W. A. Christian, *Person and God in a Spanish Valley* (New York, 1972).

– Polish Catholics had their own ministers. In Wales, in contrast, nonconformism had provided 'social cement' in mining villages and 'cut across … ethnic divisions'. Religious institutions did not attempt to rival the clubs and activities as they did in Ruhr, where society was much more 'rigidly divided'.[106]

Whatever their ideological persuasion, individuals in the coalfields mapped their beliefs onto the community. Local identity served as a battleground, for it constituted a common point of reference for different ideologies and groups. The community identity associated with originating or inhabiting a particular locality was particularly sharply drawn on the occasion of the annual feast of the patron saint of the town or village, which combined civic and 'profane' acts with masses and processions. Special two-page spreads in local newspapers attempted to capture the essence and character of the *pueblo* while young males engaged in the traditional forging of masculine bonds and affirmation of community identity by brawling with outsiders who descended on the locality to partake in the festivities.[107] The strong sense of a geographically rooted community based on residence was also betrayed by anxieties about vagrants, beggars and the unemployed from 'outside', which were expressed from left and right.[108] Yet concerns over alleged outsiders did not preclude solidarity. One of the core principles of left-wing organizations was to build solidarity between workers, whether on a local, regional or transnational level. The introduction of tourism societies to the coalfields was a strategy that sought to overcome localist impulses and encourage enlightened attitudes by arranging trips that aimed to forge fraternal bonds between towns.[109]

As a point of reference, the 'community' was also an arbiter that was invoked in the context of local political struggles and strikes. The *pueblo* had a moral authority that could confer legitimacy on conflicts. In Tudela Veguín, in the midst of the cement factory strike, a meeting was held so that

[106] James, *Politics*, pp. 34–7. See also S. H. F. Hickey, *Workers in Imperial Germany: the Miners of the Ruhr* (Oxford, 1985), ch. 3. For a comparative overview, see S. Berger, 'Difficult (re-)alignments – comparative perspectives on social democracy and religion from late-nineteenth-century to interwar Germany and Britain', *Journal of Contemporary History*, liii (2018), 574–96.

[107] E.g. *Avance*, 23 July 1932. For fights between youths in the south of Spain, see J. Pitt-Rivers, *The People of the Sierra* (London, 1954), p. 11.

[108] E.g. *Región*, 29 May 1931; *El Noroeste*, 9 March, 1 Apr. 1932. For similar anxieties in southern Spain in the 1950s, see Pitt-Rivers, *People*, p. 27.

[109] E.g. *El Noroeste*, 9, 25 July, 16 Sept. 1931. A Feminist Trip Society in Trubia organized a 400km tour of Asturias for 50 young women employed in domestic service (*Región*, 16 July 1931).

the community could judge the conduct of the strike committee, alleged by the contractors to be 'revolutionaries, troublemakers who the community [*pueblo*] hates'.[110] Appealing to the community as the ultimate guarantor of moral authority was common during the Republic and occurred not only in the context of strike action, but also when coalfield society grappled with the fallout from the repression of the Asturian October.

The springtime of the people

During the election campaign of spring 1931 it seemed highly unlikely that Spain would wake up as a Republic on 14 April. Yet municipal elections succeeded where a botched military uprising supported by a general strike organized by the Republicans and socialists had failed five months earlier. The election campaign was one of intense activity and became a de facto plebiscite on the monarchy.[111] Although the elections returned a majority for monarchist candidates, the widespread vote-rigging, intimidation and manipulation by local bosses in rural areas – a system known as *caciquismo* – meant that clear victories for the Republican–socialist slate in urban areas signalled a defeat for the monarchy. Within two days, King Alfonso XIII had fled into exile (although he believed it to be temporary) and the Republic was proclaimed. Joyous crowds celebrated the results and new regime in a 'popular fiesta' that expressed the 'redemption and emancipation' of the people.[112] The crowds destroyed monarchist symbols, as in Mieres, where portraits of the king were burnt, and renamed public spaces in honour of Republican heroes, as occurred in Sama.[113]

In the Asturian coalfields, the Republican–socialist coalition was victorious and appeared to confirm not only left-wing political hegemony, but also the socialist movement as the most influential political force. The socialists (10) were second to the left Republicans (13) in Langreo, but outnumbered their right Republican (3), monarchist (1), and Communist (3) opponents. In Mieres and Laviana, the socialists formed the largest minority on the council and in San Martín del Rey Aurelio they obtained

[110] *El Noroeste*, 13 Oct. 1931.

[111] R. Cruz, *Una revolución elegante: España 1931* (Madrid, 2014), pp. 63–6; S. Ben-Ami, *The Origins of the Second Republic in Spain* (Oxford, 1978), pp. 213–38.

[112] For the 'popular fiesta', see S. Juliá, *Madrid, 1931–1934: de la fiesta popular a la lucha de clases* (Madrid, 1984), pp. 7–21. For 'redemption and emancipation', see Cruz, *Una revolución*, pp. 74–101.

[113] *El Noroeste*, 15 Apr. 1931; *Región*, 15 Apr. 1931. For similar scenes in Madrid, see *ABC*, 16 Apr. 1931.

an outright majority with fifteen councillors out of twenty-one seats.[114] In Aller and Lena, the results were annulled due to complaints of irregularities and later repeated.[115] Yet political control did not mean a political or cultural monopoly and the underlying conflicts and pressure points at the local level along with the re-emergence of the right would be central to the emergence of radicalism in 1932.

Two-and-a-half months after the municipal elections, the wave of enthusiasm for the young Republic translated into an overwhelming victory for the Republican–socialist coalition in elections for the Constituent Cortes. Even though no party gained an overall majority, the PSOE boasted the most seats (116). The Republican deputies belonged to a number of different parties. Described as a party 'without ideas or ideals', the Radical Party led by Alejandro Lerroux, who had moderated the populist, firebrand views of his youth, followed the socialists with ninety seats. The Radicals possessed a relatively well-developed apparatus on a national level, although they were weak in Asturias. Towards the end of the year, the Radical Party withdrew from government and moved to oppose the government from the centre-right.[116] The left wing of the Radicals had peeled off in 1929 to form the Radical Socialist Party, which was characterized by anticlericalism and left-wing populist Republicanism. The Republican ranks were completed by a number of parties who combined prominent, influential leaders with a small membership, which did not bode well for binding the masses to the new Republic. Prime minister and minister of defence, Manuel Azaña, led the left–Republican party Republican Action, while veteran politicians Niceto Alcalá Zamora and Miguel Maura, who occupied the presidency of the Republic and the ministry of the interior respectively, belonged to the small Liberal Republican Right.[117]

Given the small apparatus and membership of the Republican parties, the socialist movement would provide the 'arm and support' for the Republic.[118] Yet the socialist position towards the Republic was complicated.

[114] For the results, see J. Girón, 'Elecciones y partidos políticos en Asturias, 1890–1936', cited in D. Ruiz et al., *Asturias contemporánea, 1808–1975: Síntesis histórica. Textos y documentos* (Madrid, 1981), p. 118; *La Voz de Asturias*, 14 Apr. 1931.

[115] See *La Voz de Asturias*, 14 Apr., 2 June 1931. For the rerunning of elections, see Ben-Ami, *Origins*, pp. 270–4.

[116] P. Preston, *The Coming of the Spanish Civil War: Reform, Reaction and Revolution in the Second Republic* (London, 1978), p. 98. For the Radical Party, see N. Townson, *The Crisis of Democracy in Spain: Centrist Politics under the Spanish Second Republic* (Brighton, 2000).

[117] For the Republican parties, see J. Avilés Farré, *La izquierda burguesa y la tragedia de la Segunda República* (Madrid, 2006).

[118] L. Araquistaín, *El ocaso de un régimen* (Madrid, 1930), quoted in Bizcarrondo, *Historia*, p. 2.

Reformism, moderation and reliance on the levers of state power – whether through arbitration or representation – had always been hallmarks of Spanish socialist politics, but occupying positions of political power proved a divisive issue during the Primo de Rivera dictatorship and the Republic. Indalecio Prieto, a pragmatic, centrist socialist 'who made no claims to Marxist faith', was appointed minister for the economy alongside two other socialist ministers: Francisco Largo Caballero, a veteran trade unionist leader and now minister of labour, and Fernando de los Ríos, minister of justice. Julián Besteiro, a professor of logic who held a rigid, scientific view of the road to socialism, opposed their position and strongly rejected socialist participation in Republican governments.[119]

Even as the socialists co-operated in the construction of the Republic, they were careful to explain that the Republic of 14 April was not *their* regime. The Republic was a 'kind of capitalist antechamber to Socialism'.[120] Such sentiments were expressed at both the level of national and local politics. In May, Cándido Barbón, a socialist councillor in Mieres, declared socialists to be 'the best and most enthusiastic defenders of the Spanish Republic', yet it was 'still bourgeois and we are socialists'.[121] This sentiment was echoed by González Peña two weeks later at the SOMA congress and reflected the wider position of the socialist movement.[122] Attempting to resolve this tension as the Republic was built and contested would prove to be an important component in radicalization.

Left-wing opposition to the Republic came from the Communist Party and the anarchist movement. The PCE did not have any representatives in the Constituent Cortes and was guided by the isolationist Comintern policy of the Third Period, which rejected collaboration with other parties. Whereas the dissident communists of the tiny Workers' and Peasants' Bloc (BOC) celebrated the arrival of Republican democracy, the PCE rejected the new regime and demanded 'all power to the Soviets!'[123] The anarchists' position was more complex. They welcomed the fall of the monarchy insofar as the Republic would ensure that, at least in principle, unions and

[119] P. Heywood, *Marxism and the Failure of Organised Socialism in Spain, 1879–1936* (Cambridge, 1990), pp. 112–9, the quotation at p. 112.

[120] Heywood, *Marxism*, p. 116.

[121] *La Aurora Social*, 15 May 1931.

[122] *La Aurora Social*, 29 May 1931. See also S. Juliá, '"Preparados para cuando la ocasión se presente": los socialistas y la revolución', in *Violencia política en la España del siglo XX*, ed. S. Juliá (Madrid, 2000), p. 166.

[123] For a summary, see H. García, 'De los soviets a las Cortes: los comunistas ante la República', in *Palabras como puños: la intransigencia política en la Segunda República*, ed. F. del Rey (Madrid, 2011), p. 112.

associations could operate freely.[124] Their criticism of authority, state power and formal political participation made them no friend of the Republic, although this did not stop anarchists from voting in elections, particularly in 1931 and 1936. The CNT grew to a membership of a million in 1932, even as the movement had become mired in divisions over strategy. These differences culminated at the end of summer 1931 with the signing of the 'Treintista' manifesto. The thirty signatories believed in moderation, union discipline and preparation prior to any attempt at revolution. In contrast, a sector of the CNT under the influence of the more radical yet numerically small FAI believed that revolution was nigh. The radical sector prevailed. The *Treintistas* were expelled over the following months and the CNT embarked on a process of 'revolutionary gymnastics' – priming the masses for insurrectionary action. The strategy aimed at revolution through an escalating dynamic of collective action followed by police repression. Between January 1932 and December 1933, the CNT attempted three ill-fated revolutionary movements that tested the Republican authorities.[125]

The challenge to the Republic did not emanate solely from the left. Most of the political right opposed the Republican project. The Catholic, monarchist right coalesced into two main positions: catastrophism and possibilist 'accidentalism'. The former included recalcitrant monarchists, who would form Renovación Española in 1933, and the Carlists, an ultra-conservative movement characterized by its opposition to liberalism and industrial modernity through a defence of monarchism, Catholicism and an idealization of a traditional rural socioeconomic order.[126] The Carlists would be joined by Spanish fascism, whose most prominent, yet still very small, party – Falange Española (FE) – was not founded until 1933. These groups did not believe in an accommodation with the Republic and preferred to plot its violent downfall. Carlist militias engaged in military training from 1931.[127] In contrast, the 'accidentalist' position signified participating in the Republic without actively supporting it. Parliamentary seats could be used to undermine the Republic from within. The 'accidentalist' position was occupied by the parties that coalesced into the first mass Catholic political party in Spanish history: the Confederation of Autonomous Right-Wing Groups (CEDA). Its origins lay in National

[124] Ealham, *Class*, p. 76; Casanova, *Anarchism*, pp. 3–4.

[125] Contrasting interpretations in Casanova, *Anarchism*, pp. 53–83 and Ealham, *Class*, pp. 108–31.

[126] See M. Blinkhorn, *Carlism and Crisis in Spain 1931–1939* (Cambridge, 1975); J. Canal, *El carlismo: dos siglos de contrarrevolución en España* (Madrid, 2000).

[127] Blinkhorn, *Carlism*, p. 63.

Action, an organization created at the end of April 1931 and rebadged as Popular Action (AP) from spring 1932. Under the leadership of José María Gil Robles, a lawyer from Salamanca, AP joined forces with other groups, including the Valencian Regional Right, to form the CEDA in 1933, a loose organization united by the principles of religion, fatherland, order, family, work and property.[128]

Catholicism provided a powerful unifying and mobilizing tool for the political right. That the new regime would reshape the relationship between the Catholic Church and the state was unavoidable, given the established privileges of the Catholic Church, the latter's association with the monarchy and the strong current of secularism and anticlericalism that ran through Spanish Republicanism and the left. Unsurprisingly, the Church met the new regime with apprehension.[129] The hierarchy showed initial caution, which was not always shared by parish priests, as revealed by the many letters to the press criticizing priests for anti-Republican sermons.[130] A significant watershed moment for the 'religious question' occurred on 11–13 May, when the playing of the monarchist national anthem in Madrid sparked a riot and a wave of anticlerical incendiarism that affected convents, religious schools and churches, and spread to Andalusia and the Levante.[131]

The burnings facilitated the reorganization and consolidation of the political right after the proclamation of the Republic thanks to the identified need to defend the Catholic faith, which was galvanized further by the debate over the draft Republican constitution in autumn 1931. The original draft had 'aroused deep clerical apprehension', which worsened over the course of the debate.[132] The new *carta magna* separated the Church and state. It removed state funding of the clergy, dissolved the Jesuit order and placed limitations on others; it asserted state-licensing of marriage, and restricted the public display of faith, such as religious processions. Revision of the Constitution deriving from the self-appointed defence of the Church proved to be the 'rallying cry' for the right and demonstrations took place

[128] For the CEDA, see J. R. Montero, *La CEDA: el catolicismo social y político en la II República* (2 vols, Madrid, 1977).

[129] W. J. Callahan, *The Catholic Church in Spain, 1875–1998* (Washington, D.C., 2000), pp. 276ff. See also Lannon, *Privilege*, pp. 179–80.

[130] E.g. *El Noroeste*, 23 May 1931.

[131] For a summary of incidents, see A. L. López Villaverde, *El gorro frigio y la mitra frente a frente: construcción y diversidad territorial del conflicto político-religioso en la España republicana* (n.p., 2008), pp. 195–203.

[132] Callahan, *Catholic Church*, pp. 286–92, the quotation at 287; for Asturian National Action's response, see *Región*, 8 Oct. 1931.

across Spain.[133] Over the next few months, National Action extended its organization in Asturias and across the country, with newly enfranchised women a particular target for recruitment.[134] In Asturias, women's groups formed in Gijón, Oviedo, Mieres and Avilés in January and February 1932, and female AP activists in Gijón created and ran their own combative newspaper, *Acción*.[135] This combination of right-wing reaction and left-wing anticlericalism was critical to the emergence of radicalism in 1932.

Reform of the relationship between the Church and state was one plank of the policies pursued by the Republican–socialist governments from their offices in the ministries in Madrid. Yet building the new regime was also a local affair. The crowds that celebrated the arrival of the Republic thronged the public galleries at the first municipal council meetings to observe Republican democracy in practice.[136] The new municipal councillors saw themselves as representatives of their local communities and as conduits for a new kind of democratic politics removed from the stagnation and corruption of the monarchy. It was the 'people' who had brought the Republic and they were invoked as the 'driving soul' behind the new regime.[137] Celso Fernández, the republican mayor of Langreo, explained to the press that his priority was to do away with 'old cacique-style techniques' in contracting workers in favour of 'strict justice'.[138] The municipal council chamber would be the platform for the regeneration of Spain.

In the 'red' valleys of the Asturian coalfields, beneath the belching chimneys and smog described by Arlt, mayors and councillors attempted to combine constructing the Republic with negotiating competing pressures from their constituents and the responsibilities of office as workers, political groups and communities agitated and petitioned in favour of their own

[133] Preston, *Coming of the Spanish Civil War*, p. 35. For rallies in Salamanca, see Vincent, *Catholicism*, pp. 180–3.

[134] For the decision to expand in Asturias, see *Región*, 10 Jan. 1932. For Galicia, see E. Grandío Seoane, *Los orígenes de la derecha gallega: la CEDA en Galicia (1931–1936)* (Sada, 1998), pp. 102–6 and for Salamanca, see M. Vincent, 'The politicization of Catholic women in Salamanca, 1931–1936', in *Elites and Power in Twentieth Century Spain: Essays in Honour of Sir Raymond Carr*, ed. F. Lannon and P. Preston (Oxford, 1990), pp. 115–26. See also I. Blasco Herranz, '"Tenemos las armas de nuestra fe y de nuestro amor y patriotismo; pero nos falta algo": la Acción Católica de la Mujer y la participación política en la España del primer tercio del siglo XX', *Historia social*, xlviii (2002), pp. 15–19.

[135] *Acción*, 27 Feb. 1932.

[136] E.g. in Mieres, *Región*, 25 Apr. 1931.

[137] J. M. Macarro Vera, *Socialismo, República y revolución en Andalucía (1931–1936)* (Seville, 2000), p. 21. See also Juliá, *Madrid*, p. 7.

[138] *El Noroeste*, 23 Apr. 1931.

objectives. The coalfield communities were far from homogenous. A number of factors, including industrial development and company paternalism, had shaped a landscape of largely small communities in which political rivals cohabited and coexisted at the workplace, in the bar and in cultural institutions. The communities were crisscrossed by tensions and pressure points, as well as different axes of identification and potential mobilization. This image of intimate communities, in which individuals engaged in bitter conflict but also occupied common ground and shared a political idiom, provides the foundation for understanding the development of radicalism during the rest of the Republic.

2. Building and contesting the Republic (1931–2)

To celebrate the proclamation of the Republic, the government declared 15 April a national holiday. That morning, a festive 1,200-strong column bearing Republican banners, flags and red, yellow and purple streamers set out to walk the fifteen kilometres from the arms-manufacturing town of Trubia to Oviedo. They were greeted by the political authorities and a municipal band on the outskirts of the capital before joining the crowds thronging the streets, mirroring celebrations that were taking place across Spain.[1] Two years later, another group of citizens from Trubia repeated the journey, although this time by train and for a different reason. On arriving in Oviedo, the crowd, which included many women, unfurled banners and marched through the centre of the city to the courthouse. Eighty of them entered and the remainder shouted 'freedom for Josefa!' outside. Josefa Álvarez, a twenty-three-year-old from Trubia, was on trial for stabbing and killing her ex-fiancé, who had abandoned her after she became pregnant with their child.[2] Whereas in 1931 the troupe of *trubiecos* celebrated the promise of the new Republic, in 1933 they demanded it uphold its promise of justice, which in this case meant advancing women's rights. In demonstrations like these, citizens across Spain expressed their own vision of Republican reform.

The Republic was not simply rolled out from Madrid, but a product of the interaction of the conflicts and mobilization that occurred at a local level. Citizens and workers, energized by the new political context, presented demands to employers and municipal authorities that pursued the promise of justice associated with the Republic. This chapter examines arenas and forms of political practice in order to probe how the interaction of citizens and authorities gave shape to the Republic at a local level and the tensions and conflicts that emerged, such as over the use of the police force. Tensions over policing would be central to radicalism in 1934, but an examination of the aforementioned factors in 1931 and 1932 exposes the lack of radicalism at the beginning of the Republic. The episodes of conflict show a desire for moderation and the peaceful conciliation of interests.

1 *La Voz de Asturias*, 16 Apr. 1931; *El Noroeste*, 16, 17 Apr. 1931.

2 Josefa was acquitted and was greeted by applause on leaving the courthouse. N. Aresti, 'El crimen de Trubia: género, discursos y ciudadanía republicana', *Ayer*, lxi (2006), 261–85.

Community was an important foundation for political action. Demonstrations and delegations of petitioners claimed to speak for and embody collectives, whether citizens, members of a political party or trade union, or residents of a given locality. Republican justice was also imagined through local frames of reference regarding community justice. Such an approach complicates the tendency to divide forms of collective action – or 'repertoires' – into so-called 'modern' and 'pre-modern' categories or, as recently formulated by Cruz in the Spanish context, 'communitarian' and 'cosmopolitan'. Whereas the former focused on the local sphere of politics and involved 'rigid' and 'violent' tactics, the latter involved claims made on national and international politics and employed non-violent strategies like strikes, demonstrations and petitions.[3] At the heart of such a classification of collective action is how politics is conceptualized, particularly whether the political is restricted to the more formal aspects of political participation or widened to the relationships of power within social relations. As Kaplan and Radcliff have shown in the context of Spain, mobilizing on behalf of the local community – the bread riots, for example – was an important form of political engagement.[4] It was neither limited to rural areas, nor necessarily localist in focus. While the strike was the predominant form of collective action in the coalfields during the 1930s, the forms of political engagement were much wider, richer and resist reduction to categories of rural and industrial, pre-modern and modern. Casting the net wider and understanding the relationship between forms of action is necessary to understand the dynamics of radicalization.

The promise of the Republic

In early 1932, *Avance*, the Asturian socialist daily, commented that communities had 'awoken' under the Republic in an 'explosion of sleeping desires and repressed impulses'.[5] Energized by the new political context, citizens presented petitions and demands to municipal councillors. In so doing, they gave voice to community demands and attempted to wrest the Republic into being in their daily lives. Their demands tended to centre on improvements in infrastructure and services, such as roads, washhouses, schools or street lighting. The petitions were often framed in terms of the

[3] R. Cruz, *Protestar en España* (Madrid, 2015), p. 18.

[4] See T. Kaplan, *Red City, Blue Period: Social Movements in Picasso's Barcelona* (Berkeley, Calif., 1992) and P. Radcliff, *From Mobilization to Civil War: the Politics of Polarization in the Spanish City of Gijón, 1900–1937* (Cambridge, 1996).

[5] *Avance*, 14 Jan. 1932. Councillors in Aller were inundated with demands by July 1931 (*La Aurora Social*, 10 July 1931).

alleged neglect or abandonment of a neighbourhood or village, particularly when compared to the surrounding districts. Criticizing councillors for neglecting to bring certain villages into the light of scientific modernity could be a potent way for rivals to score political points by drawing on inter-town rivalries or harnessing anxieties about being left behind in the progress towards industrial modernity.[6] The arrival of 'Edison's discovery' could be a major source of local satisfaction. It was feted in Hueria de San Tirso (Mieres) with a 'succulent banquet', speeches and toasts.[7] The combination of municipal councillors articulating their duty to represent their communities and the association of the Republic with progress and modernity meant that the demands presented by citizens tended to receive a sympathetic hearing.

The desire to represent the community's interests led to municipal councils adopting a mediating role between citizens and the mining companies, for many of the demands concerned the effects of mining activities. Roads were often blocked by spoil heaps or the water supply suddenly disappeared. Republican and socialist councillors, who saw themselves as guardians and protectors of the local community's interests, responded to complaints by groups of citizens by negotiating with the companies on the community's behalf. Councils requested the assistance of the mining companies to mitigate the effects of the industry and contribute to improvements to infrastructure. This made sense in the light of the companies' financial clout and the legacy of paternalism, but it was also a moral question. For socialist and Republican councillors, it was the companies who had created the problems that communities faced. In Mieres, councillors demanded that Fábrica de Mieres took responsibility for 'depriving the local communities of water' and reminded the company that the municipal authorities were not going to solve the problem.[8] Councillors did not present an uncompromising attitude or seek to open up a front in the class struggle. There was nothing radical about the mediating role that they adopted. Instead, councillors, backed by citizens' demands, attempted to maintain a fragile social contract whereby companies' investment in infrastructure compensated for the damage industry caused to the environment of the coalfields.[9]

The Republic provided an opportunity for communities to link improvements with the wider project of Republican 'justice'. A case from

[6] E.g. *El Noroeste*, 30 Jan. 1932.

[7] *El Noroeste*, 4 Aug. 1931.

[8] Archivo de Mieres (AM), Actas municipales, 8 Aug. 1931 to 10 March 1932, fo. 4.

[9] E.g. Archivo de Langreo (AL), Actas municipales, 29 Jan. 1931 to 10 Sept. 1931, fo. 62; Archivo de Aller (AA), Actas municipales, 2 Oct. 1930 to 3 Oct. 1931, fos. 184–5.

1932 involving residents of Langreo and Laviana illustrates how defence of the community, ideas of the Republic and community justice were interlinked, and how the former could lead to frictions over the exercise of state authority. On 14 April 1932, a year after celebrating the proclamation of the Republic, residents of Sama joined politicians in the central square of the town. A jet of water spouted twenty metres into the air and was greeted with 'delirious displays of enthusiasm'.[10] The date of the inauguration was significant. It marked the first anniversary of the proclamation of the Second Republic, and the unveiling of the water supply formed part of the festivities held in Sama and across Spain. The Republic had delivered the town clean water via modern infrastructure. The political intent to link the supply with the regime was underlined by the fact that it was inaugurated before it was even ready. Engineers had made the ceremony possible in April, but only in July did the supply enter regular service.[11] The inauguration was the culmination of socialist councillor Enrique Celaya's decades-long campaign for a new water supply. For Celaya, his campaign derived from his duty as both 'a socialist and a citizen'. He had fulfilled the will and needs of the local community, as he had aimed to do since his election as a councillor eighteen years earlier.[12]

Construction of the new supply had not been without problems. The source of the water lay in Laviana and there had been friction between the councils since work on the pipeline began in 1930. Simmering tensions boiled over in early 1932. Civil guards had to be deployed to protect the construction workers and a strike was called in Laviana in protest.[13] Twenty-three diverse organizations from Laviana, encompassing shopkeepers, socialist and anarchist groups, the Ateneo and musicians, united to send a telegram to the minister of the interior demanding that he remove the civil governor (his representative in the province), who bore responsibility for public order. The defence of community assets brought diverse associations and political groups together in an impassioned defence of a resource that they believed belonged to the local community. They should be justly compensated for access to a resource that was their inheritance as Laviana residents and they appealed to the government to recognize and negotiate

10 *Avance*, 15 Apr. 1932.

11 *El Noroeste*, 1 July 1932.

12 *Avance*, 15 Apr. 1932. See also the interview with Celaya, *Avance*, 23 July 1932.

13 *Región*, 15, 16 March 1932; *Avance*, 15 March 1932. A. Fernández García, *Langreo: industria, población y desarrollo urbano* (Gijón, 1980), pp. 266–7; A. R. Felgueroso Durán and A. Fernández García, 'La gestión de los socialistas en el Ayuntamiento de Langreo entre 1909 y 1936', in *Historia del socialismo en Langreo 1897–1997*, ed. A. Fernández García and J. Girón (Gijón, 1997), pp. 168–9.

with the local community as an entity in its own right. Their protest was motivated in particular by the deployment of the Civil Guard, a move they considered completely unwarranted.[14]

Municipal authorities were not simply a channel for responding to demands, arenas for party political squabbles or bureaucratic mechanisms for managing construction permits or local taxes. Councillors also assumed a proactive role in constructing the new Republic, which could even mean pushing the boundaries of legality, as occurred in the case of cemeteries. Burial grounds and funeral processions had long been a contentious issue and a focal point for Republican and anticlerical agitation prior to 1931. There were three kinds of cemetery in Spain in 1931: municipal, parish and private. While municipal cemeteries were notionally under public control, keys were usually in the hands of the parish priest, who controlled whether bodies were buried in the Catholic or civil area – the latter commonly a small, badly kempt zone adjoining the Catholic cemetery. Yet prior to the approval of a clear legal framework to deal with municipal and parish cemeteries in 1932, municipal authorities, emboldened by the publication of a bill to secularize parish cemeteries, removed the walls between Catholic and civil cemeteries in places that included Cuenca, Zaragoza and Barcelona. The council in Langreo ordered the removal of the wall between the Catholic and civil areas of the municipal cemetery even earlier – in October 1931 – after the parliamentary debate on the articles relating to religion in the Constitution, but prior to the publication of the cemetery bill in December. Enthusiasm for building the Republic was such that authorities enacted legislation faster than legislators worked, although councillors were careful to flex their muscles regarding municipal cemeteries rather than Church property. Tearing down the wall was a barometer of the progress of the Republican project. By removing barriers, they symbolically emancipated the dead.[15]

The secularization of public life across the country extended to the substitution of religious street names in favour of a nomenclature invoking the Republic, freedom, the Republican martyrs of the December 1930

[14] Telegram from Laviana to the minister of the interior, 14 March 1932, Archivo Histórico Nacional (AHN), Gobernación (A), folder 7A, file 19.

[15] For a detailed discussion, see M. Kerry, 'The bones of contention: culture wars and the secularisation of cemeteries and death practices in the Spanish Second Republic', *European History Quarterly*, xlix (2019), 73–95. For details of Barcelona, see *ABC*, 8 Dec. 1931. For background, see J. Jiménez Lozano, *Los cementerios civiles y la heterodoxia española* (Barcelona, 2008 [1978]) and M. Martorell Linares, '"The cruellest of all forms of coercion": the Catholic Church and conflicts around death and burial in Spain during the Restoration (1874–1923)', *European History Quarterly*, xlvii (2017), 657–78.

rising, or even Karl Marx.[16] Councils also attempted to tax church bells, as occurred in Langreo, although the decision was overturned.[17] Even so, the self-appointed secularizing missions of municipal authorities were not an immediate frontal onslaught of the Church at the local level. Religious education and the display of religious images were no longer compulsory in primary schools from May 1931, but little changed in the Asturian coalfields despite the power Republicans and socialists wielded on municipal councils. Religious images initially removed from schools in Mieres were reinstated by October and religious education continued, while in Aller it simply moved to the end of the school day.[18] This relative moderation in 1931 was the result both of a Republic that was still in the process of being defined and of municipal authorities that sought to balance the competing demands of different constituencies. The implementation and struggles over secularizing policy would be a critical factor in radicalization in 1932, as left-wing activists became increasingly frustrated at the lack of a tangible secular Republic in their everyday lives.

The politics of labour

Petitioning the municipal authorities was a common form of collective action in the 1930s, but the pre-eminent tool of working class political practice was the strike. Asturias – and the coal valleys in particular – was a hotspot for labour conflict during the Second Republic. The province led the country in total number of strikes in 1932 and 1933 and in the number of strikers in 1932.[19] Strike action was a rich phenomenon; the workforce and the unions differed in their interpretations of what it meant and how it should be employed.

[16] E.g. J. M. Macarro Vera, *Socialismo, República y revolución en Andalucía (1931–1936)* (Seville, 2000), p. 250; A. L. López Villaverde, *El gorro frigio y la mitra frente a frente: construcción y diversidad territorial del conflicto político-religioso en la España republicana* (n.p., 2008), p. 204; M. Thomas, *The Faith and the Fury: Popular Anticlerical Violence and Iconoclasm in Spain, 1931–1936* (Eastbourne, 2013), p. 52.

[17] AL, Actas, 24 Dec. 1932 to 30 Sept. 1933, fos. 9, 95. For Aragón, see M. P. Salomón Chéliz, *Anticlericalismo en Aragón. Protesta popular y movilización cívica (1900–1939)* (Zaragoza, 2002), pp. 356–9.

[18] *El Noroeste*, 21 Oct. 1931. See also M. del M. Pozo Andrés and B. Hortañón González, 'El laicismo en la escuela pública', in *Laicismo y catolicismo: el conflicto político-religioso en la Segunda República*, ed. J. de la Cueva Merino and F. Montero García (Alcalá de Henares, 2009), pp. 296–7.

[19] A. Shubert, *The Road to Revolution in Spain: the Coal Miners of Asturias, 1860–1934* (Urbana, Ill., 1987), p. 149.

There were different kinds of stoppage in the coalfields during the 1930s. A fatal accident in a pit sparked an automatic stoppage as a collective gesture of mourning (and a chance to investigate the cause). Other spontaneous stoppages were quite different; workers downed tools in a wildcat strike if wages went unpaid or they considered a disciplinary action taken by foremen or the employer to be unjust.[20] Such strikes were not under union control and differed from planned strikes, which were officially declared with a list of demands and usually involved a union. Strikes were also accompanied by a range of ritualized activities, including propagandizing missions in the streets, articles in the press to win the battle for public opinion, and raising strike funds by visiting other places of work on payday.[21]

At the level of union ideology and strategy, there was a clear difference between the UGT and the CNT. The UGT placed its faith in the state. Socialist moderation and reformism focused on growing the UGT as an organization and using the state to do so; this had been the strategy followed by Largo Caballero during the Primo de Rivera dictatorship and it continued under the Republic with Largo Caballero now minister of labour.[22] The 'mixed juries' introduced by Largo Caballero – a new iteration of the 1920s arbitration committees – were intended to channel demands through the mechanisms of the state, thereby tying the masses to the system and increasing socialist prestige by growing the movement and confirming the efficacy of socialist strategy. The socialist position at the beginning of the Republic was thus to eschew strike action.

Cleaving the masses to the Republican system was also a way to undermine the CNT. The anarchist principles of the CNT meant that they preferred direct action, placing their faith in workers' collective strength to force an employer's hand, rather than channelling their demands through the state. Yet anarchists' rejection of arbitration committees and preference for direct action did not preclude mediation. During a lengthy conflict at the Fondón pit in autumn 1932, striking anarchists were willing to negotiate via the mayor and civil governor; indeed, it was the former who found

[20] For a similar desire to assert control of the labour process in Wales, see L. James, *The Politics of Identity and Civil Society in Britain and Germany: the Miners in the Ruhr and South Wales, 1890–1926* (Manchester, 2008), p. 27.

[21] For different forms of stoppage, see R. Church and Q. Outram, *Strikes and Solidarity: Coalfield Conflict in Britain, 1889–1966* (Cambridge, 1998), pp. 10–13.

[22] See P. Preston, *The Coming of the Spanish Civil War: Reform, Reaction and Revolution in the Second Republic* (London, 1978), pp. 7–9 and J. Aróstegui, *Largo Caballero: el tesón y la quimera* (Barcelona, 2013), pp. 259–99.

the solution to the strike.[23] As occurred elsewhere in Spain, the role of the mayor as a mediator was often central to the resolution of labour conflicts.[24] However, the 1932 Law of Associations made this task difficult, as it forced anarchist associations to seek legal authorization in order to operate. During a nine-month strike at the Duro-Felguera steelworks between 1932 and 1933, councillors were unable to mediate in a dispute between the CNT and the company because the civil governor refused to allow them to do so unless anarchists followed the requirements of the Law.[25]

The first major strike of the Republic exemplified the differences between the socialists and anarchists and constituted the most important struggle between the SUM and the SOMA for hegemony over the workforce during the Republic. The root of the strike lay in a desire for the reinstatement of the seven-hour working day in the mines. The SUM called for its immediate, direct implementation while the socialists preferred government mediation. The SUM prepared a general strike for June 1931, which the SOMA criticized as an attack on the Republic. This set the scene for a test of their respective strength and influence at the beginning of the new regime. As a general strike, the stoppage failed. On the first day, 7,000 mineworkers followed the SUM's call to down tools while 20,000 entered the pits. The conflict became deadlocked. In an attempt to extend the strike, SUM activists engaged in sabotage, and shootouts occurred between strikers and those still working.[26] The strike did not result in a clear victory or defeat for either socialists or anarchists. The SUM failed to achieve the immediate re-introduction of the shorter working day and at the end of the summer Largo Caballero, the socialist minister of labour, decided to impose it by decree.[27]

The June strike was exceptional for its scale – as conflicts in 1931 tended to be localized and short – but not for its objectives. Improving working conditions and increasing wages tended to be the focal point of workers' demands during the first year of the Republic, but as the economic situation evolved, so did the nature of the demands. From the beginning of 1932, the

[23] M. Castejón Rodríguez, 'La patronal hullera asturiana en la Segunda República' (unpublished UNED PhD thesis, 2009), pp. 380–1.

[24] F. Cobo Romero, *De campesinos a electores: modernización agraria en Andalucía, politización campesina y derechización de los pequeños propietarios y arrendatarios: el caso de la provincia de Jaén, 1931–1936* (Madrid, 2003), p. 225.

[25] Negotiations were also hamstrung by Duro-Felguera's intransigence (*Región*, 25 Feb., 26 Apr. 1933).

[26] Telegram from the civil governor to the minister of the interior, 1 June 1931, AHN, Gobernación (A), folder 7A, file 7; *El Noroeste*, 3, 5, 11 June 1931; *La Aurora Social*, 5 June 1931.

[27] *El Noroeste*, 27, 29 Aug. 1931; Castejón Rodríguez, 'La patronal', p. 351.

coalfields faced significant economic problems, which companies blamed on the high levels of unsold coal stocks, wage increases, the seven-hour day and the cost of Republican labour legislation, including holidays. A small number of mining companies closed or went bankrupt, including El Caudal, which owed its workers five months' wages, and Hulleras de Riosa, which left 800 unemployed.[28] Others implemented short-time working and reduced piecework rates.[29] These were the first symptoms of problems that plagued the industry during the second half of 1932 and throughout 1933.

The SOMA hierarchy constantly exhorted its members not to strike in accordance with the socialist strategy of avoiding strike action so as not to undermine the Republic. Yet the socialist rank and file consistently went on strike in 1931 and 1932. On one occasion, a strike in Barredos (Laviana) was actually called by the local SOMA section, while on another, mineworkers refused to enter the Sotón mine in protest at accidents, a decision which was praised by a SUM official because it defied the exhortations of the SOMA officials.[30] SOMA leaders attributed such strikes to the 'spirit of youth', 'irresponsible elements' or 'people of little or no responsibility', who spread 'confusion' and deceived the rank and file.[31] Socialist officials thus recognized that socialists did go on strike, even as they reinforced the anti-strike message and the self-image of socialists as moderate and sensible in their politics. In fact, the SOMA leadership had already shown concern at the prospect of rank-and-file militancy. At the SOMA congress in May 1931, the Executive Committee modified the union's statutes in an attempt to restrict the ability of local sections to call strikes. In theory, they could no longer do so.[32]

The unintended consequence of the SOMA's anti-strike attitude was to encourage strike action. For socialists, strike action could be an expression of support for the Republic as mineworkers attempted to press for the social justice associated with the regime through higher wages, better working conditions and an assertion of working-class power. Condemnation of the rank and file for striking did not prevent SOMA officials intervening in disputes. Rather, the union quickly involved itself in strikes in order to accelerate their resolution.[33] Paradoxically, the combination of a socialist at

[28] *Avance*, 3, 17 Jan., 19 Feb., 14 Apr. 1932; *Región*, 10 May 1932.

[29] *Región*, 19, 20 Feb. 1932.

[30] *El Noroeste*, 1, 3, 15 July 1931.

[31] *Avance*, 10, 11 May, 7 Sept. 1932.

[32] *Región*, 8 May 1931; Shubert, *Road*, pp. 143–4; *El Noroeste*, 26 May 1931.

[33] E.g. conflicts at the Llamas and Mariana pits and in Olloniego (*La Aurora Social*, 6 Nov. 1931; *Avance*, 20 Nov., 4, 5, 6, 13 Dec. 1931).

the helm of the ministry of labour, the arbitration mechanisms fashioned by this ministry, and a socialist desire to avoid strikes, created the ideal opportunity for strike action.

The strike was the quintessential tool of political practice in the coalfields, but not everyone could strike. Across the country, unemployment was an increasingly pressing issue.[34] Unemployed workers in Oviedo and the coalfields held meetings and organized demonstrations in 1931 demanding 'bread and work', and in early 1932 a commission of women petitioned the municipal council in Aller to find work for the former employees of El Caudal.[35] These demands were targeted at the municipal authorities, which, along with the provincial deputation, organized public works that were the traditional solution to unemployment. Under the Republic, the ministry of labour also tasked councils with creating local labour exchanges to aid the placement of unemployed workers. Public works were initially forthcoming, but councils soon ran out of funding. The council in Mieres did not renew the contracts of its labourers and in Oviedo public works halted. Over 200 workers from the 250-strong workforce of temporary workers were laid off.[36] The acuteness of the situation was compounded by a rise in the price of bread to its peak in 1932, sparking protests in Mieres and further afield.[37]

One solution to unemployment and rising prices was to labour illegally. The case of the *chamiceros*, who extracted coal from surface mines [*chamizos*] on mining companies' property, provides an insight into how mineworkers imagined the local economy. In the summer of 1932, the Civil Guard increasingly harassed a number of *chamiceros* operating in San Martín del Rey Aurelio, with some cases ending up in court.[38] The *chamiceros* responded by organizing assemblies and electing a committee to defend their interests, with which the socialist-led council refused to engage, despite there being a socialist member on the otherwise Communist-dominated committee.[39]

[34] Interwar unemployment in Europe has been the subject of a recent wave of scholarship, e.g., M. Perry, *Prisoners of Want: the Experience and Protest of the Unemployed in France, 1921–1945* (Aldershot, 2007) and *Unemployment and Protest: New Perspectives on Two Centuries of Contention*, ed. M. Reiss and M. Perry (Oxford, 2011).

[35] E.g. *Región*, 28 Apr. 1931; *El Noroeste*, 30 July 1931; letter from Aurora García (and others) to the municipal council of Aller, 19 June 1932, AA, box 532, folder: Asuntos obreros 1932; *Avance*, 3 Jan. 1932.

[36] C. Benito del Pozo, *El ayuntamiento republicano de Oviedo, 1931–1936* (Oviedo, 1989), pp. 88–9; *El Noroeste*, 22 July 1932.

[37] *Región*, 30 Apr., 4 May 1932; Preston, *Coming of the Spanish Civil War*, p. 39; J. Casanova, *Anarchism, the Republic and Civil War in Spain (1931–1939)* (Abingdon, 2004), p. 23.

[38] See AHPA, AP, box 78434, files 174, 176, 177, 183 (1932).

[39] *El Noroeste*, 15 Oct. 1932; *Avance*, 18 Oct. 1932.

The *chamiceros* offered a solution to the problem they themselves posed. They offered to sell the coal they mined to the company for an agreed fee.[40] In essence, they sought to formalize their activities such that they would be, in effect, freelance workers.

The *chamiceros*' solution was underpinned by a particular notion of a moral economy at the local level.[41] In the face of material urgency, they argued that the market should be remoulded in order to afford an equitable distribution of work for miners. The imperative of employment justified the *chamericeros*' infringement of property rights. This was a moral economy in its broadest sense of attempting to change the priority of the market to the employment of local workers over the profit margins of businesses. There was a moral and economic imperative to make the best use of natural resources for the collective good of the local community. The *chamiceros* demanded the social justice promised by the Republic, whether sincerely or, from a Communist position, in an attempt to place the authorities under pressure using maximalist demands to unmask the bourgeois nature of the Republic. In any case, there was little radical in how the *chamiceros* acted. They attempted to reach a negotiated settlement that did not fundamentally disturb the relationship between capital and labour. Rather than socializing the means of production, they were willing to pay the mining company a fee for the right to mine coal.[42] For the mining companies, however, it was an attack on their right to manage their property as they wished.

The underlying logic in the moral economy of the *chamiceros* paralleled practices in rural areas in other parts of Spain where peasants undertook agricultural tasks without the consent of the landowner and demanded payment afterwards.[43] From autumn 1931, these incidents increased, with '[a] n astonishing number of occupations and "illegal cultivations" of properties [taking] place in provinces such as Huesca and Teruel'. In Puebla de Valverde (Teruel), groups entered an estate and ploughed the land, cut trees and collected wood. They stopped when the mayor appeared, 'on condition that the authorities agreed to obtain the title deeds from the proprietor, as the locals believed that the village had a rightful collective claim to the

[40] *Avance*, 8 Oct. 1932.

[41] The foundational text is E. P. Thompson, 'The moral economy of the English crowd in the eighteenth century', *Past & Present*, l (1971), 76–136.

[42] *Avance*, 8 Oct. 1932.

[43] E.g. in Bujalance (Córdoba) (R. Cañete Marfil and F. Martínez Mejías, *La Segunda República en Bujalance (1931–1936)* (Córdoba, 2010), p. 177). E. Majuelo Gil traced the process in Navarra through the Republic in *Luchas de clases en Navarra (1931–1936)* (Pamplona, 1989).

property'.[44] Sometimes the demands were more radical, as citizens opened up a new front in decades-long local conflicts over the sale and privatization of common land. This distinguishes the cases of the land invasions from the *chamiceros*, even if both formed part of a longer tradition of transgressive actions that reordered the market in line with a local understanding of a moral economy.[45]

Cases of poverty-stricken workers undertaking direct action to gain food were not unheard of in interwar Europe and consumer protests were particularly in evidence at the end of the First World War. In Weimar Germany, hungry citizens engaged in direct action during periods of economic distress, such as forcing the 'sale of foodstuffs at lower prices' during the early 1920s or plundering fields during the Great Depression.[46] Therein lies a key difference between Germany and Spain. Spanish agricultural workers operated in the favourable political and legal context offered by the Republic, rather than the crises of the early 1920s and the Depression. Under the Republic, 'for the first time the balance of legal rights swung away from landowners to the rural proletariat'.[47] Invading estates responded to hunger and a desire for land, but also the opportunities opened up by the creation of the Republic.

The solution proposed by the *chamiceros* was not the only one sought by workers within the existing framework of capitalist relations in the coalfields. As the coal companies struggled with falling demand for coal, workforces proposed collective contracts to avoid the closure of mines.[48] Under collective contracts, mineworkers took charge of the labour and extraction process and sold the coal back to the company. Such a solution located industry's woes in the organization of production rather than market forces. Removing the company's representatives – the foremen and deputies – would allegedly resolve the company's economic problems. As with the *chamiceros*, there was little militant in these proposals. Instead, rank-and-

[44] Casanova, *Anarchism*, pp. 21–2.

[45] See P. Radcliff, 'Women's politics: consumer riots in twentieth-century Spain', in *Constructing Spanish Womanhood: Female Identity in Modern Spain*, ed. V. Lorée Enders and P. Radcliff (New York, 1999), pp. 301–23.

[46] Schumann argued these acts were simply direct action prompted by material need rather than necessitating an explication based on sophisticated notions of a moral economy (D. Schumann, *Political Violence in the Weimar Republic, 1918–1933: Fight for the Streets and Fear of Civil War* (New York, 2012), pp. 11–4, 238–9).

[47] E. Malefakis, *Agrarian Reform and Peasant Revolution in Spain: Origins of the Spanish Civil War* (New Haven, Conn., 1970), p. 170.

[48] E.g. at Industrial Asturiana (*Avance*, 13, 21 Sept. 1932); Carmona mine in Mieres (*Avance*, 13 May 1932).

file discontent at the SOMA's response to the problems in the coal industry would give rise to radicalism in labour matters at the end of 1932.

Property

Trespassing onto private property in times of economic need, whether to extract coal or plough land, was not the only way in which property was at the centre of conflict during the 1930s. The distribution of land was one of the central preoccupations of the Republican–socialist government. The nature of agricultural property and farming practices in Spain meant there were a large number of landless labourers on the *latifundia* of the south, who struggled to subsist thanks to seasonal underemployment and low wages. The Republican–socialist government planned a substantial land reform for fourteen provinces across Extremadura, Castile, Andalusia and La Mancha, in which land would be subject to compulsory purchase and distributed to peasants. The September 1932 law was limited in practice and by the end of 1933, only 4,399 families had settled on 24,203 hectares of land.[49] Spain was not the only European country to enact land reform 'to bolster … legitimacy and stave off social unrest', nor was it the only one to fail. In eastern Europe, the Baltic and the Balkans, governments failed to address 'the power and influence of large [land]owners' or 'establish a group of moderately prosperous peasants who would have been the lynchpins of social and political stability'.[50]

Access to land was one facet of the struggle for property. A further problem was posed by housing. Housing shortages had long been a problem in cities and industrial areas across Europe, from the Ruhr industrial region to Barcelona, where housing was insalubrious and overcrowded.[51] In Europe, the lack of housing became particularly acute at the end of the First World War, thanks to a number of factors, including migration to the cities, the removal of rent controls, lack of construction during the war and an increase in marriages in its aftermath.[52] In Asturias, the quality and

[49] Malefakis, *Agrarian reform*, p. 281. For recent reflections, see J. Carmona, J. R. Rosés and J. Simpson, 'The question of land access and the Spanish land reform of 1932', *Economic History Review*, lxxii (2019), 669–90.

[50] L. Boswell, 'Rural society in crisis', in *The Oxford Handbook of European History, 1914–1945*, ed. N. Doumanis (Oxford, 2016), p. 253.

[51] J. R. Shearer, 'Shelter from the storm: politics, production and the housing crisis in the Ruhr coal fields, 1918–24', *Journal of Contemporary History*, xxxiv (1999), 19–47; C. Ealham, *Class, Culture and Conflict in Barcelona, 1898–1937* (Abingdon, 2005), p. 5.

[52] For Vienna and Paris, see H. Gruber, *Red Vienna: Experiment in Working Class Culture, 1919–1934* (New York, 1991), pp. 45–73 and T. Stovall, *Paris and the Spirit of 1919: Consumer Struggles, Transnationalism and Revolution* (Cambridge, 2012), pp. 36–48, 193–212. For

adequate supply of homes was a long-running issue.[53] The Jesuit Sisinio Nevares heaped praise on the SHE for the homes it built in Aller, but the thirty-three '*cuarteles*' containing 465 dwellings and the fifty 'single-family houses' were clearly insufficient for 4,000 miners.[54] The situation was so desperate that those who migrated to the coalfields to work had to sleep in barns and *hórreos* (traditional Asturian granaries).[55]

During the Republic, discontent and agitation over housing in the coalfields centred on rent, rather than the supply or quality of housing stock. Struggles over rent occurred across Spain during the first year of the Republic, including in Barcelona, Huelva, Cádiz and Seville. In the Catalan capital, agitation against rents had surfaced prior to the Republic and, under the stewardship of anarchist activists, mushroomed into a strike in the summer of 1931.[56] The dynamic was different in the Asturian coalfields, where there was no strike but a significant wave of activism in 1932 that emerged in response to a government decree in December 1931. The new legislation allowed tenants to petition for a reduction in rent. Tenants' leagues (*Ligas de inquilinos*) emerged in the coalfields – as they did across the country – to press for reductions.[57] Some of the leagues predated the Republic, such as in Oviedo and Gijón, but the new political context facilitated their creation and growth. By May 1932 an Asturian regional federation had been formed, with the participation of seven coalfield leagues (Turón, Boo, Moreda, Pola de Lena, Mieres, Sama, Laviana), along with Trubia, Gijón and Avilés.[58] The coalfield leagues featured prominent socialist involvement and were often based at the local Casa del Pueblo. The speedy organization of the leagues, along with the mobilization and results they achieved cannot be understood without a look at the pre-existing traditions of community activism and organizational frameworks in the coalfields.

Berlin, see E. Rosenhaft, *Beating the Fascists? The German Communist Party and Political Violence, 1929–1933* (Cambridge, 1983), pp. 10–11.

[53] See J. M. Jove y Canella, *Topografía médica del concejo de San Martín del Rey Aurelio* (Madrid, 1923).

[54] S. Nevares, *El patrono ejemplar: una obra maestra de Acción Social* (Madrid, 1936), p. 211.

[55] Fernández García, *Langreo*, p. 262.

[56] Ealham, *Class*, pp. 93–5, 100; N. Rider, 'The practice of direct action: the Barcelona rent strike of 1931', in *For Anarchism: History, Theory, and Practice*, ed. D. Goodway (London, 1989), pp. 88–94; Cruz, *Protestar*, p. 86.

[57] *Gaceta de Madrid*, 30 Dec. 1931. The decree was later modified (*Gaceta de Madrid*, 12 March, 18 June 1932). Leagues existed across Spain (e.g., see details in *Noticiero de Soria*, 16 June 1932).

[58] *Región*, 23 May 1932.

The leagues provided a new vehicle for citizens to fight for the social justice they identified with the Republic. As banners held aloft by demonstrating members of the league from Muros del Nalón, a town near the coast, proclaimed: 'We demand justice' and 'The law must be fulfilled'.[59] Activism in Asturias attempted to exploit the opening provided by legislation in contrast to protests against evictions in post-First World War Paris or the Communist-organized rent strike in 1930s Germany, which were defensive reactions to a quickly deteriorating economic situation.[60]

Women played a prominent role in rent activism both as organizers and as a target for support. At league meetings in Trubia and Oviedo most of the audience was made up of women and two women were appointed to a neighbourhood committee in the provincial capital.[61] In Aller and Trubia, organizers spoke in the name of and appealed to working-class mothers: 'As women, as proletarian mothers, it hurts us to see our children barefoot and poorly fed because of the excessive RENT THAT WE PAY [*sic*]'.[62] Women's activism drew on pre-existing traditions of women mobilizing at the local level in defence of community-based justice.[63] Nevertheless, orators at meetings were men, reflecting male predominance in positions of power in local politics.

Whereas CNT activists in Barcelona favoured direct action due to their lack of 'faith in Republicans' and the 'notoriously intransigent landlord class', coalfield leagues instead emphasized their desire for the harmonious conciliation of interests through reaching 'friendly' agreements between tenants and property owners.[64] The league in Mieres declared its pride at having negotiated lower rents while maintaining good relationships with the owners. They preferred to channel tenants' demands through the courts if an agreement was not possible. The league in Aller took pride in having 'triumphed in every case dealt with by the justice system'.[65]

[59] *La Voz de Asturias*, 22 June 1932.

[60] P. Swett, *Neighbors and Enemies: the Culture of Radicalism in Berlin, 1929–1933* (Cambridge, 2004), p. 45.

[61] *Avance*, 15, 21 July 1932.

[62] *Avance*, 10 July 1932. For the same phrasing in Trubia, see *Avance*, 15 July 1932. French tenants framed their demands in terms of wartime sacrifice (Stovall, *Paris*, p. 202).

[63] See Radcliff, 'Women's politics', pp. 301–23 and T. Kaplan, 'Female consciousness and collective action: the case of Barcelona, 1910–1918', *Signs*, vii (1982), 545–66. For women's prominence in Berlin rent strikes, see Swett, *Neighbors*, p. 45.

[64] Ealham, *Class*, p. 101.

[65] *Avance*, 1 June, 10 Oct. 1932.

If the leagues were moderate in practice, the language was often bullish and asserted the collective power of the working class. The league in Mieres scoffed at landlords who 'badly counselled … think justice will not be done' and warned that the league would make sure that it was.[66] The problem lay in the fact that reaching 'friendly' agreements was not easy. Landlords defended their interests and even fuelled conflict by evicting tenants or raising rents.[67] Tensions ran high in some areas. One league leader was arrested in Pola de Laviana for punching a landlord who had insulted him. The landlord in question was accused of refusing to respect both the legislation and the 'correct instructions' of the league. Instead, he had announced an increase in rents. The league protested at the arrest by gathering outside prison before assembling in front of the landlord's home in a menacing manner. The landlord took refuge in the home of the socialist deputy mayor. Ironically, it was the secretary of the tenants' league who protected the landlord from the crowd by personally escorting him home.[68]

Rent activism was an arena in which citizens – and women in particular – mobilized to construct the justice they associated with the Republic in their everyday lives, through their own actions. For landlords, the wave of requests for rent reduction could be symptomatic of how the Republic meddled in their affairs and destabilized the traditional social order. Resistance to rent reduction meant that tenants also became very aware of the limits of Republican reform. In 1932, tenant activism was moderate and conciliatory rather than radical, although disputes over rents would become increasingly bitter over the next couple of years.

Governance

The state was a key actor in the dynamics of conflict. It did not exist as a monolithic entity, but a network of channels and institutions, formed by different layers of administrative responsibility and power.[69] The policing of society lay in the hands of multiple levels of the state, including the mayor as the immediate authority at the local level, the civil governor

[66] *Avance*, 1 July 1932.

[67] E.g. *Avance*, 28 May, 2, 10 July 1932.

[68] *Avance*, 2 July 1932. The league later protested at the landlords' 'campaign' against the leaders (*Avance*, 12 July 1932).

[69] My approach to the state is influenced by M. Mann, e.g., his 'The autonomous power of the state: its origins, mechanisms and results', *European Journal of Sociology*, xxv (1984), 185–213. For a sociological perspective on the state in relation to collective action, see *Breaking Down the State: Protestors Engaged*, ed. J. M. Jasper and J. W. Duyvendak (Amsterdam, 2015).

(the government's delegate in the province) and the state security forces themselves. The Spanish state security force's actions played a key role in the dynamics of collective action. The state security forces were often an agent that escalated protest to the point of violence, thanks to the particular political culture and training of the security forces, even as they attempted to uphold law and order.[70]

Historically, the Spanish left had had an uneasy relationship with the principal arm of law enforcement, the Civil Guard, which had been created in 1844 as a rural gendarmerie to deal with brigandage. The Civil Guard was not well equipped to police mass protests and strikes, even as it was increasingly called upon to do so. Far from neighbourhood police officers, civil guards were stationed in municipalities away from their place of origin and housed in barracks with their families that were isolated from the community, although they often maintained ties with the local elite.[71] In the Asturian coalfields, the SHE had paid for the construction of Civil Guard barracks and many company security guards were ex-civil guards.[72]

The corps itself cultivated a strong sense of 'honour' and closely identified with its mission to protect the *patria* and the social order, which was imagined in terms of traditional social hierarchies.[73] The Civil Guard had not been willing to intervene to prevent the fall of the monarchy, but there was nevertheless 'an underlying sensation that the corps was incompatible with the new political order' due to its 'ultraconservative' mentality.[74] At the beginning of the Republic, the Mieres municipal council agreed to solicit the dismissal of civil guards stationed in the district for their 'many crimes' and to draft regulations for a new 'republican guard' with a 'civic character'.[75] There was also an immediate campaign in Asturias for the removal of Lisardo Doval, a Civil Guard commander in the province, for the torture and mistreatment of prisoners during the Primo de Rivera dictatorship. At the first council meeting in Gijón, councillors agreed to demand his

70 E.g. Cruz, *Protestar*, pp. 89–90; Casanova, *Anarchism*, p. 18; E. González Calleja, *En nombre de la autoridad: la defensa del orden público durante la Segunda República española (1931–1936)* (Granada, 2014).

71 See F. Chamberlin, 'Honor-bound: the military culture of the Civil Guard and the political violence of the Spanish Second Republic, 1931–1936' (unpublished UCSD PhD thesis, 2017).

72 Nevares, *El patrono*, pp. 29, 23.

73 On these themes, see G. Blaney, 'The Civil Guard and the Spanish Second Republic (1931–1936)' (unpublished University of London PhD thesis, 2007) and Chamberlin, 'Honor-bound'.

74 Blaney, 'Civil Guard', pp. 105–6, 110; González Calleja, *En nombre*, pp. 90–1.

75 AM, Actas, 16 May 1928 to 1 Aug. 1931, fos. 104, 112.

transfer out of the province – a move that was supported by a motion from their counterparts in Mieres – and they later organized a commission to collect denunciations of Doval's conduct. The provincial press published a flurry of letters denouncing his behaviour or else springing to his defence.[76] Doval was removed from Asturias, but he would return to direct the police operation in the province after the revolutionary insurrection.

The government had recognized the potential problems posed by the Civil Guard at the beginning of the Republic, but had little choice but to rely on it. Tentative plans for a people's 'civic guard' were finally shelved in favour of creating a new corps – the Assault Guard – to supplement the Civil Guard.[77] Envisaged as a more modern force for policing urban disorder that would show 'hardness without brutality', the Assault Guard was modelled on other European forces, including the German Schutzpolizei and the French Garde Republicaine Mobile. Assault guards operated in squads, as opposed to in pairs, were trained in crowd control and armed with truncheons and machine pistols. Despite the prestige and money invested in the Assault Guard – who numbered 12,000 by the end of 1932 – they failed to offer a fundamentally different policing strategy to the Civil Guard.[78] The government also developed legislative measures to protect the Republic, namely the Law for the Defence of the Republic that was promulgated in October 1931. The law authorized restrictions on civil liberties in order to defend the constitutional order. Over the next couple of years – before the Law of Public Order replaced it in July 1933 – the law was deployed against those agitating against the Republic, including the conspiring monarchist right and the rebellious left, particularly the anarchist movement.[79]

The policing of Spanish society in the new Republic constituted a thorny matter for the state, as underlined by a number of violent clashes that occurred between the security forces and crowds at the end of 1931 and beginning of 1932. While these episodes did not happen in Asturias, they are important for what they reveal about the exercise of state power at the local level in Spain in the 1930s. The most emblematic occurred in Castilblanco and Arnedo. In both cases violence erupted when security forces attempted to break up a demonstration. In Castilblanco, a remote, poverty-stricken

[76] *Región*, 17 Apr., 12 May 1931; AM, Actas, 16 May 1928 to 1 Aug. 1931, fo. 104; *El Noroeste*, 19 Apr., 2, 22 May 1931.

[77] González Calleja, *En nombre*, pp. 131–3.

[78] González Calleja, *En nombre*, pp. 140–6. On France, see J. M. Berlière, 'The difficult construction of a "Republican" police', in *Policing Interwar Europe: Continuity, Change and Crisis, 1918–1940*, ed. G. Blaney (Basingstoke, 2007), pp. 14–30.

[79] Discussion in González Calleja, *En nombre*, pp. 190–9. On implications for the anarchists, see Ealham, *Class*, pp. 69–70.

village of 3,000 inhabitants located in Badajoz province, socialist-authorized marches took place on 30 and 31 December 1931 in the context of a strike. When the mayor ordered the dissolution of the demonstration, a tussle led to a shot being fired by the four civil guards present which killed a member of the crowd. Demonstrators jumped on the guards, beat them to death, mutilated them and destroyed their weapons.[80] Days later, on 5 Januaury – and before public consternation had receded – civil guards opened fire on demonstrators in Arnedo, in La Rioja province. There had been a lengthy prelude to this, consisting of friction between Faustino Muro (a shoe factory owner), workers and trade unionists in 1931. Muro had encouraged votes for the monarchist slate in the April municipal elections and sacked workers for political reasons. After the proclamation of the Republic, workers had repeatedly protested about the working conditions and dismissals at his factory. An arbitration committee found in the workers' favour, but Muro refused to acknowledge the ruling. The sacking of a worker led to a general strike in January 1932. A peaceful demonstration was held in the town to celebrate an agreement reached between governor, socialists and local bosses. The shouting, dancing protestors converged on the main square. A shot was fired wounding a civil guard, and his fellow guards opened fire without warning. Eleven were killed and thirty injured, from a one-year-old child to a man in his sixties.[81]

The violence in Castilblanco and Arnedo contributed twelve of the 103 deaths caused by the Civil Guard between 14 April 1931 and 5 January 1932.[82] Explanations of these episodes tend to focus on two factors. First, the culture of the Civil Guard, namely its rigidity and emphasis on upholding its honour and the unsuitability of its weaponry for crowd control.[83] Second, the rapid politicization of rural areas that posed a challenge to municipal and provincial authorities in managing competing interests and demands at the local level. In many areas of Spain, councillors who had never exercised political power before occupied council chambers. This dramatic shift in municipal politics, particularly in rural areas, coupled with the massive growth in unionization translated into a formal

[80] On Castilblanco, see M. Baumeister, 'Castilblanco or the limits of democracy – rural protest in Spain from the Restoration monarchy to the early Second Republic', *Contemporary European History,* vii (1998), 1–19; R. Trullén Floría, 'Castilblanco como sinécdoque: el discurso contrarrevolucionario de interpretación de la Segunda República', *Historia social,* lxxxiii (2015), 55–71; González Calleja, *En nombre*, pp. 98–105.

[81] This summary is based on C. Gil Andrés, *La República en la plaza: los sucesos de Arnedo de 1932* (Logroño, 2002).

[82] Figures from González Calleja, *En nombre*, p. 113.

[83] As argued by Chamberlin, 'Honor-bound', particularly pp. 167–73.

politicization of towns and villages across the country. As new forms of politics and a new balance of power emerged in the countryside due to the politicization engendered by the Republic, rural elites responded with force.[84]

In narratives of the Second Republic, episodes like Castilblanco and Arnedo often appear as localized phenomena that punctuated national political life. Such a view overlooks the tensions over state power at the local level and the importance of community as a framework for making sense of political developments and as a framework for action. The strength of feeling invested in the local community combined with the historically weak articulation of the Spanish state meant that local communities tended towards 'self-policing' or self-governance. This extended beyond remote areas of Badajoz. As a socialist councillor in Langreo said when discussing a proposal for the council to stop paying the Civil Guard's telephone bill: '[we] socialists are those who need the Civil Guard the least'.[85] In a similar manner, when the different organizations in Laviana united to telegram the government to protest against the construction of the water supply in early 1932, they singled out the deployment of the Civil Guard for particular criticism. They expressed indignation in the name of the community at the threat of force. The government was acting in a 'dictatorial' manner that was completely unwarranted.[86] Over the coming years, this principle would be asserted even more strongly. While the socialists believed in participating in the state and using the levers of state power to implement reform, this could coexist with traditions of the self-policing pueblo at the local level. The following years saw frequent assertions that the local left could better police public order, and this rhetoric turned into reality, as the coexistence of the state security forces and the left became increasingly difficult in the coalfields.

Such uneasiness, if not opposition, at what was considered to be the intrusion of the state into working-class communities was a sentiment not limited to the coalfields or Spain. In Berlin, residents of working-class districts 'universally' regarded police with 'suspicion'.[87] In the Ruhr and South Wales, cuts in welfare or intrusion into the family home to assess a family's claim to benefit payments triggered a 'rising cycle of protest',

[84] The dynamics also reflect longer traditions of rural revolts and riots (Baumeister, 'Castilblanco', pp. 11–17).

[85] AL, Actas, 17 Sept. 1931 to 21 Apr. 1932, fo. 118.

[86] Telegram from Laviana to the minister of the interior, 14 March 1932, AHN, Gobernación (A), file 7A, document 19.

[87] Swett, *Neighbors*, p. 215.

exacerbated by mass unemployment in these industrial areas.[88] The state was an active player in the unfolding dynamics of protest. In Spain, the promise of Republican justice and corresponding investment of moral authority in the state meant that allegations of 'betrayal' by agents of the state were keenly felt, particularly in 1934. This was not just a question of Republican reform, but also a dispute over the reach and exercise of state power.

The construction of the Republic at a local level occurred through the interaction of pressure from competing interest groups, administration of laws and orders emanating from Madrid by the municipal authorities, and oversight and policing from the civil governor and Civil and Assault Guard. Between 1931 and 1932, the Asturian coalfields saw increasing agitation as citizens and residents seized the opportunity to assert the interests of their community and other groups with whom they identified. The Asturian coalfields proved to be an area with a high capacity for organization and struggle, thanks to the political traditions forged over many years and, in particular, the dense network of political and union institutions, such as Casas de Pueblo and neighbourhood associations. These institutions and associations were foundations for projecting claims about the community.

There were moments of tension in strikes, tenant activism and over the actions of the police forces, but there was little radicalism in these episodes. Radicalism emerged from friction between rival groups on the left and the cleavage between left and right as moulded by the context of the Republic, namely the way it reconfigured the place of religion in Spanish society. If the classic view proposes that radicalization was a frustrated response to employer and right-wing intransigence in the face of Republican reform, the story requires greater sensitivity to the shifting political context of the Republic during the 1930s, as well as the dynamics of politics at the local level.

[88] A. Zukas, 'Explaining unemployed protest in the Ruhr at the end of the Weimar Republic', in *Unemployment and Protest: New Perspectives on Two Centuries of Contention*, ed. M. Reiss and M. Perry (Oxford, 2011), the quotation at p. 160. For Britain, see S. Ward, *Unemployment and the State in Britain: the Means Test and Protest in 1930s South Wales and North-East England* (Manchester, 2013).

3. Anticlericalism, dissidence and radicalization (1932–3)

> You said that I had a church wedding ... Criticize me when you see my children saturated with clericalism or when my father kneels on the cold slabs of the church ... If citizens' private lives interest you so much, why, you great cynic, did you not object to your brother Socrates applying for a post office licence under the Primo de Rivera dictatorship? Your family observes church marriages, applies for posts during the dictatorship and you are a pretender for a thousand *beatas* ... Where is your radicalism now, when not long ago you offered your hand to a priest?[1]

José Estrada penned this torrent of disparaging remarks in response to criticism published by Communist rivals. For Estrada, a socialist, their behaviour did not match the radical political ideal they claimed to espouse. His scorn, underpinned by a charge of hypocrisy, was typical of the mudslinging between leftists that was prevalent in the first years of the Republic. Anticlericalism was an important way of showing one's radical mettle and played a prominent role in rivalry within the left, between socialists, Communists and anarchists. Attacking the Church, whether rhetorically or physically, was also a way of reacting to a re-emerging and re-organizing political right in 1932. The importance accorded to religion in Spain might appear to set the country apart from wider Europe, but religion played a role in political struggles more widely. In the crisis of the Weimar Republic, Communists foregrounded militant anticlericalism in order to mobilize working-class support and undermine the German Social Democratic Party, while in France 'the clerical/anticlerical division remained an important structurant of political life' between the world wars.[2] The cleavage over religion was particularly marked and at times noted as an important feature of struggles in towns and villages across Spain, yet its role in fuelling radicalization in the Second Republic has been largely neglected.

[1] *Avance*, 24 July 1932.

[2] T. Weir, 'The Christian front against godlessness: anti-secularism and the demise of the Weimar Republic, 1928–1933', *Past & Present*, ccxxix (2015), 201–38; K. Passmore, *From Liberalism to Fascism: the Right in a French Province* (Cambridge, 1997), p. 45. See also D. H. Bell's emphasis on friction over religion in Italy in *Sesto San Giovanni: Workers, Culture and Politics in an Italian Town, 1880–1922* (New Brunswick, N.J., 1986).

'Anticlericalism, dissidence and radicalization (1932–3)', in M. Kerry, *Unite, Proletarian Brothers! Radicalism and Revolution in the Spanish Second Republic, 1931–6* (London, 2020), pp. 71–96. License: CC-BY-NC-ND 4.0.

Between 1932 and 1933, a current of radicalism developed in the coalfields. It had its roots in conflicts over the role of religion at a local level, both as an element of intra-left rivalry and as a symptom of the revival of the right and the lack of progress in constructing a secular Republic. However, religious divisions were not the sole drivers of radicalism. As the coal industry continued to struggle, the SOMA attempted to respond through pivoting in strategy to embrace strike action. Rather than the union radicalizing into line with the grassroots, its solutions to ameliorate the situation of the workforce only widened the growing breach between the rank and file and the union hierarchy, entrenching dissidence and fomenting greater radicalism. This was particularly evident in younger activists, whose role in spearheading radicalism is widely acknowledged.[3] Radicalism was expressed in two ways. Rank-and-file activists sought new ways of building working-class unity and re-appropriating the 'radical' label. From late 1932, socialists responded to a shift in the political mood in the coalfields by explicitly refashioning radicalism such that it did not contradict moderation and reformism. A year later, this radical impulse shifted further to the crystallization of a particular vision of the Republic, as a militant and uncompromising 'social Republic'.

Religion, rivalry and radicalism

On 8 October 1931, the debate in the Republican Constituent Cortes on the draft constitution turned to the role that the Church would play in the new state. As this phase of parliamentary debate loomed, Juan Pablo García, a young Asturian socialist lawyer, had written in the socialist weekly *La Aurora Social* that 'the clerical problem [was] the true touchstone of radicalism and democracy for Spanish politicians (men and parties)'. Recent parliamentary votes had served to 'unmask' those claiming to be radicals.[4] The debate was 'emotional and divisive' and positions hardened in parliament.[5] Beyond the walls of the Cortes, rejection of Catholic belief and practice was also a significant marker of radical zeal. Since August, citizens had regularly denounced parish priests for anti-Republican sermons in the provincial press or in person to the civil governor.[6]

[3] See work by S. Souto Kustrín, particularly *Paso a la juventud: movilización democrática, estalinismo y revolución en la república española* (Valencia, 2013).

[4] *La Aurora Social*, 18 Sept. 1931.

[5] For a summary, see W. J. Callahan, *The Catholic Church in Spain, 1875–1998* (Washington,D.C., 2000), pp. 274–94, the quotation at p. 288. For more detail, see V. M. Arbeloa, *La semana trágica de la Iglesia en España (8–14 octubre de 1931)* (Madrid, 2006).

[6] Such denunciations were claimed to be a daily occurrence (*Avance*, 15 Dec. 1931; *El Noroeste*, 13 Jan. 1932).

Alleging religious belief or practice was an important way of slurring rivals and thereby asserting one's own radical credentials. Accusations, counteraccusations and denials of religious practice flew back and forth between rival newspapers in Asturias in 1932. An article in anarchist *Solidaridad* singled out a Communist for selling religious images, while one individual wrote to *El Noroeste* denying a report in socialist *Avance* that he had given money to the parish priest of Baíña (Mieres). He retorted that socialists received payments from the priest and sent their members to confession in return.[7] One young socialist used the forum afforded by the provincial press to boast that he had convinced his wife-to-be to reject the 'pack of wolves' intent on using her to claw him back to Catholicism.[8] These claims – for example, that a socialist had taken his daughter to a different village in order to baptize her – and counterclaims should be treated carefully.[9] Rather than providing unambiguous evidence of actual religious practice, the slurs informally regulated the public and private conduct of leftists by reinforcing values and delineating the limits of acceptable behaviour. The desire to distance themselves publicly from rumours reveals how damaging the taint of religiosity could be to leftist reputations at the local level.

There was radicalizing potential in these prying eyes and public slanders. The pride in anticlericalism and desire to display radical zeal led to political groups formalizing this policing mechanism through internal procedures to eject members who were not sufficiently anticlerical. The PCE in Turón expelled one of its members for religious observance, proclaiming 'that is how we communists react to those who humiliate themselves before the Church'.[10] In a similar vein, the Socialist Youth (JS) in Asturias proposed a formal ban on its members 'attending and practising religious acts' and that 'atheist, antireligious and materialist tasks [be made] obligatory', though the proposal was rejected after fierce debate.[11] This was not restricted to Asturias. In Jaén, in Andalusia, the JS agreed that members should not have relationships with young women 'proud of their religiosity'.[12] Whether the policy was enforced or not, it demonstrated a commitment to upholding its anticlerical – and therefore radical – self-image.

7 *Solidaridad*, 18 July 1931; *El Noroeste*, 18 June 1932.

8 *Avance*, 24 Nov. 1932.

9 *La Aurora Social*, 6 Nov. 1931.

10 *El Noroeste*, 13 Nov. 1932.

11 *Avance*, 16, 18 July 1933.

12 A. M. Moral Roncal, *La cuestión religiosa en la Segunda República española: iglesia y carlismo* (Madrid, 2009), p. 64.

The nature of anticlerical rivalry on the left was moulded by the secularizing context of the new Republic. The Republic decreed the separation of church and state and secularizing legislation signalled that 'the Church was to be a voluntary association for those willing to subscribe instead of the guardian of Spain's identity and conscience'.[13] The measures introduced by the Republican–socialist government removed the Church's control over key aspects of citizens' lives, including marriage, education and death. Crucifixes were removed from school walls and civil burials were provided for. In practice, the implementation of government legislation depended on the nature of local politics. In Salamanca, which was a stronghold of Catholicism and conservatism, weddings continued to be religious affairs and there was no growth in civil burials.[14] In the left-wing coalfields of Asturias, meanwhile, the impulse to undermine the 'Catholic compass' was strong and activists continued to push the boundaries of secularism in order to present themselves as the most radical.[15] Criticizing past contact with the Church was a way of smearing one's opponents and positioning oneself in the radical vanguard.

The official secularism of the Republic fuelled and complicated the spiralling race to reject religion. The change in the national political landscape recalibrated what it meant to be radical. Secular values were no longer as radical as they had been prior to 1931. In order to appear radical in 1932, activists had to surpass state secularism. At the same time, espousing militant anticlericalism meant that an activist might be vulnerable to attacks from rivals, as many – if not most – activists' pasts did not meet the new exacting standards. Prior to 1931, it had not been easy to avoid a church wedding, baptism or simply contact with a priest. As José Estrada pointed out, it was unfair to judge an individual's radical credentials according to their past actions when avoiding the Church's control of rites of passage had been very difficult prior to the Republic.[16] But such occasions could nevertheless now be used to besmirch a rival's reputation.

Leftists did not solely measure their radical mettle against one another. Tensions existed within the left, but also started growing between leftists and Catholics as the secularizing project of the Second Republic started

[13] F. Lannon, *Privilege, Persecution and Prophecy: the Catholic Church in Spain, 1875–1975* (Oxford, 1987), p. 181.

[14] M. Vincent, *Catholicism in the Second Spanish Republic: Religion and Politics in Salamanca, 1930–1936* (Oxford, 1996), p. 68.

[15] On the 'compass', see M. Thomas, *The Faith and the Fury: Popular Anticlerical Violence and Iconoclasm in Spain, 1931–1936* (Eastbourne, 2013), pp. 32–3.

[16] *Avance*, 24 July 1932.

to impact on the everyday lives of citizens in 1932. Announcements in the provincial press trumpeted the first civil marriages and civil burials in towns and villages as victories over tradition and superstition. Parents in Tiraña (Laviana) of a baby registered without a baptism were congratulated for 'having liberated the child from the clerical dunking', while speeches at a civil wedding in Boo emphasized the 'civic value of the act, calling on those present [at the reception] to imitate their example' and not be stifled by 'clerical despotism'.[17] Such ceremonies were interpreted as marking the arrival of secular Republican modernity. Religious ceremonies no longer defined the nature of the local community. A riot occurred in Villarubia de Santiago (Toledo) when a girl was baptized against her parents' will.[18]

Catholics had already voiced their criticism of the Republican project in 1931 through the modern weapons of an 'aggrieved interest group': petitions and rallies.[19] The Church mobilized Catholics to make monetary donations to replace reduced state funding of the Church, and parents' associations were created to defend Catholic education.[20] Catholic women visited the homes of (young) women in their communities to press them into following the dictates of Catholic doctrine, a practice denounced by articles in *Avance*. Catholic women were accused of repeatedly pressuring a woman in Ciaño-Santa Ana to demand a church wedding ceremony and of insulting young female socialists in La Cuesta (San Martín del Rey Aurelio), Carbayín and Laviana.[21] The tone of such episodes indicates the bitterness of the atmosphere in the towns and villages and how Catholic reaction to secularization served to stimulate more militant, stubborn and outraged expressions of anticlericalism locally (and vice versa).

The friction between Catholics' expression of identity and the leftist proclamation of secular values is particularly evident in struggles over crucifixes. In early 1932, crucifixes were removed from school classrooms across Spain in accordance with a ministerial order.[22] In many areas, including Castile, Andalusia and Galicia, Catholics organized public

[17] *Avance*, 21 Jan., 10 Apr. 1932.

[18] Thomas, *Faith*, pp. 57–8.

[19] Vincent, *Catholicism*, p. 183. For petitions, see e.g., J. M. Macarro Vera, *Socialismo, República y revolución en Andalucía (1931–1936)* (Seville, 2000), p. 259.

[20] E.g. *Región*, 13, 16, 17 Feb., 13 Apr., 2 July, 28 Sept. 1932; *Hoja parroquial de Santa María la Real de la Corte*, 7 Feb., 11 Sept., 4 Dec. 1932.

[21] *Avance*, 21 Feb., 8 Apr., 20 May, 16 Aug. 1932. For similar accusations in Valencia, see S. Valero, *Republicanos con la monarquía, socialistas con la República: la Federación Socialista Valenciana durante la II República y la Guerra Civil (1931–1939)* (Valencia, 2015), p. 85.

[22] *Gaceta de Madrid*, 14 Jan. 1932.

demonstrations to protest or even reverse the removal of crucifixes from schools, sometimes destroying the Republican symbols that had replaced the religious image.[23] Such demonstrations did not occur in the Asturian coalfields, where Catholic organization was much weaker. Instead, Catholics expressed their dissent towards the secularizing regime on an individual level by wearing crucifixes around their necks – a practice applauded by *Acción*, a new weekly newspaper run by Catholic women in Gijón, and encouraged by the Asturian AP leader Cernuda.[24]

The proliferation of crucifixes around the necks of Catholics sparked a reaction from leftists. A socialist in Tuilla appealed for young men to ignore women sporting crucifixes 'when strolling, when dancing, in everything to do with daily life', while the JS in Turón declared themselves 'not prepared to tolerate' what they described as a Jesuit-inspired 'ignominious campaign'. They demanded the authorities act.[25] Elsewhere the crucifix was mocked. A group of people waited outside mass in La Felguera in June accompanied by a dog wearing a crucifix, while youths in Mieres and Sama rang bells to ridicule young women wearing crucifixes as they passed on their evening stroll.[26] In doing so, the youths adapted the mocking tradition of the *cencerrada* – a form of rough music frequently employed to taunt remarrying widows or widowers, or someone marrying outside the community – that was the Spanish variant of European *charivari*.[27] On this occasion, youths retooled the *cencerrada* for contemporary political needs. The young women were censured for transgressing the new moral standards of the community. Catholicism was not welcome, nor was it representative of the Asturian coalfields. The *cencerrada* and the crucifix-wearing dog were an assertion of a local secular hegemony believed to be under threat in the face of a reorganizing Catholic right in 1932.

Leftists pressured authorities and teachers into observing secularism in 1932 as a way of exhibiting their own radical zeal. This policing ranged from entering a municipal school and demanding a teacher hand over books and the wall-mounted image of Christ, to reporting a parish priest to the civil

[23] Vincent, *Catholicism*, p. 185; Macarro Vera, *Socialismo*, p. 261; E. Grandío Seoane, *Los orígenes de la derecha gallega: la CEDA en Galicia (1931–1936)* (Sada, 1998), p. 116; M. González Probados, *O socialismo na Segunda República (1931–1936)* (Sada, 1992), p. 129.

[24] *Acción*, 26 March, 16 Apr., 14, 21 May, 4 June 1932; *Región*, 24 Feb. 1932.

[25] *Avance*, 16, 30 Apr. 1932.

[26] *Región*, 22, 25 June 1932; *El Noroeste*, 13 Apr. 1932.

[27] On *charivari* and rough music, see N. Zemon Davis, 'The reasons of misrule: youth groups and charivaris in sixteenth-century France', *Past & Present*, l (1971), 41–75; E. P. Thompson, 'Rough music reconsidered', *Folklore*, ciii (1991), 3–26.

governor for criticizing the Republic.[28] Denunciation was more common than direct action. Young militants, who tended to be the most active in these cases, tried to place pressure on municipal and provincial authorities to uphold their more radical vision of the Republic. At times, they backed their demands with veiled threats. The JS in Aller requested that the municipal authorities enforce the prohibition on public demonstrations of faith – as mandated by article 27 of the Constitution – and warned otherwise of 'greater evils that favour no-one, as we youths are not going to consent to the trampling on any articles of the current Constitution, especially by those who merit the repulsion of all citizens of liberal spirit'.[29] These young militants policed both the parish priest and the Republican authorities to demand that secularization be enacted more quickly and deeply than it had been thus far. As in the case of crucifixes, criticism centred principally on the public exhibition of Catholic faith. Militants sought to curtail the way Catholic symbols sacralized the public space of streets and squares.[30]

Public space was therefore central to struggles over religion. The Constitutional requirement that the authorities approve religious processions, such as during Holy Week and on local feast days, provided opportunities for anticlerical mayors to ban them in the name of the law or over fears for public order. While for Catholics a procession expressed a parish's devotion and affirmed local identity and tradition, preventing a procession was a Republican – or anticlerical – victory. The degree to which processions were banned varied a great deal. Thirty-nine were banned in La Rioja in the spring/summer of 1932, while the situation was less restrictive in Andalusia.[31] In Salamanca, processions occurred as usual outside the provincial capital, but not in the city itself.[32]

Schools operated by mining companies were a battleground over religious symbols and the nature of education itself. Relative moderation in 1931 gave way to conflict in 1932 and the consequent radicalization and hardening of positions on the part of parents and the mining companies. In autumn 1931, the ministry of education banned those without teaching qualifications from working in schools and later reiterated the secular

[28] *El Noroeste*, 8 Jan., 30 March 1932.

[29] *Avance*, 7 Jun. 1932; AA, Actas, 30 May 1932 to 9 Feb. 1933, f. 39.

[30] M. Delgado Ruiz, 'Anticlericalismo, espacio y poder. La destrucción de los rituales católicos, 1931–1939', *Ayer*, xxvii (1997), *passim*.

[31] C. Gil Andrés, *Echarse a la calle: amotinados, huelguistas y revolucionarios (La Rioja, 1890–1936)* (Zaragoza, 2000), p. 382; A. L. López Villaverde, *El gorro frigio y la mitra frente a frente: construcción y diversidad territorial del conflicto político-religioso en la España republicana* (n.p., 2008), p. 214.

[32] Vincent, *Catholicism*, p. 186.

character of education in a ministerial circular in mid January 1932.[33] The ban meant that the Dominican school in San Martín del Rey Aurelio owned by Duro-Felguera was closed for much of the 1931–2 school year because the teachers lacked the required teaching qualifications and the company was unwilling to substitute them. The municipal authorities requested that the company cede them the school, but were unsuccessful. Workers threatened a strike if the schools did not reopen and offer a secular education in March 1932.[34] In defiance, Duro-Felguera reopened the school with suitably qualified Dominicans – citing a petition that the company had in fact gerrymandered – and 2,000 workers responded with a ten-day strike.[35] The strike revealed both the strength of conviction of the workforce and the importance of religious schooling to the mining companies.

The strike would prove to be the only victory over a mining company in the matter of religious education. Companies reasserted their authority in the schools they owned at the beginning of the next school year. Hulleras del Turón demanded proof of baptism in order to register pupils and SHE made it clear that the confessional nature of schooling was non-negotiable; 'and this is occurring in a secular state?' asked *Avance*.[36] The newspaper claimed to have been inundated with letters of protest, although it hoped the matter would not spiral into strike action. Undeterred, SHE refused to back down and instead closed the schools, a decision which affected nearly 2,000 children.[37] Some 2,000 people attended a rally on 25 September in defence of secular education. When a busload of attendees passed through Cabañaquinta, their shouts in defence of secular schools were met with a cry of 'down with the Republic'. Youngsters had to be restrained from leaving the bus to give the individual 'what he deserved'. Even though the civil governor claimed to have solved the matter by ensuring that religious education classes would be optional, the schools remained closed.[38]

Despite the pressures from left-wing activists at the local level, leftist councillors and mayors in the coalfields remained cautious. They attempted to balance respect for different beliefs and upholding Republican secularism.

33 *Gaceta de Madrid*, 14 Jan. 1932. For complaints, see e.g., *Región*, 24 Feb. 1932.

34 *El Noroeste*, 17 March 1932.

35 M. V. Álvarez Fernández, *La escuela del paternalismo industrial asturiano (1880–1937)* (Gijón, 2006), pp. 281–2; Á. Mato Díaz, *La escuela primaria en Asturias (1923–1937): los procesos de alfabetización y escolarización* (Oviedo, 1992), p. 267; *El Noroeste*, 24 Apr. 1932.

36 *Avance*, 10, 13 Sept. 1932.

37 *Avance*, 13 Sept. 1932 ; Álvarez Fernández, *La escuela*, p. 284.

38 *Avance*, 27 Sept., 4 Oct. 1932; Álvarez Fernández, *La escuela*, pp. 284–5; Mato Díaz, *La escuela*, p. 197.

While some councils placed restrictions on Catholic funeral processions, which they interpreted as contravening the constitutional prohibition of public displays of faith, Catholics could express their religious identity by placing crosses on tombs or funeral carriages.[39] Likewise, the provincial deputation removed chaplains from welfare institutions, but made it clear that chaplains funded by private donations would be allowed to practise. The deputation was 'non-denominational' not anticlerical.[40] Toeing this line was difficult when the authorities were under pressure from both Catholics and left-wing activists, who were dissatisfied with the pace of secularization for opposing reasons.

Frustration at the continued presence of Catholicism in public life and a resurgent right – along with unrealistic expectations at the extent to which religion would disappear from public life – was manifest in episodes of violence against shrines from mid 1932. Such attacks on Church property often occurred just before the feast day of the local patron saint. This served to disrupt the occasion as a Catholic collective performance, in which the parish and local community were affirmed as coterminous.[41] In mid September, an explosion destroyed an image of Christ at a hermitage in Turón and similar assaults occurred on religious images in Sobrescobio, Santa Rosa (Mieres) and beyond Asturias in 1932.[42] The turn to violence was a marked contrast to 1931, when feast days had been relatively peaceful. The desecration of images attempted to accelerate Republican secularizing legislation and enforce an image of the local community as secular. *Avance* claimed the attack in Turón resulted from rumours that the priest had planned an unauthorized procession that 'was opposed by the *pueblo*'. The newspaper thus justified iconoclasm for reflecting the community's desires.[43] According to this view, the community was consubstantial with anticlericalism.

These attacks on Catholic images in late summer 1932 also occurred in the specific context of a failed military coup. In August 1932, General Sanjurjo and a group of fellow plotters initiated an uprising in Seville in

[39] The authorities in Mieres routinely authorized the erection of crosses at graves while the 1933 regulations on funeral processions in Aller allowed religious and political symbols (AA, Actas, 18 Feb. 1933 to 6 Jan. 1934, ff. 182–3).

[40] AHPA, Actas de la comisión de la Diputación Provincial, 29 Dec. 1931 to 12 Sept. 1933, ff. 196–9, 208–9.

[41] See Delgado Ruiz, 'Anticlericalismo'. For a similar emphasis on disruption coinciding with Holy Week in Aragón, see M. P. Salomón Chéliz, *Anticlericalismo en Aragón. Protesta popular y movilización cívica (1900–1939)* (Zaragoza, 2002), pp. 281, 288.

[42] *Región*, 18 June, 17 Aug. 1932; Thomas, *Faith*, pp. 54–6.

[43] *Región*, 15 Sept. 1932; *Avance*, 14, 15 Sept. 1932.

the traditional style of a *pronunciamiento* by declaring a state of war and expecting the government to step aside. The conspirators were critical of the direction being taken by the Republic, particularly the statute of autonomy that attempted to fulfil the aspirations of Catalan nationalists.[44] The poorly supported coup was easily suppressed by the government and led to a wave of revenge attacks, which were frequently directed at the Church.[45] Targeting the Church was an established form of demonstrating political discontent, as occurred in Barcelona in 1909, and May 1931 in Madrid and southern Spain.[46] There were attempts to set fire to churches and convents in Seville, and in the Asturian coalfields, councillors in Langreo singled out 'churches and convents' and a Duro-Felguera confessional school as 'centres' of conspiracy. The chairman assured the council that such centres had been under surveillance for a while. Communist councillors presented a motion with fifteen demands covering local and national politics – seven of which centred on the Church.[47] The failed coup also stimulated a new wave of restrictions on religious practices by municipal authorities in the south of Spain, including taxes on the tolling of church bells and the banning of Catholic funeral processions.[48]

The Communist motion in Langreo was voted down, but the response from socialist councillors shows how the coup helped to propagate a radical mood. Belarmino Tomás, speaking for the socialists, asserted their combativeness. Like the Communists, socialists were 'radical', but they were also a party of government and would abide by the government's plan of action.[49] This statement was not significant in itself, but it was symptomatic of how socialists embraced self-identification with the label 'radical' over the course of 1932, which represented a distinctive shift from 1931. Local divisions and rivalries pushed socialists to adopt the radical label, even if this was limited to rhetoric over an actual shift in political practice.

In 1931, socialists had loudly proclaimed their moderation and responsibility in contrast to Communist and anarchist 'extremists', whose attitude was portrayed as dangerous, unrealistic and immature. Socialists

[44] For the coup, see E. González Calleja, *Contrarrevolucionarios: radicalización violenta de las derechas durante la Segunda República, 1931–1936* (Madrid, 2011), pp. 81–106.

[45] P. Preston, *The Coming of the Spanish Civil War: Reform, Reaction and Revolution in the Second Republic* (London, 1978), p. 73.

[46] See J. C. Ullman, *Tragic Week: a Study of Anticlericalism in Spain* (Cambridge, Mass., 1968).

[47] Macarro Vera, *Socialismo*, p. 251; AL, Actas, 28 Apr. 1932 to 17 Dec. 1932, ff. 98–99, 100.

[48] Macarro Vera, *Socialismo*, p. 252.

[49] AL, Actas, 28 Apr. 1932 to 17 Dec. 1932, ff. 98–9.

sarcastically mocked those who interrupted a meeting in Sama for being 'the real revolutionaries' and derided Communists in Aller for striking 'for sport'.[50] Yet by 1932, socialists were claiming to be the 'true revolutionaries'. In Olloniego they drew a clear line between themselves and the Republican bourgeoisie, 'no matter if [the latter] call themselves radical'.[51] There had been a shift in the mood among rank-and-file militants. To be a Communist was now fashionable – or so an activist from Ujo claimed – while mineworkers at La Cobertoria complained that 'he who makes the most outrageous comments [at workplace assemblies] is the one who comes out best'.[52] Attempting to wrest back the labels 'radical' and 'revolutionary' from Communists and anarchists was the socialist response to this, possibly out of a fear of being outflanked on the left. The voguishness of radicalism was due in part to those who had joined a different political group during the Republic needing to prove themselves to their new comrades. The zealousness of the converted was remarked upon in Turón and Bazuelo (Mieres), where the non-unionized and former members of Primo de Rivera's right-wing political movement, Unión Patriótica, now fashioned themselves as 'the most revolutionary'.[53]

Yet the socialist attempt to wrestle back the label of 'radical' in 1932 was little more than rhetoric. The strategy pursued by the SOMA in mining conflicts did not change. Socialists still condemned strike action, which was 'a very revolutionary tactic for "simpletons", idiots and the naïve'. Strikes would 'undoubtedly' harm workers if not deployed responsibly.[54] In his criticism of a CNT-led strike at the Fondón pit in Sama, SOMA leader Graciano Antuñac learly spelled out the distinction between radicalism and strike action:

> One is not more radical or more revolutionary for being an early riser and declaring strikes for trifling reasons. It is necessary to choose the right moment for the fight against capital. But it is also necessary to know what are the demands, because otherwise, instead of victories, there will be failures.[55]

As a socialist from Mieres clarified at the end of 1932, to be a 'revolutionary' worker could not 'be understood in the negative sense that certain individuals extol, for whom hold-ups and crime are fully justified'. Rather, he defended

[50] *La Aurora Social*, 14 Aug., 11 Sept. 1931.

[51] *Avance*, 17 Apr. 1932.

[52] *Avance*, 25 Aug., 6 Dec. 1932.

[53] *Avance*, 23 March, 15 July 1932.

[54] *Avance*, 15 March, 30 July 1932.

[55] *Avance*, 24 Sept. 1932.

'persevering action, daily conquests, consolidating positions taken from the bourgeoisie, in order to continue along the road to emancipation' because 'the opposite would mean cultivating our own ruin'.[56] Socialists were radicals for they desired the transformation of society, but this did not necessarily entail confrontational strategies. Rather, socialists reconfigured radicalism to denote restraint – and thus responsible socialists had always been radical. This attempt to reconcile radicalism and moderation meant socialists still distinguished themselves from Communists and anarchists.

Militancy grew over the following year. Rhetorical radicalism continued, but the vigorous appeals for action and a more combative style of politics meant that strategic moderation eventually disappeared. In October 1933, the JS from Hueria de San Andrés (San Martín del Rey Aurelio) called for more *controversias*, as they were 'the best way of propagating socialist ideals and educating the masses in a Marxist and revolutionary way, inciting, thus, the rebellious spirit innate in all proletarians'.[57] Rather than simply contesting the categories 'radical' and 'revolutionary', the appeal was for a militant attitude to be actively instilled in the working class.

The coal crisis

Socialist participation in government made it difficult for them to redefine radicalism. They did not have the same freedom to adopt a militant, oppositional attitude as anarchists or communists. This cut to the heart of a major problem facing social democratic parties in Europe, which was particularly acute in Germany but also apparent in other countries where social democratic parties held government office, such as France and Britain. Governing within a capitalist system while attempting to defend the demands of their working-class constituency was a challenging combination at the best of times, but it was made even more so by the Great Depression. Social democratic ministers were often reluctant to challenge the prevailing liberal economic orthodoxy, which counselled cuts in expenditure to balance the books.[58] The German Social Democratic Party was unable to change course economically and the association of socialists with the defence of the Weimar Republic became a hindrance, as disgruntled voters turned to extreme options adept at channelling the radical mood into a rejection of Weimar democracy.

[56] *Avance*, 29 Dec. 1932.

[57] *Avance*, 4 Oct. 1933.

[58] But see French socialists' desire to 'stimulate demand', J. Jackson, *The Politics of Depression in France, 1932–1936* (Cambridge, 1985), pp. 40–1.

Germany had been hit particularly hard by the shockwaves from the Wall Street crash in 1929. In the industrial heartland of the Ruhr, unemployment climbed rapidly. Half the workforce – 187,000 men – was dismissed between 1930 and 1932, by which point there were six million jobless nationally.[59] Unemployment was also high in British mining regions. In July 1931, nearly 40 per cent of the insured population were unemployed in County Durham and 41 per cent in Glamorgan, while in certain areas unemployment was higher still, including Jarrow on Tyneside, where it reached 73 per cent.[60] Across Europe, ten million were unemployed in 1931. In Spain, the situation was different. The effects of the crash hit later and did not have the same rapid, deep impact, although the economy slowed and unemployment remained an endemic problem during the Republic. This was due in part to the effects of Primo de Rivera's massive investment in public works during the 1920s along with the structural underemployment that formed part of Spain's agricultural economy.

The Asturian coal industry did not experience the same level of unemployment seen in the German and British mining areas – or even the Basque iron mines, where the number of workers dropped by a third between 1929 and 1933 – even as it faced difficulties.[61] Piecework rates were reduced, the workforce at Hulleras de Riosa shrunk by two-thirds, and Hulleras del Turón introduced short-time working.[62] Rather than symptoms of a worldwide economic slump, workers interpreted the difficulties through a political lens, which is testament to the level of politicization of Spanish society during the Republic. In Turón the finger was pointed at the 'the attitude of a certain person of great influence in … Altos Hornos de Vizcaya [the owner of Hulleras del Turón], who showed himself to be against the regime', a sentiment later echoed in Figaredo.[63]

Mineworkers' frustrations prompted the proliferation of small-scale conflicts. *Avance* lamented that cases such as a twenty-four-hour strike in protest over a disciplinary matter in Barredos (Laviana) were 'frequently repeated' while a socialist from Caborana expressed his frustration at the 'atmosphere of conflicts in … peaceful [Aller]', which 'sometimes come

[59] A. Zukas, 'Inscribing class struggle in space: unemployed protest in the Ruhr in late Weimar Germany', *Labour History Review*, lxxx (2015), 31–62, at p. 39.

[60] S. Ward, 'The means test and the unemployed in South Wales and the north-east of England, 1931–1939', *Labour History Review*, lxxiii (2008), 113–32, at p. 113.

[61] R. Miralles, *El socialismo vasco durante la II República: organización, ideología, política y elecciones, 1931–1936* (Bilbao, 1988), p. 114.

[62] *El Noroeste*, 9 Sept. 1932; A. Shubert, *The Road to Revolution in Spain: the Coal Miners of Asturias, 1860–1934* (Urbana, Ill., 1987), pp. 144–5.

[63] *Avance*, 9 March, 27 Aug. 1932.

from the flippancy of the workforce, though more often they are due to the clumsiness and impertinence of the bosses'.[64] The SOMA hierarchy continued to pursue a strategy of avoiding strike action, although socialists often participated in locally organized strikes in defiance of SOMA orders, including a twenty-hour solidarity strike with Industrial Asturiana workers threatened with the company's closure and the resultant loss of 1,200 jobs.[65] These seeds of rank-and-file dissent flowered into internal opposition within the socialist mining union over the following year.

Pressure on the SOMA continued to grow as the economic situation deteriorated. The SOMA appeared to be slowly changing position. The union joined the rank and file in criticizing the mining companies' 'offensive' against the workers in August and the Executive announced a general strike soon afterwards.[66] Yet the strike was cancelled twice after employers made promises to address the union's demands.[67] The announcement that Fábrica de Mieres, Duro-Felguera and Hulleras del Turón were to close their mines indefinitely in mid November left the reluctant union with no choice. The SOMA called a general strike and 25,000 downed tools for six days, even as the socialists continued to emphasize their moderation. The solution they proposed included a number of measures to increase the consumption of coal.[68]

The November general strike seemed to confirm SOMA's hegemony in the coalfields. It received mass backing and an attempt by anarchists and Communists – who were swept up in the strike – to prolong the stoppage failed. Even in Turón, where the SUM's call received most support, only 25 per cent continued the strike.[69] While anarchists and Communists were unable to resist being drawn into socialist strikes, the reverse was not true.[70] Even so, rather than confirming the SOMA's dominance, the strike served to legitimize the rumbling dissent within the socialists' own ranks. For the leadership, the November strike was a means of responding to rank-and-file demands and quelling dissent, not a curtain-raiser for further militancy. The SOMA considered the negotiated solution to the strike as a legitimation

[64] *Avance*, 9 July, 15 March 1932.

[65] For the strike, see *El Noroeste*, 24 Sept. 1932.

[66] *Avance*, 9 Aug. 1932.

[67] *Avance*, 18 Sept., 23 Oct. 1932.

[68] Shubert, *Road*, p. 145.

[69] *Avance*, 22 Nov. 1932; *Región*, 22 Nov. 1932.

[70] E.g., see a CNT-organized solidarity strike to support Duro-Felguera metalworkers in December (*Avance*, 10 Dec. 1932; *Región*, 10 Dec. 1932; M. Castejón Rodríguez, 'La patronal hullera asturiana en la Segunda República' (unpublished UNED PhD thesis, 2009), p. 382).

of their state-centred, moderate approach to conflicts between capital and labour. The rank and file held a different view. They considered it a signal that their long-running discontent was legitimate and that the union was aligning itself with the more militant grassroots. The SOMA even felt the need to quash publicly rumours that they were going to collaborate with other unions in a general strike.[71]

The solution to the general strike was short-lived and did not prevent a further decline in the fortunes of the mining industry. At the beginning of 1933, mining companies announced further closures and dismissals and *El Noroeste* observed that the situation was ruining shopkeepers' businesses.[72] Faced with this panorama, the SOMA balloted its members on a second general strike. They voted overwhelmingly in favour: 15,128 for strike action and 113 against. Again, the strike appeared to be a success. It received widespread support in the coalfields and the SOMA managed to negotiate a settlement, which was overwhelmingly ratified by 15,105 votes to 410. The agreement aimed to reduce coal production through a 10 per cent reduction in the labour force. This would be achieved through an early retirement and subsidy scheme that paid workers not to work.[73] Retirement would be voluntary, but forced retirement would follow if there were not enough volunteers.[74]

Yet not only was the solution insufficient to improve the fortunes of the struggling coal industry, it also contributed significantly to the radicalization of the wider workforce. When details of the lay-offs emerged, they proved unpalatable to the mineworkers. Subsidies for those dismissed would be far lower than wages, young mineworkers would lose their jobs as well as older miners and the companies would decide who was to be removed from the workforce if there were not enough volunteers.[75] Faced with the unattractive pensions and unemployment subsidies, there were too few volunteers for redundancy or retirement and so companies were obliged to paste up their own lists of those to be dismissed.

The publication of lists of workers deemed excess to requirements led to a wave of strikes.[76] Mineworkers had their own criteria as to who should retire. *Avance* published their articles criticizing the lack of volunteers in their pits – in Vegadotos (Mieres) purportedly only 20 per cent of eligible

[71] *Avance*, 4 Dec. 1932.

[72] *El Noroeste*, 5, 15, 21, 26, 27 Jan. 1933.

[73] Shubert, *Road*, p. 146.

[74] *Avance*, 3 March 1933.

[75] *Revista Industrial Minera Asturiana*, 16 March 1933.

[76] *Avance*, 8, 18, 21 March 1933.

older mineworkers had solicited retirement – even as the newspaper scolded the authors for their impatience.[77] The SOMA leadership censured unhelpful rumours spread by 'extremists' and tried to reassure workers, aided by *Avance*. The socialist daily reported that most workers favoured the retirement and subsidy scheme and that there were many volunteers. Yet the need for these reports, several articles penned by SOMA president Amador Fernández, official SOMA press releases and an extensive speaking tour by SOMA leaders to explain the measures is revealing of the widespread opposition and discontent in the coalfields.[78]

The scheme did achieve its objective in reducing the workforce – 2,795 workers were either retired or receiving subsidy payments by the end of June 1933.[79] Yet the process had not been smooth. Young mineworkers in particular spearheaded protests. Indignation at the dismissal of young workers while those over sixty continued to work sparked wildcat strikes in Siero and the Nalón valley.[80] A lyrical article in *El Noroeste* explained that 'young and strong' mine workers' desperation was manifest in a plunge towards revolution and a desire for violence. The author augured a threatening future: 'a deaf and black storm of repressed courage, of restrained impetus, is dragging itself aggressively and obstinately, relentless and rough, intoxicated by explosions and liberated cries. Why this suffering?'[81] Even those who had kept their jobs resented the levy on their wages to pay for the subsidies, which meant that 'a revolutionary wave … [was] being born again in the depths of the mines'.[82]

In Germany, too, unemployment hit young workers particularly hard. Some young males withdrew from society while others, humiliated and angered at losing their status and independence, gravitated towards the Communists and Nazis in search of 'material assistance, the sense of belonging and order, [and] the action-first mentality of radicalism'. These groups provided them with a 'reconstructed "family"' and a sense of purpose.[83] The politics of 'action' espoused by movements that engaged in

[77] *Avance*, 17 March 1933.

[78] *Avance*, 15, 14, 17 March 1933.

[79] *Revista Industrial Minera Asturiana*, 16 Aug. 1933.

[80] *El Noroeste*, 26, 28 March 1933.

[81] *El Noroeste*, 6 Apr. 1933.

[82] *El Noroeste*, 9 Apr. 1933.

[83] P. Swett, *Neighbors and Enemies: the Culture of Radicalism in Berlin, 1929–1933* (Cambridge, 2004), pp. 109–13. See also S. Reichardt, 'Violence and community: a microstudy on Nazi Storm Troopers', *Central European History*, xlvi (2013), 275–97. For a broader survey of how unemployment can result in protest, as opposed to nihilism and passivity, see

street violence attracted those seeking the redemption of class or nation and who rejected or were tired of 'sterile' democratic politics.[84] The particular Asturian context led to a different effect. Young socialists did not move to the Communist ranks in great numbers. They channelled their anger and resentment into 'action-first' radicalism within socialism. Socialism was refashioned as the radical and revolutionary option. The Asturian JS claimed that Lenin was more aligned with Spanish socialists than Communists by publishing a commentary on an extract from his 1905 text 'Social-democracy and the provisional revolutionary government'. Five months later, a delegate from the JS National Committee observing a plenary meeting of the Asturian JS accused the Asturians of being obsessed by the 'dictatorship of the proletariat' and using the language of communists.[85] Claiming Lenin for socialism was a clear bid to position themselves as the revolutionary vanguard and emphasize the radical character of their politics. The national JS followed with extracts from Lenin's *The State and Revolution* in its mouthpiece *Renovación* during the first few months of 1934.[86]

Militancy was not confined to younger workers. It quickly erupted in the autumn in the wake of a third general mining strike organized by the SOMA. Called in response to the companies' cancellation of payments to the retirement fund created after the previous general strike, the strike was peaceful. It resulted in a provisional extension of the agreement that had ended the previous conflict while the government worked towards a definitive solution.[87] Yet simmering resentment soon re-emerged via numerous wildcat strikes in October and November when mineworkers did not receive their wages. Reporting on a spontaneous strike of 2,000 mineworkers at Fábrica de Mieres, *El Noroeste* asked for what had the last mining strike been fought.[88] The solution negotiated by the SOMA had done little to alleviate the overall situation of the coal industry while the union continued to refuse to sanction wildcat strikes. The Mieres SOMA

Unemployment and Protest: New Perspectives on Two Centuries of Contention, ed. M. Reiss and M. Perry (Oxford, 2011).

[84] On politics as action in interwar Europe, see M. Vincent, 'Political violence and mass society: a European civil war?', in *The Oxford Handbook of European history, 1914–1945*, ed. N. Doumanis (Oxford, 2016), pp. 388–403. For the importance of youth and radicalism, see E. Rosenhaft, *Beating the Fascists? The German Communist Party and Political Violence, 1929–1933* (Cambridge, 1983), p. 193; S. Whitney, *Mobilizing Youth: Communists and Catholics in Interwar France* (Durham, N.C., 2009).

[85] *Avance*, 6 Dec. 1932, 9 May 1933.

[86] Souto Kustrín, *Paso*, p. 57.

[87] Shubert, *Road*, p. 146; *Avance*, 29 Sept. 1933.

[88] *El Noroeste*, 13, 26 Oct. 1933; *Avance*, 13 Oct. 1933.

regional committee advocated patience, blaming strikes on 'irresponsible elements' who were 'taking advantage of the discontent'.[89] Patience was little consolation for mineworkers owed wages, not least as rank-and-file militancy achieved results. After 2,000 went on strike in Mieres, Fábrica de Mieres quickly announced that October's wages would be paid the following day. Grassroots pressure achieved more immediate results than the SOMA. The radical attitude among the rank and file was hardening. Even as Fábrica de Mieres paid workers at some pits, two mines remained on strike in solidarity with those still waiting.[90]

Frustrated with the deteriorating situation of the coal industry and the SOMA's inability to provide a vision or strategy to improve the state of affairs, mineworkers of different ideologies were turning to workplace unity to defend their interests collectively. The new initiatives drew on the traditions of pit-based assemblies in which workers from different unions debated and elected their representatives during disputes, but extended them further towards a more vigorous form of rank-and-file unity that had been catalysed by the general mining strikes. Back in February, joint strike committees had been formed at pit-level without the sanction of the SOMA and were relevant enough for *Avance* to pour scorn on them, labelling them a 'comedy'.[91] Further committees followed during the September general strike. At La Nueva pit, it was formed by representatives of the socialists, anarchists, Communists and unaffiliated, while in Ciaño-Santa Ana workers of 'all tendencies' attended a 'huge [*magna*] assembly'.[92] These rank-and-file initiatives threatened the authority and strategy of the SOMA.

Much more challenging for the SOMA than pit-based initiatives was the creation of the cross-union Pro-Workers' Unity Committee (CPUT: Comité Pro-Unidad de los Trabajadores) in Blimea at the beginning of 1933.[93] The CPUT committee was formed of delegates representing the socialists, anarchists, Communists and the non-unionized. This inclusion of the unaffiliated was novel. It indicated the desire for all workers to have a voice in the urgent circumstances facing the industry and marked a departure from the existing strategy of trying to capture the unaffiliated

[89] *Avance*, 12 Nov. 1933.

[90] *Avance*, 15, 18 Nov. 1933.

[91] *Avance*, 5, 19, 21, 23 Feb. 1933.

[92] *El Noroeste*, 26 Sept. 1933; see also 13, 29 Sept. 1933.

[93] The CPUT only receives a brief mention or footnote in the historiography (see D. Ruiz, *Insurrección defensiva y revolución obrera: el octubre español de 1934* (Barcelona, 1988), p. 88; E. Izquierdo, 'Hacia la unidad sindical, 1933–1934', *Estudios de Historia Social*, xxxi (1984), 113–22, at p. 117.

or members from rival unions. The CPUT reportedly had the 'enthusiastic backing' of twenty-one of the twenty-three sections of the SOMA regional committee in San Martín del Rey Aurelio, which was traditionally a bastion of socialism, and also enjoyed the support of Communists in Requejo (Turón).[94] The CPUT was symptomatic of a desire for a new direction for the left that put unity above the interests of individual parties and trade unions and recognized that convergence between them was unlikely.

The socialist representative on the CPUT was José Estrada, the same man who six months earlier had engaged in a public exchange of slurs with his Communist rivals. Estrada was an important socialist in San Martín del Rey Aurelio. He had been president of the Socialist group in Blimea and secretary of the SOMA regional committee in 1932.[95] Now Estrada appealed for 'the fusion of all workers for the defence of common interests and rights, without anyone giving up their ideology or tendency and without having to leave their respective Unions'.[96] In effect, Estrada had put his finger on the problem. The respective mining unions made regular, routine calls for working-class unity, but achieving the collapse and absorption of a rival union was unrealistic. Estrada declared this strategy 'absurd'; instead, 'unity ha[d] to be made beyond ideological tendencies and beyond, moreover, all of your leaders'.[97]

Seeking an alliance at the level of the rank and file was a challenge to the SOMA and its principle of leaving strategic questions to the union leadership. Unsurprisingly, the socialist hierarchy was not interested. The Socialist Group and SOMA Regional Committee met to discuss the 'indiscipline' of Estrada for conspiring with 'external and enemy elements' and quickly expelled him. Estrada hit back, criticizing the 'spiritual myopia' of the SOMA bureaucracy.[98] Little more about Estrada appears in the archival record. It is possible that he had converted to Communism and attempted to subvert the SOMA from within. In any case, the events of 1932 had pushed him to engage with his rivals in Blimea.

Unity initiatives at a local level were not a phenomenon limited to Asturias, but were a feature of political activity on the left in Europe at the time, including in southern France and the Welsh coalfields.[99] Neighbourhood

[94] *El Noroeste*, 1, 5 Feb. 1933.

[95] A. Fernández Pérez, *Tiempos heroicos: diccionario biográfico del socialismo asturiano* (Oviedo, 2013), pp. 282–3.

[96] *El Noroeste*, 4 Jan., 1 Feb. 1933.

[97] *El Noroeste*, 11 Feb. 1933.

[98] *Avance*, 8 Jan. 1933; *El Noroeste*, 1 Feb. 1933.

[99] For France, see G.-R. Horn, *European Socialists Respond to Fascism: Ideology, Activism*

networks and kinship links could serve to forge alternative paths of solidarity in a crisis. However, evidence is fragmentary and, as Stephanie Ward pointed out in the context of British mining areas, the co-operation of different political groups – including those beyond the left – could be fragile and did not mean that previous fractures had been overcome.[100]

The consolidation of workplace-based assemblies and committees as mechanisms for unity and dialogue led to growing dissent in the socialist ranks. At an assembly chaired by a SOMA member in September 1933, workers agreed not to return to the mines until the SOMA solution had been debated at a workplace assembly, and strongly criticized the socialist mayor of San Martín del Rey Aurelio for preventing them from holding meetings.[101] Spasms of dissidence had manifested themselves throughout the year. SOMA members were thrown out of the section in Piñeres (Aller) for criticizing the leadership.[102] There was a growing rift between the hierarchy and grassroots in the Asturian socialist movement in 1933, something which is frequently highlighted by historians for the rest of Spain.[103] Across the country, thousands of members left the UGT. Its membership shrank to 400,000 in 1933 after a high point of over a million in 1932.[104] Yet in Asturias, even as the SOMA lost touch with its members, the union did not implode or collapse as an organization, whereas in the Ruhr tens of thousands of voters switched from the German Social Democratic Party to the Communists in the summer of 1932.[105] In Asturias, however, there was no viable alternative in the coalfields. For SOMA members, moreover, sharp criticism of the leadership did not necessarily contradict union membership. The union could still be an effective vehicle for militancy. Besides, if unity was the solution to the problems of the working class, why leave the socialist ranks?

---

and Contingency in the 1930s (New York, 1996), pp. 138–9. There was also a failed attempt by the Second (social-democratic) and Third (Communist) Internationals to 'reach an understanding' in early 1933 (p. 37).

[100] S. Ward, *Unemployment and the State in Britain: the Means Test and Protest in 1930s South Wales and North-East England* (Manchester, 2013), pp. 170–1.

[101] *El Noroeste*, 26 Sept. 1933.

[102] *Avance*, 14 May 1933.

[103] E.g. Preston, *Coming of the Spanish Civil War*, p. 80; J. Aróstegui, *Largo Caballero: el tesón y la quimera* (Barcelona, 2013), p. 297; H. Graham, *Socialism and War: the Spanish Socialist Party in Power and Crisis, 1936–1939* (Cambridge, 1991), pp. 43–7.

[104] M. Bizcarrondo, *Historia de la UGT*, iii: *Entre la democracia y la revolución, 1931–1936* (6 vols, Madrid, 2008), pp. 18, 24.

[105] As emphasized by Shubert in *Road*, p. 149. For the Ruhr, see D. Harsch, *German Social Democracy and the Rise of Nazism* (Chapel Hill, N.C., 1993), p. 205.

Frictions and growing militancy formed part of a wider radicalizing climate in coalfield towns and villages in 1933, driven by tensions over other community pressure points. Conflicts between tenants and landlords were increasingly bitter. In Oviedo, the Tenants' League expressed its satisfaction over the reduction in rents achieved over the past year, yet it also wrote to the minister of justice demanding the cessation of a judge who was alleged to favour the landlords.[106] The Tenants' League in Sama warned landlords to stop evicting tenants and follow the procedures established by the law. A month later, three firecrackers [*petardos*] were thrown onto the roof of the home of a lawyer who advised landlords in Langreo.[107] Even though it is not possible to draw a strong causative link between rent activism and this particular attack, the fractious atmosphere was clear. In Aller, the league's anger at a landlord's 'intransigence' and 'reprehensible methods' in a case that had already gone to trial sparked a boycott of a theatre owned by the landlord. The boycott had 'the support of all working class organizations in the municipality, without exception'.[108] This militancy deriving from tenant activism was also evident nearly 2,000km southwest of Asturias on the island of Tenerife. In the spring-summer of 1933, members of the Tenants' League went on strike when a court ruled in favour of an eviction. The conflict escalated. The authorities closed union and tenants' centres and arrested their leaderships, demonstrations erupted in protest and a warehouse full of straw was set on fire.[109]

Mining companies mirrored the resistance shown by landlords. Hulleras del Turón demonstrated obstinacy in its resistance to Republican secularism. School inspectors confirmed a socialist denunciation that the company demanded proof of baptism in order to register at the school and made a number of recommendations, including that religious education be optional and timetabled outside of normal class hours. Days later, the mayor's district representative reported that the school staff had taken the children to mass against the orders of the school inspector and, after the de la Salle brothers refused to co-operate, the mayor of Mieres ordered the arrest of one of the teachers.[110]

[106] *Avance*, 16 March 1933.

[107] *Avance*, 19 Feb. 1933; *Región*, 18 March 1933.

[108] *Avance*, 27 Apr. 1933.

[109] *Heraldo de Madrid*, 6, 7 July 1933. See also C. D. Aguiar García and Y. Hermida Martín, 'Techo y dignidad. La lucha del Sindicato de Inquilinos de Tenerife durante la Segunda República', in *Culturas políticas en la contemporaneidad: discursos y prácticas políticas desde los márgenes a las élites. Culturas políticas y acción colectiva desde la izquierda durante el S. XX*, ed. J. A. Caballero Machí, R. Mínguez Blasco and V. Rodríguez-Flores Parra (Valencia, 2015), pp. 115–18.

[110] *Avance*, 16, 22 Feb., 1 March 1933.

The implicit social contract between the mining companies and residents of the coalfields was eroding. Municipal councils were frustrated at the inertia and lack of co-operation from mining companies. After months of fruitless battling with them, the council in Langreo decided to take Carbones La Nueva to court for not repairing damage to public services and in a separate case called for the arrest of the director of Carbones Asturianos.[111] The difficulties in fulfilling their role as guarantors and defenders of the local community and their own workforces led in some cases to a more militant and aggressive statement of municipal power. During the September mining strike, socialist and Republican councillors in Langreo reached the point of questioning property rights. They demanded 'new legislation' on the 'property of mines' in which mineworkers would take precedence over the owners. As one councillor reasoned, 'mining concessions represent a leasehold contract and when one of the parties fails to uphold the agreement, the contract is broken and should then be rescinded'. The radicalism of the motion surprised Communist councillors, who claimed that it would achieve nothing and failed to answer working class demands.[112] For supporters of the motion, the companies' inability to offer stable employment meant they had broken a social contract with the mineworkers and local communities. Property rights and the relationship between the local community and the companies were now open to renegotiation.

In the context of the same September mining strike, striking miners in Mieres used coercion to prevent the transportation of coal and further disrupt the local economy. The SOMA Executive Committee distanced itself from this use of violence, yet at the same time instrumentalized it as a warning: 'the companies and authorities would do well to interpret it as the firm resolve and intent to take the movement to the limits of resistance'.[113] Whereas in 1932 the SOMA leadership had embraced the radical label yet rejected violence, towards the end of 1933 its position was now more ambiguous. This attitude is inextricably linked to the context of political upheaval due to the collapse of the Republican-socialist coalition and the new militancy in the rhetoric of the president of the PSOE and minister of labour, Francisco Largo Caballero.

The rhetoric of radicalism

Largo Caballero's militant turn came as Republican-socialist collaboration in government neared its conclusion. The government had come under

[111] AL, Actas, 7 Oct. 1933 to 16 June 1934, ff. 29–30, 39–40.

[112] AL, Actas, 24 Dec. 1932 to 30 Sept. 1933, ff. 181–2.

[113] *Avance*, 23 Sept. 1933.

increasing pressure for a variety of reasons, including obstructionism in parliament, a deepening division within the Radical Socialist party that formed part of the governing coalition, mounting economic difficulties and right-wing success in municipal elections held in parts of central Spain. A particular problem was posed by events in a small village in Cádiz province in January 1933. A nationwide anarchist-organized revolutionary insurrection failed across the country, but in Casas Viejas libertarian communism was proclaimed. Three guards were killed and eight peasants died, six of whom were burned inside a shack. The Assault and Civil Guard killed fourteen peasants they arrested after defeating the insurrection.[114] Information slowly emerged detailing the actions of the Assault Guard and parliamentary questions and investigations ensued. The government was cleared of responsibility, but the affair was very damaging and became a 'Calvary' for the cabinet. The final blow to the Republican-socialist government came in September, when results of the elections to the Court of Constitutional Guarantees confirmed the resurgence of the right and widespread support for Radical Party, who sat in opposition to the government parties in Cortes.[115] When the Republican-socialist government fell, President Alcalá Zamora turned to the Radical Party. Lerroux's cabinet failed to obtain the confidence of the Cortes and instead his fellow Radical, Diego Martínez Barrio, produced a government that shepherded the legislature towards national elections in November.

Frustrated reform, rank-and-file discontent and the fracturing of the Republican-socialist government formed the backdrop to Largo Caballero's change in rhetoric. In the summer of 1933, he gave two key speeches as part of his attempt to reconnect with the socialist grassroots. He reiterated the socialist movement's commitment to socialism and, significantly, in a speech at the JS summer school on 12 August, he stated that it was impossible to build socialism within a bourgeois Republic.[116] Even as the final destination was socialism – as it had always been – there were now two roads available: gaining power through elections or the use of force. In this 'double scenario', the latter was to be employed if the former was blocked or if the socialists' enemies broke with legality. Largo Caballero continued

[114] The canonical study is J. Mintz, *The Anarchists of Casas Viejas* (Bloomington, Ind., 1994 [1982]). See also J. Casanova, *Anarchism, the Republic and Civil War in Spain (1931–1939)* (Abingdon, 2004), pp. 68–72.

[115] For detailed analysis, see N. Townson, *The Crisis of Democracy in Spain: Centrist Politics under the Spanish Second Republic* (Brighton, 2000), pp. 152–79, the quotation at p. 156.

[116] See Aróstegui, *Largo Caballero*, pp. 314–16.

to sketch this 'double scenario' through the election campaign.[117] In his speeches, he repeatedly justified the socialist trajectory during the Republic, criticized the Republicans for allegedly expelling the socialists from power and demanded power for the socialists in order to build a 'social Republic'. Largo Caballero, however, talked himself into a corner. Electoral defeat in November reduced his double scenario down to one.

Radicalization affected not only the veteran trade unionist and his followers, but also broad swathes of the socialist movement. A more aggressive assertion of socialist identity and the delineation of a sharper 'social Republic' are palpable in Asturias from much earlier than the election campaign. The attempted coup by Sanjurjo a year previously had sparked a national 'wave of pro-Republican fervour' and in Sama workers declared themselves prepared to 'take to the streets' to defend the Republic.[118] The coup served to strengthen the affective bonds between socialists and the regime, and started to shape a particular idea of the Republic as more assertive and left wing. Councillors in Oviedo demanded the Constitution be implemented to deepen the regime, while *Avance* insisted the Republic make 'a sharp turn to the left'.[119] A more muscular Republic was needed, rather than engagement with the Republic's opponents.

The radical rhetoric was a more assertive expression of socialist ideology and strategy, but portraying it as a straightforward rejection of Republican democracy is simplistic. The militant mood in 1932 and 1933 actually served to sharpen Republican loyalty, although this allegiance was to a particular vision of a 'social' Republic. The crystallization of this understanding of the Republic was reflected in *Avance*'s editorial the day before the Republican-socialist government fell:

> The idea of a 'Republic for all' makes sense for those who want a Republic, but there are people who do not want it, as occurs with every new regime. Well, these people should not be taken into count in the progress of the regime. The Republic has to be introduced against them.[120]

The struggle against the Republic's enemies was framed in more aggressive terms. The Republic had to be introduced in a more radical manner,

[117] S. Juliá, 'Los socialistas y el escenario de la futura revolución', in *Octubre 1934: cincuenta años para la reflexión*, ed. G. Jackson et al. (Madrid, 1985), pp. 103–30; Aróstegui, *Largo Caballero*, pp. 327–8.

[118] Preston, *Coming of the Spanish Civil War*, p. 73; *Avance*, 12 Aug. 1932. See, e.g., pro-Republican demonstrations in Galicia (González Probados, *O socialismo*, pp. 133–4).

[119] *Avance*, 12, 13 Aug. 1932.

[120] *Avance*, 7 Sept. 1933.

disregarding those who opposed the Republican-socialist project of the first biennium. The language was more militant, but it was far from a decided rejection of the Republic, still less a call for an immediate revolution. Socialists continued to ridicule anarchists who had been engaged in a months-long strike in La Felguera for thinking they could defeat Duro-Felguera or carry out a social revolution.[121]

When the Republican-socialist coalition collapsed in September 1933 and the president entrusted the centre-right Radical Party with forming a government, the socialist rank and file did not reject the Republican framework, as was clear in the appeal to action by the Turón JS:

> Before they change the course of the Republic towards the right, we will exhaust ourselves in the struggle to prevent it. This is not a threat. We are determined to throw ourselves into the struggle, no matter how hard it is, before they take the direction of the current revolution away from us.[122]

The Socialist Youth was the first line of defence of the Republican 'revolution', which echoed Largo Caballero's rhetoric that combined criticism of the Republican parties with a defence of Republican state interventionism and the achievements of socialist ministers between 1931 and 1933.[123] Indeed, the vision of a more sharply defined social Republic reflected the demands agreed at the national congress of the UGT in autumn 1933 in which the socialist union demanded more state intervention in the economy, including the nationalization of industry.[124]

The militant defence of the Republic and the socialist rediscovery of a radical identity meant that the vision of the Republic was increasingly conceptualized in class terms.[125] *Avance*'s rhetoric became ever more militant and the newspaper instructed its readers that:

> IF THEY SPEAK TO YOU OF A REPUBLIC FOR ALL, REPLY: Republic for me, because I work. Not for everyone. Not the capitalist who lives at my expense. No to equal defence for his misappropriation and my rights. I want my Republic, the Social Republic.[126]

[121] *Avance*, 1 Aug. 1933.

[122] *Avance*, 17 Sept. 1933.

[123] Aróstegui, *Largo Caballero*, pp. 326–7.

[124] Bizcarrondo, *Historia*, p. 53.

[125] See also a renewed enthusiasm for socialism in Andalusia, in Macarro Vera, *Socialismo*, p. 281.

[126] *Avance*, 16 Nov. 1933. Emphasis as in the original.

To an extent, *Avance*'s rhetoric was electioneering. Through polarizing brinkmanship, the socialist newspaper attempted to solidify its core support, warning of the dangers of voting for other political options. Yet this radical vision also reveals that the socialists had developed a bold, assertive vision for the future. In a deteriorating economic situation and now freed from the responsibility of national government, they could begin to project a new future of a 'social' Republic.

By autumn 1933, the socialist position had shifted away from the self-proclaimed moderation and pointed criticism of Communist and anarchist radicalism that had characterized it in 1931. During 1932 socialists had moulded 'radicalism' to fit their strategy of moderation in response to a change in the political mood in the coalfields, which itself had been conditioned by the new Republic. The new secularizing context of the Republic instigated the repositioning of oppositional political identities, while the resurgence of the right made 1932 a year of much greater conflict at the local level than 1931. At the same time, conditions in the mining industry deteriorated further, yet the SOMA was reluctant and unable to respond in a way that satisfied rank-and-file mineworkers. In fact, the SOMA's position only served to alienate sections of the mining workforce, particularly young workers. The grassroots radicalism was channelled into piecemeal rank-and-file unity initiatives and evident in the more militant and aggressive rhetoric, both in Asturias and from the socialist leadership.

Electoral defeat in November 1933 closed the parliamentary road to a social Republic, at least in the short term. According to Largo Caballero's rhetoric, the only option was an ill-defined revolutionary movement and over the following months, he directed the planning of such a movement. While the factors outlined in this chapter were at the heart of the emergence of radicalism in the coalfields, they do not provide the whole picture of the radicalizing dynamic, nor do they explain the revolutionary insurrection. Radicalism would continue to combine rivalries and tensions on a micro level over an individual's reputation and place in the community, and projections about the wider nature of the community itself, but between 1933 and 1934 two new radicalizing factors came to the fore: the perceived emergence of 'fascism' in 1933 and the actions of the security forces in 1934. These local struggles channelled and accelerated radicalization and would leave Asturias on the threshold of revolution.

4. Fascism and the politics of policing (1933–4)

In June 1934, L. Vega publicly admonished his neighbours in Tuilla for their complacency towards fascism and issued a rallying call to action:

> There are those who think that in Tuilla there are no fascists and this is a serious mistake as this *pueblo* cannot be an exception, especially taking into account its political history. What is happening is that those individuals are so comfortable that they adapt to political circumstances admirably, as we had occasion to see when the Republic arrived … Tuilla, we must not cross our arms deluding ourselves that it is a paradise, as our enemies are taking up positions cautiously and astutely, taking advantage of our excessive confidence and good faith.[1]

Fascism had to exist in Tuilla for it accommodated a pre-existing right-wing presence, yet as a shadowy, conspiratorial threat, there was also something qualitatively different about it. Vega's appeal for urgent action formed part of a wave of articles during the eighteen months prior to October 1934 that focused on fascism in the coalfields. The articles reveal the steady incorporation of fascism into political language and associated imaginaries of the social and political order at the local level. The rise of fascism was not simply the international backdrop to radicalization, but an integral part of the radicalization process, thanks to the alleged emergence and growth of fascism in the coalfields. Vega's interpretation of fascism as a transmutation of traditional reactionary politics was typical, even as doubts abounded as to what constituted – or could constitute – Spanish fascism.[2]

Anxieties over fascism injected urgency into political action particularly after the defeat of the divided forces of the former Republican-socialist coalition in elections in November 1933. Fears were compounded – and appeared to be corroborated – by the actions of the new conservative administration. The government was not fascist, but the change in policing strategy stoked fears about the possible implementation of authoritarianism

[1] *Avance*, 7 June 1934.

[2] Rivers of ink have been spilled defining fascism. Much less has been written on leftists' understanding of fascism, although work on the response of the British left is more comprehensive (K. Hodgson, *Fighting Fascists: the British Left and the Rise of Fascism, 1919–1939* (Manchester, 2010) and D. Stone, *Responses to Nazism in Britain: Before War and Holocaust* (Basingstoke, 2003)).

or fascism from above. Stricter and more assertive policing by the security forces unleashed waves of protest in the coalfields in 1934, which constituted the pre-eminent way in which the change in the direction of the Republic was experienced in daily life. The dynamic of protest and more aggressive policing sparked an upward spiral of radicalization and a growing alienation of the coalfield communities from the state. For *Avance*, only a revolution could resolve this situation.

Militancy in the face of crisis was one response to the dark panorama unfolding for the left in Europe in the mid 1930s. The continued rise of the extreme right prompted a period of soul-searching, rethinking and realignment within the left between 1933 and 1935. Leftists experimented with new economic ideas, including the Belgian 'Plan de Man' and left-wing unity initiatives, aided by the Communist abandonment of the isolating 'class against class' policy of the 'Third Period' (1928–35) in favour of Popular Frontism.[3] Even in stable democratic states like the Netherlands, social democrats debated the strategy of political violence.[4] The year 1934 stands out as being one of particular rebelliousness and restlessness – and the year the left 'finally recorded a success'.[5] In addition to the failed Austrian socialist rising, the year saw a failed revolutionary general strike in Portugal, mass left-wing demonstrations in France, the emergence of violent street politics in Britain and several days' rioting in the Jordaan neighbourhood of Amsterdam. Each episode responded to national dynamics, so similarities should not be overstated, but they do indicate a deepening political crisis, to which left-wing organizations often struggled to respond. The Asturian revolutionary insurrection formed part of this international context, even if nothing approached the scale of events in northern Spain.

Identifying the fascist threat

The first 'fascist' posters were pasted on walls in Oviedo in March 1933, although left-wing organizations appeared untroubled by this.[6] *Avance* ridiculed the posters, the Socialist Youth summer school programme did

[3] See G.-R. Horn, *European Socialists Respond to Fascism: Ideology, Activism and Contingency in the 1930s* (New York, 1996).

[4] K. Mennen, 'Necessary evil, last resort or totally unacceptable? Social Democratic discussions on political violence in Germany and the Netherlands', in *Political Violence and Democracy in Western Europe, 1918–1940*, ed. C. Millington and K. Passmore (London, 2015), pp. 98, 100.

[5] G. Eley, *Forging Democracy: the History of the Left in Europe, 1850–2000* (Oxford, 2002), p. 263.

[6] *El Noroeste*, 19 March 1933.

not reference fascism and antifascism was not central to PCE policy in 1933.[7] Certainly, there were few or no avowed fascists in the coalfields in 1933, and fascism was still a minor player in Spanish politics. The party most closely identified with fascism in Spain, Falange Española, was not formed in Madrid until October 1933 (and formally constituted in Asturias six months later), by which point FE had become FE-JONS. Nevertheless, over the course of 1933 fascism increasingly featured in articles sent in from towns and villages in the coalfields with activists like L. Vega identifying it in pre-existing political divisions, while simultaneously worrying that fascism was a new, hidden, growing threat.[8]

The dramatic increase in the use of the term 'fascist' in 1933 was sparked by Hitler's accession to power and the subsequent destruction of the powerful German labour movement, but as a term it was hardly new. Labelling something or someone as 'fascist' was a common rhetorical tool to slur enemies prior to 1933. Both Communists and anarchists denounced socialists as 'social fascists' and Asturian socialists made a swipe at the anarchist FAI by claiming that only spelling differentiated *faístas* from *fascistas*.[9] Nor was employing the term in such a loose way limited to Spain. The British Independent Labour Party paradoxically labelled the bill for a Public Order Act a 'fascist bill to stop fascism', while a British Communist described mass unemployment as a characteristic of fascism.[10]

The conceptual looseness of fascism was part of the process of constructing a nascent antifascist culture. Demanding a clear definition from disparate individuals in the Asturian coalfields would be unfair, not least as socialist leaders themselves understood fascism in very different ways.[11] The task of translating fascism from the international arena into

[7] *Avance*, 8, 12 March, 11 Aug. 1933; *El Noroeste*, 22, 30 March, 6 Apr., 12 May 1933; F. Erice, 'El PCE en Asturias, de los orígenes a la guerra civil', in *Los comunistas en Asturias (1920–1982)*, ed. F. Erice (Gijón, 1996), p. 61.

[8] For similar simultaneous discussion in the Basque socialist movement, see R. Miralles, *El socialismo vasco durante la II República: organización, ideología, política y elecciones, 1931–1936* (Bilbao, 1988), p. 189.

[9] G. Álvarez Chillida, '*Negras tormentas* sobre la República. La intransigencia libertaria', in *Palabras como puños: la intransigencia política en la Segunda República*, ed. F. del Rey (Madrid, 2011), p. 82; *Avance*, 30 July 1933.

[10] T. Buchanan, 'Beyond Cable Street: new approaches to the historiography of antifascism in Britain in the 1930s', in *Rethinking Antifascism: History, Memory and Politics, 1922 to the Present*, ed. H. García, M. Yusta, X. Tabet and C. Clímaco (New York, 2016), p. 66.

[11] See F. Gallego, *Barcelona, mayo de Barcelona: la crisis del antifascismo en Cataluña* (Barcelona, 2007), ch. 2; H. García, 'Was there an antifascist culture in 1930s Spain?', in García, Yusta, Tabet and Clímaco, *Rethinking*, p. 96.

the Spanish domestic context and the everyday reality of the coalfields was difficult. The lack of fascist organizations in the coalfields meant that it was applied to existing local political divisions, which could mean adding it to existing epithets like 'clerical monarchist reaction'.[12] Fascism existed as the transmutation of a pre-existing threat, yet at the same time there was something distinctive about it that prompted activists to wrestle with identifying fascists at the local level. This required defining their politics.

Particularly vexing for the Asturian left was the relationship of fascism to Catholicism, and an attempt to clarify the issue in *Avance* only muddied the waters. It first described fascism as a 'reactionary movement' that sought a strong, centralized state and should not be confused with 'clericalism', only to later predict that Spanish fascism would be based on Catholicism, as Spain did not exhibit the 'combination of circumstances' necessary for 'authentic fascism'.[13] For those observing the movements of the political right in Asturias, Catholicism appeared to be entangled with the incipient Falange. Asturians could sign up to FE at the offices of CEDA-supporting *Región*, while a cathedral canon was one of the first Falangist organizers in the province.[14]

The lack of clarity was comprehensible given the wider national context. The founder of FE, José Antonio Primo de Rivera, proceeded from the 'mainstream of conservative Spanish politics' and was elected to the Cortes in November 1933 on a right-wing list that included CEDA and Carlist candidates.[15] The CEDA's own position appeared ambiguous to left-wing activists as it oscillated between a 'prudent distancing and an admiration which was not always hidden'.[16] José María Gil Robles had admired the Nazi aesthetic at the Nuremberg rallies in autumn 1933 – and its influence would be visible on the aesthetics and pageantry of the rallies of CEDA's youth wing (JAP) in 1934 – but he criticized the position of Nazism on religion. Yet determining a pure, 'authentic' fascism was not necessarily important in identifying a threat to left-wing politics. Engelbert Dollfuss's

[12] *Avance*, 5 Sept. 1933. The lack of clarity is noted by many, e.g., S. Souto Kustrín, 'Octubre de 1934: historia, mito y memoria', *Hispania Nova. Revista de Historia Contemporánea*, xi (2013), 477–81, at p. 488.

[13] *Avance*, 6 Sept. 1933.

[14] M. Suárez Cortina, *El fascismo en Asturias* (Gijón, 1981), pp. 125, 154–6.

[15] M. Vincent, 'Spain', in *The Oxford Handbook of Fascism*, ed. R. J. B. Bosworth (Oxford, 2009), p. 365.

[16] J. Jiménez Campo, *El fascismo en la crisis de la Segunda República española* (Madrid, 1979), p. 71. See also P. Preston, *The Coming of the Spanish Civil War: Reform, Reaction and Revolution in the Second Republic* (London, 1978), p. 47.

Catholic-infused right-wing authoritarianism in Austria was closer to the Spanish CEDA than Nazism, a point not lost on the Spanish left.[17]

Criticism of the cinema at the Casa del Pueblo in Sotrondio for showing 'another fascist film' illustrates how the fascist threat was dependent on existing ways of imagining political and cultural enemies. The management of the theatre at the Casa del Pueblo was subcontracted to a businesswoman who had conspired with an 'important fascist' to project the film, which 'belonged to a Jesuit company' who allegedly sold them at half the price of other films. The classic anticlerical trope of the Jesuits operating in a shadowy underhand – 'Jesuitical' – manner combined with fascism, which, like the Society of Jesus, was depicted as an international conspiracy. The tentacles of fascism had surreptitiously reached into the heart of socialist organization – 'the Casa del Pueblo serves for all kinds of fascist propaganda' – and could prey on the unsuspecting rank and file. Fortunately, 'the working class community [*pueblo*], the community with the greatest socialist faith in the province, will not allow this type of show to be projected in the salon of the Casa del Pueblo again'.[18] To label something or someone as fascist was to issue a rallying call to action. The working-class community was called upon to oppose the growth of fascism in their towns and villages.

The context of the Asturian coalfields was different to that of Berlin or Paris. In these metropoles, political struggle was often tied to the capture or defence of particular urban spaces, whether streets or neighbourhoods. Taverns, which were meeting places and headquarters for political groups, were central to the struggle to control districts in the German capital and Nazi Stormtroopers pursued a deliberate policy of disputing particular districts in the capital. Similarly, street fighting between the left and right in Paris centred on the control of particular urban spaces. Newspaper sellers were a particular target, as political groups asserted their claim to control a given space.[19] In the Asturian coalfields, the context of leftist hegemony and lack of avowed fascists, or at least organized right-wing paramilitary street politics, meant that fascism manifested itself in leaflets slipped into magazines at the ateneo, propaganda thrown from a car or alleged secret meetings.[20] Fascism was still an encroachment on leftist territory, but it was not a physical presence that invaded from the outside; rather, it emerged

[17] Souto Kustrín, 'Octubre', pp. 488ff.

[18] *Avance*, 26 Oct. 1933.

[19] C. Millington, 'Street-fighting men: political violence in interwar France', *English Historical Review*, cxxix (2014); E. Rosenhaft, *Beating the Fascists? The German Communist Party and Political Violence, 1929–1933* (Cambridge, 1983), especially pp. 22, 111–27.

[20] *Avance*, 1 Aug., 20 Sept. 1933.

from within the valleys themselves. Fascism was a conspiratorial threat that could destroy the unsuspecting left from within, just as fascism had cannibalized European democracies from the inside. The left would only realize this when it was too late. Identifying the emergence of fascism thus entailed leftists demanding that it be driven from their communities.

By the election campaign of autumn 1933, the term 'fascist' was common currency in the Asturian left-wing press, although much more so in articles sent in from towns and villages than *Avance*'s editorials.[21] Fascism had become an important frame for understanding politics, yet socialist activists dismissed the threat posed by right-wing political mobilization. CEDA campaigners in San Martín del Rey Aurelio were jeered as 'those catechizing ladies' and '*beatas*'.[22] Ridicule centred on their inferior numbers, age and gender, revealing a flash of misogyny, even if the latter did not represent all on the left, nor extend to their own female activists.[23] The term *beata* referred to religious older women and was implicitly contrasted with youthful radicalism. The latter was the harbinger of progress while the *beatas* embodied the old world of obscurantism and superstition. Nor did these women have much agency. 'Friars and priests' directed the *beatas* in their electioneering activities, an allegation which echoed the fears that had divided the PSOE during the parliamentary debate over women's suffrage in autumn 1931. Many continued to believe that women's votes would be dictated from the lectern.[24] Right-wing activists did not represent the local community as understood by socialists in the autumn of 1933. Socialists were still confident in the left-wing character of the coalfields. Ultimately, this confidence was not well founded.

The election was fought in very different circumstances to 1931. The right was resurgent while the Republican-socialist alliance had collapsed. The electoral law favoured broad coalitions and the CEDA entered into alliances with several different parties, including centrists and those further

[21] E.g. *Avance*, 16 Nov. 1933.

[22] *Avance*, 28 Oct., 2, 10 Nov. 1933.

[23] Women were heavily involved in campaigning in Asturias and more widely. For Asturias, see M. A. Mateos, *¡Salud, compañeras! Mujeres socialistas en Asturias (1900–1937)* (Oviedo, 2007), pp. 152–7. For female rightist mobilization, see I. Blasco Herranz, *Paradojas de la ortodoxia: política de masas y militancia católica femenina en España (1919–1939)* (Zaragoza, 2003) and M. Vincent, 'The politicization of Catholic women in Salamanca, 1931–1936', in *Elites and Power in Twentieth Century Spain: Essays in Honour of Sir Raymond Carr*, ed. F. Lannon and P. Preston (Oxford, 1990). For the anticlerical depiction of the *beata*, see M. P. Salomón Chéliz, 'Beatas sojuzgadas por el clero: la imagen de las mujeres en el discurso anticlerical en la España del primer tercio del siglo XX', *Feminismo/s*, ii (2003), 41–58.

[24] *Avance*, 28 Oct. 1933.

to the right. In Asturias, the CEDA formed a joint slate with the Liberal-Democratic Republican Party (PRLD). The PRLD maintained a following in Asturias but had not capitalized on the arrival of the Republic despite its historical role as a prominent player in Spanish Republicanism during the Restoration monarchy. The party had shifted towards the right and was vocally anti-socialist. While the right sought alliances, the situation was more complicated for the centre-left and left. The fracturing of the previous government coalition between socialists and left Republicans and the embitterment of the relationship between them impeded collaboration, although a few electoral alliances were formed in certain provinces. In Valencia, the weakness of the socialists meant they united with the left Republicans, while in Malaga, the Communists joined the socialists.[25] In Asturias, a proposal for an electoral alliance with the Communists at the congress of the FSA was hotly debated and received support from coalfield delegates. The Executive Committee did not favour the idea and managed to deflect it into a vote authorizing the Committee to enter an alliance if necessary.[26]

The elections were 'one of the most bitter-fought and violent in Spanish electoral history', though 'probably the fairest of all', despite 'serious fraud' in some areas.[27] Abstention was high in areas of anarchist support thanks to anarchists' campaign against participation in the ballot. The results were a catastrophe for the PSOE and left republicans. The number of socialist deputies halved from 116 to fifty-nine, while the number of deputies for Azaña's Republican Action dropped from twenty-six to five. The Radical Socialist party, which had suffered breakaways, collapsed from sixty representatives to a single deputy, who was elected thanks to an alliance with the Radical Party in León province. The Radical Party added a further twelve deputies to finish in second place with 102 seats, thanks to co-operating in the second round with the CEDA, who returned the highest number of deputies in the new Cortes (115).

25 S. Valero, *Republicanos con la monarquía, socialistas con la República: la Federación Socialista Valenciana durante la II República y la Guerra Civil (1931–1939)* (Valencia, 2015), p. 101.

26 J. Girón, 'Asturias, Octubre de 1934: el fracaso de un intento de alianza electoral entre socialistas y comunistas', in *Octubre 1934: cincuenta años para la reflexión*, ed. G. Jackson et al. (Madrid, 1985), pp. 199–201.

27 E. González Calleja, *Cifras cruentas: las víctimas mortales de la violencia sociopolítica en la Segunda República española (1931–1936)* (Granada, 2015), p. 246; N. Townson, *The Crisis of Democracy in Spain: Centrist Politics under the Spanish Second Republic* (Brighton, 2000), p. 193. For allegations of fraud and coercion in Asturias, see *Avance*, 23, 24 Nov. 1933 and *El Noroeste*, 23 Nov. 1933.

The results generated consternation and intense debate within the socialist leadership. The keys to power now lay in the hands of their opponents from the first biennium, the Radicals and the CEDA. For socialists and left Republicans, the proximity of the CEDA to power threatened the Republic itself. Between the first round of elections on 19 November and the end of the year, the executive committees of the PSOE and UGT held a succession of meetings in which they debated how to proceed. Acute differences lay between Largo Caballero and Besteiro, who presided over the PSOE and UGT respectively. Largo Caballero now favoured the preparation of a revolutionary movement that could respond to the perceived threat of a new administration dismantling the Republic. Building on his proposals, Prieto fleshed out a manifesto for a socialist government in January 1934. Besteiro rejected these plans, as he did any voluntarist strategies. When Besteiro's own ideas were voted down at successive meetings of the PSOE and UGT executives in January, he had little choice but to resign the presidency of the UGT. Caballeristas replaced the Besteiristas. Planning the movement could now begin in earnest.[28] Over the next few months, Largo Caballero oversaw preparations with the aid of a mixed UGT, PSOE and JS committee.

The election results were a shock for socialists in the Asturian coalfields. The CEDA-PRLD alliance won the most votes on a regional level. In the coalfields, the socialists won clear victories, although results higher up the valleys were split more evenly or else favoured the right. In El Condado (Laviana), where tensions ran high during the elections, the CEDA-PRLD obtained 244 votes, while the socialists and Communists received 145 and 140 respectively.[29] Aller was divided between socialists in the lower valley and the CEDA-PRLD in the mountains, although 'the Communists obtained many votes in the whole municipal district'.[30]

The belittlement of rightist campaigning prior to the elections contrasted sharply with the number of votes deposited in ballot boxes and the results caused consternation among the socialist grassroots. Activists turned to analysing their own communities in an attempt to account for the results. Votes for the right did not fit a Marxist interpretative schema of what *should* happen in predominantly working class areas, nor did they match the image of community held by local leftists. Unable to account for the

[28] This account is based on J. Aróstegui, *Largo Caballero: el tesón y la quimera* (Barcelona, 2013), pp. 340–51; S. Juliá, 'República, revolución y luchas internas', in *El socialismo en España: desde la fundación del PSOE hasta 1975*, ed. S. Juliá (Madrid, 1986), pp. 238–40; M. Bizcarrondo, *Historia de la UGT*, iii: *Entre la democracia y la revolución, 1931–1936* (6 vols, Madrid, 2008), pp. 97–103.

[29] *Avance*, 22 Nov. 1933.

[30] *El Noroeste*, 23 Nov. 1933.

number of CEDA-PRLD votes in Trubia, an activist blamed a coalition of treasonous workers and women, both devout older women and the daughters of workers.[31] Likewise, in Murias (Aller) – the 'largest centre of reactionaries you will ever come across' – votes for the right were attributed to 'disorganized and disoriented' workers, women ('you do not get fed [by your mothers] if you do not go to mass') and the SCOM. Abstention was ascribed to threats.[32] Women were now assigned agency, albeit the ability to coerce men into voting against their interests. Voting for the right was not the result of a democratic choice; voters had been duped or coerced.

The election results led to a radical reaction, which manifested itself in the form of a militant backlash. The SOMA called on citizens in Turón to boycott a shop for 'praising our sweat and then laughing at us', showing 'disrespect' and desiring a regime similar to Nazism or fascism.[33] Between December and the end of January, shots were fired at the homes of young Catholics, at an AP meeting behind closed doors and an address in Oviedo denounced publicly for electoral fraud.[34] The first two episodes of frustration and dissent occurred in areas of Aller with a high percentage of votes for the CEDA-PRLD. Tensions resulting from the election results were also apparent in other areas of Spain, but manifested differently according to local political dynamics. In Ciudad Real province, the socialists appear to have borne the brunt of violence, but in an expression of jubilation rather than disappointment. In Torre de Juan Abad the Civil Guard beat up socialists who had confronted an individual shouting support for fascism and the king, and in February a Casa del Pueblo and a socialist mayor were both attacked.[35]

There was a distinct shift in the political winds in towns across Spain, and the changes were felt on an individual level. While evidence is slim and fragmentary due to the nature of the sources and available testimonies, a letter in *Avance* from Julia Morán, a resident of Pola de Laviana, gives an indication of the sense of a shifting political equilibrium at the local level and the pressures that accompanied it. Morán was the secretary of the local women's section of the Socialist Group and the widow of a prominent local socialist.[36] Morán lambasted rumours that circulated in Laviana regarding

[31] *Avance*, 25 Nov. 1933.

[32] *Avance*, 17 Jan. 1934.

[33] *Avance*, 7 Dec. 1933.

[34] *Avance*, 28 Nov. 1933; *Región*, 3, 27 Jan. 1934.

[35] F. Rey, *Paisanos en lucha: exclusión política y violencia en la Segunda República española* (Madrid, 2008), pp. 343, 346.

[36] *Avance*, 15 June, 9 Nov. 1932; Mateos, *¡Salud, compañeras!*, p. 129. For her biography, see

her and her family in a manner that revealed how a person's local standing was based on a combination of personal and political issues. Although the gossip was not directly related to politics, she framed her indictment of those whispering about her in a defiant declaration of socialist identity:

> In Laviana, like everywhere else, it seems that being a socialist is a crime … I affirm [*hago constar*] that I am a socialist revolutionary and I am not ashamed of it. I would be much more ashamed to be a hypocrite and deceitful like those *señoras* who label me thus … We have to be rebels because that is what these times require. The day we have to go out into the streets, [we] female revolutionaries and rebels will respect those who respect us, but those who slander and libel us – they will receive what they deserve.[37]

Morán felt corralled and under pressure in the intimate community of Pola de Laviana due to the change in the political atmosphere after the elections. She reacted not by withdrawing, but by reaffirming her identity in a militant manner.

Morán did not frame her criticism in terms of fascism, but fascism had become an important way of understanding right-wing opposition in the coalfields. Importantly, because of the election results, fascism now had to exist. The results provided a new impetus for trying to locate the hidden, conspiratorial threat of a force that posed an existential danger to the left in the coalfields and the provincial capital. During 1934, leftists reported fascism 'emerging' in towns and villages across the coalfields, even if it remained a shadowy presence.[38] 'Viva *el fascio*' was daubed on walls in La Felguera, fascism 'classes' were supposedly taught in Trubia and a priest allegedly wanted to create a 'fascist trade union'.[39] There was a now greater urgency in the fight against fascism. Leftists issued warnings, and confrontation in the streets became more commonplace. Socialists passed on the names of some 'monarchist lads' who reportedly shouted 'viva fascism' at 'comrades' in Caborana and warned that if the situation continued to deteriorate 'our patience will run out and it will end in tragedy'.[40] And leftists did respond to the threat of fascism. The first copies of the Falangist newspaper *FE* on sale in Oviedo were burned in the street, which led to a scuffle, and a month

the 'Diccionario biográfico del socialismo español' <http://www.fpabloiglesias.es/archivo-y-biblioteca/diccionario-biografico/biografias/17680_moran-sanchez-julia> [accessed 25 Oct. 2018].

37 *Avance*, 23 Feb. 1934.

38 *Avance*, 9 Jan. 1934.

39 *Avance*, 16, 17 Feb., 15 Mar. 1934.

40 *Avance*, 16 Jan. 1934.

later communists burned an effigy of Hitler on Shrove Tuesday in a twist on traditional transgressive carnival celebrations.[41]

The domestic fascist threat was now no longer identified purely with a semi-hidden local threat. The election of a conservative administration beholden to the CEDA meant that there was great sensitivity to a possible gradual slide towards authoritarian rule or even fascism. Fears in Spain reflected those in Britain and France, where leftists were concerned about the trajectory of their governments; indeed the French government was depicted as pre-fascist in February 1934.[42] Such concerns are understandable given that Hitler had been appointed to power through the mechanisms of the Weimar Republic, rather than by storming the Reichstag. It was unsurprising, therefore, that the newspaper of the Spanish Socialist Youth labelled the November 1933 elections a 'German disaster'.[43] Nor was Nazi Germany the only example. By mid February, *Avance* was beginning to talk of Austria, where Dollfuss had cemented his authoritarian, corporatist rule through gradual, legalistic means, as an example of what could happen in Spain.[44]

This interest in international affairs was not new, but there was a greater awareness of what was occurring beyond the Pyrenees in 1934. Lectures at *ateneos* discussed European politics and *Avance* published appeals for left-wing unity in France and Belgium.[45] The imprisoned German Communist leader Ernst Thaelmann was a particular object of interest and support, thanks to the 1934 Comintern campaign for his release.[46] Organizations across the left sent telegrams to the German embassy appealing for his freedom and the PCE in Oviedo even called on the Asturian left to take advantage of a passing German circus to do so.[47] International politics filtered down to family celebrations, such as weddings. At a civil ceremony

[41] *Avance*, 18 Jan., 14 Feb. 1934; *Región*, 14 Feb. 1934; *El Noroeste*, 15 Feb. 1934.

[42] Buchanan, 'Beyond Cable Street', pp. 65–6; B. Jenkins and C. Millington, *France and Fascism: February 1934 and the Dynamics of Political Crisis* (Abingdon, 2015), p. 3.

[43] S. Souto Kustrín, *'Y ¿Madrid? ¿Qué hace Madrid?': movimento revolucionario y acción colectiva (1933–1936)* (Madrid, 2004), p. 56.

[44] *Avance*, 15 Feb. 1934.

[45] *Avance*, 6, 20 May, 31 Aug. 1934. The Madrid-based Communist-turned-socialist student Manuel Tagüeña recalled discussing international affairs with his neighbourhood cell (M. Tagüeña Lacorte, *Testimonio de dos guerras* (Barcelona, 1978), p. 34).

[46] See A. Rabinbach, 'Freedom for Thälmann: the Comintern and the orchestration of the campaign to free Ernst Thälmann, 1933–39', in García, Yusta, Tabet and Clímaco, *Rethinking*, pp. 23–42 and S. McMeekin, *The Red Millionaire: a Political Biography of Willy Munzenberg, Moscow's Secret Propaganda Tsar in the West* (New Haven, Conn., 2003).

[47] E.g. *Avance*, 3, 13, 22, 27 July 1934; *El Noroeste*, 8 July 1934.

in Olloniego, a speech was given in memory of the 'brave Austrians' who had rebelled against Dollfuss.[48] Remarks at a wedding perhaps came easier than downing tools. A solidarity strike in February to support the plight of the Austrian socialists garnered uneven support.[49]

The politics of policing

The election results marked the beginning of a new cycle in Spanish politics. The legislature was less stable than during the first biennium. There were ten different governments between December 1933 and February 1936. President Alcalá Zamora's lack of faith in the Republican credentials of the CEDA, which had the highest number of seats in the Cortes, meant that he tasked Radicals with forming governments. First, Radical-led governments relied on the CEDA's backing in the Cortes in order to wield a parliamentary majority. From October 1934 onwards, Gil Robles' party also gained control of ministerial portfolios.

The policies of the new governments were a significant departure from the first biennium. Governments did not engage in the wholesale derogation of legislation, but did roll back or paralyse emblematic laws closely identified with the spirit of the Republic of the first biennium. State financial support for the Church was partially reinstated, the law of municipal boundaries was removed, mixed juries, which adjudicated on labour issues, were modified. Land reform, in which Republican ambitions had so far outweighed results, was paralysed. The death penalty was reintroduced and an amnesty was issued for those involved in the failed 1932 coup.[50] Radical-led governments pressured municipal authorities to come into line with the national government while council halls also became platforms for dissent, from the Basque defence of their traditional economic rights against a new wine tax to Langreo's direct communication of its opposition to government policies via telegram.[51] The government removed a number of councils that opposed government policy, although the largest wave of removals would only occur after the revolutionary insurrection of October 1934.

The change in the nature of the Republic was manifest in citizens' daily lives. Holy Week processions – absent in some areas of Spain in previous years – returned to the streets. Emblematic of Catholicism's renewed visibility

[48] *Avance*, 23 Feb. 1934.

[49] A. Shubert, *The Road to Revolution in Spain: the Coal Miners of Asturias, 1860–1934* (Urbana, Ill., 1987), p. 152; *Avance*, 20 Feb. 1934.

[50] Townson, *Crisis*, pp. 204, 223–4.

[51] For the Basques, see summary in Townson, *Crisis*, pp. 253–6. AL, Actas, 7 Oct. 1933 to 16 June 1934, ff. 132–4, 147–8.

in Salamanca was the emergence of Jesuits from hiding to participate in public life.[52] Backed by a more conservative administration, landowners and industrialists flouted labour legislation. Discrimination in contracting that targeted unionized labourers was the clearest and most common change in rural areas.[53] Pay dropped and unemployment climbed.[54] In the south, the lack of rain reduced the olive harvest and councils distributed bread to the hungry. While widespread protest did not emerge, a current of resentment coursed beneath the surface of rural society.[55] The situation in the Asturian coalfields was not quite so grave. Employment levels in the mines were stable. The principal manifestation of the changed political climate in the coal valleys was a shift in policing strategy, although there were also reports of landlords taking advantage of the new context to evict tenants.[56]

The government experienced the country's state of effervescence on its doorstep. Madrid had never been closer to a general strike than during the first few months of 1934, due to strikes in construction, hostelry and printing and metal trades.[57] The state of unrest was exacerbated by the emergence of street violence. The publication and sale of Falange's newspaper led to confrontation between supporters and opponents in the streets of the capital. FE-JONS, although a minor player in Spanish politics until 1936, attempted to flex its muscles by demonstrating its influence among students in attacks on left-wing centres. On 9 February, a member of the JS shot dead a Falangist leader, Matías Montero, who became their first 'martyr', and street violence between left- and right-wing youths continued to be a feature on the streets of the capital over the following months.[58]

Under pressure from this combination of circumstances – and the CEDA's demand for a sterner public order policy – the government responded

[52] M. Vincent, *Catholicism in the Second Spanish Republic: Religion and Politics in Salamanca, 1930–1936* (Oxford, 1996), pp. 214–15.

[53] F. Cobo Romero, *De campesinos a electores: modernización agraria en Andalucía, politización campesina y derechización de los pequeños propietarios y arrendatarios: el caso de la provincia de Jaén, 1931–1936* (Madrid, 2003), p. 280.

[54] Preston, *Coming of the Spanish Civil War*, p. 103; Townson, *Crisis*, p. 204. For examples of pay, see J. M. Macarro Vera, *Socialismo, República y revolución en Andalucía (1931–1936)* (Seville, 2000), p. 319.

[55] Macarro Vera, *Socialismo*, pp. 320–2.

[56] *Avance*, 11 Feb. 1934.

[57] S. Juliá, *Madrid, 1931–1934: de la fiesta popular a la lucha de clases* (Madrid, 1984), p. 351.

[58] E. González Calleja, *Contrarrevolucionarios: radicalización violenta de las derechas durante la Segunda República, 1931–1936* (Madrid, 2011), pp. 202–5. For a firsthand account, see Tagüeña Lacorte, *Testimonio*, pp. 42–4.

with a crackdown on the possession of arms and explosives.[59] The frisking of workers proliferated across the country. Anarchists and Communists in Bilbao organized a general strike to protest against police attempts at the searches.[60] On the same day, the Badajoz city council protested that the wave of searches was stoking 'alarm'.[61] In the Asturian coalfields, they became a daily occurrence and a very personal experience of the assertion of state power. Security forces stopped mineworkers on their way to work on the main road through the Nalón valley. *Avance* claimed that those who objected to the searches were beaten.[62]

The searches added to tensions in the coalfields. In Laviana, a series of incidents that escalated from the arrest of two men for carrying knives reveals the interplay of protest and policing, particularly how left-wing activists were willing to contest state power and assert their own vision of justice. The two men were jailed in Pola de Laviana for possessing knives that *Avance* alleged were of 'common usage' and habitually carried due to the nature of mine work. On the day of their arrest, inhabitants of Pola de Laviana planned to march on the prison to demand the men's release, but a socialist persuaded them to desist. When two days later it was reported that the men would be subjected to a summary trial, a 400-strong demonstration forced their release from the prison, which was only guarded by four civil guards. The governor sent Assault and Civil Guard reinforcements to the town, where rumours spread of orders for the arrest of left-wing leaders and a general strike was declared. When the governor heard that the strike was to protest at the arrival of security forces, he withdrew them and peace returned.[63] Mineworkers returned to work only to down their tools again on hearing news of the arrest of a socialist councillor, Luis Camblor, who was accused of heading the demonstration that released the men. Strikers announced they would not return to work until Camblor was freed, and women planned a demonstration in protest at further arrests.[64] The strike ended when a letter from Camblor recommending a return to work was read at an assembly authorized by the governor.[65]

This complex dance of strikers, police and the civil governor reveals how the arrests had concentrated fears over the direction of the government while

[59] Preston, *Coming of the Spanish Civil War*, p. 103.

[60] *Heraldo de Madrid*, 12 Feb. 1934; *El Sol*, 13 Feb. 1934.

[61] *El Socialista*, 14 Feb. 1934.

[62] *Avance*, 13 Feb. 1934.

[63] *Avance*, 20 Feb. 1934.

[64] *Avance*, 21, 22 Feb. 1934; *Región*, 21 Feb. 1934.

[65] *Avance*, 23, 24 Feb. 1934.

also providing an opportunity to resist the new policing policy. Different notions of justice clashed. Initially, leftists disputed that carrying a knife warranted arrest and a summary trial, but the situation worsened further when extra security forces arrived in the town. For the protestors, the state was intrusive and its use of force excessive; they were capable of keeping peace in Pola de Laviana. The incident also shows the crucial role played by political actors in diffusing incidents. Both the governor and socialists in Laviana took steps to de-escalate protest, even if this meant the removal of security forces. This mediation is important for it would be absent over the following months, even though the office of the civil governor did not change hands. The lack of dialogue combined with police searches would feed a radicalizing spiral through the spring.

The potential for escalation increased markedly in early March due to the appointment of a new minister of the interior. Diego Martínez Barrio, who had sought a preventative approach to public order incidents, resigned, as he was uncomfortable with government policy. He was replaced by Rafael Salazar Alonso, who pursued an assertive, confrontational policing strategy, which included militarizing public order and placing restrictions on civil liberties through use of the state of alarm. The latter suspended constitutional guarantees and authorized the security forces to enter homes without a warrant in certain circumstances.[66] Salazar Alonso's policy was informed by his 'Manichean view of politics', which showed 'sympathy for the right'.[67] His memoirs published after October 1934 reveal a tendency to see revolution in every incidence of labour conflict and an adversarial attitude in which (his) authority was to be upheld at all costs.[68]

A more assertive policing strategy could be effective in quashing protest.[69] But in the Asturian coalfields it was counterproductive. In late March, a spiral of action-counteraction-action by security forces and leftist organizations revealed the underlying tensions in the coalfields and served to fuel increasing resentment, which translated into militancy. The wave of searches for arms in left-wing cultural and political centres strengthened rather than weakened the resolve of the left. The searches combined with the police's response to protest eroded the affective links between citizens in the coalfields and the wider Republican state. Between 22 and 24 March,

[66] E. González Calleja, *En nombre de la autoridad: la defensa del orden público durante la Segunda República española (1931–1936)* (Granada, 2014), pp. 204, 224–6 and *Cifras*, pp. 177–8.

[67] Townson, *Crisis*, pp. 222–3.

[68] R. Salazar Alonso, *Bajo el signo de la revolución* (Madrid, 1935).

[69] E.g. in Valencia (Valero, *Republicanos*, p. 123).

security forces carried out searches of Casas del Pueblo, union centres and even the home of the Republican mayor of Langreo. Workers responded to these searches with a number of localized wildcat strikes.[70] A few days later police attention turned from union centres to workers themselves. Security forces stopped mineworkers on their way to the pit and rummaged through their food baskets. While they were at work, the Assault Guard 'invaded' the villages and searched their homes – even seizing a sewing machine. Crossing the threshold into workers' homes was particularly offensive. Women protested at the intrusion, which led to four arrests, and mineworkers left the mines early in protest.[71] Checking food baskets may have been humiliating, but entering the household transgressed into the intimacy of the home and was an attack on the masculine authority of the male head of the household.

Councillors in Langreo raised their voices in protest at the searches for targeting the Republic's supporters and, in particular, at the nature of the searches. The socialists criticized the security forces for not showing 'the right level of respect to citizens and organizations': 'what is most disgraceful is that those who are the target of body and house searches are those people and social and political organizations who worked the hardest and sacrificed the most in the service of the Republic'. By repeatedly searching the very citizens who formed the backbone of the Republic and targeting their private property – even breaking furniture and locks – the central state transgressed the usual boundaries of its actions and broke a social contract between local society and state institutions. Such measures could receive approval when used against the Republic's enemies, but now the security forces focused on those whose 'loyalty to the Republic ha[d] been proven'.[72]

Holy Week loomed, with the prospect of the fractious situation escalating further as political anger transferred to the Church. Whereas in previous years sporadic iconoclastic acts had targeted remote shrines, attacks on the Church now occurred in town centres. On Holy Wednesday, dynamite was thrown into the patio of the parish church in Sama. The following day youths tried to disturb the religious service, leading to a skirmish with young Catholics, and stones being thrown at the parish priest.[73] Rumours of a possible religious procession in Mieres sparked a demonstration that was broken up by the Assault Guard, who fired a hundred rounds. The security forces arrested left-wing leaders across the coalfields, which fuelled

[70] *Avance*, 25, 27, 29, 30 March 1934.

[71] *Avance*, 28 March 1934.

[72] AL, Actas, 7 Oct. 1933 to 16 June 1934, ff. 141–2.

[73] *Región*, 31 March, 1 Apr. 1934.

strikes and protests that received massive support. A stoppage by 1,500 at the Mariana pit in Mieres spread to Aller and Lena, leading to 15,000 out on strike. The sharp escalation prompted trade unions in Mieres to issue a joint appeal for the strikers to return to work.[74] It seems unlikely that the arrested leaders committed the iconoclastic acts. Rather these were preventative detentions to dampen protest. Instead, the arrests were denounced as 'arbitrary' and accompanied by wide-ranging strikes. The arrests appeared to confirm *Avance*'s narrative of an unjust, persecutory state.[75] Protest had become larger and more militant than in previous years.

The security forces' actions were a deliberate demonstration of authority, and even intentionally provocative. When a Langrean Republican association complained to the prime minister that the searches were 'counterproductive' and would not calm 'spirits', their own centre was searched.[76] The civil governor stated airily that he 'was sure that this excitation would not have any consequences' and refused to change tack even as the situation escalated.[77] In marked contrast to his approach to the February conflict in Laviana, there would be no change in strategy.[78]

The initial clampdown by the state security forces in February had coincided with the 'Austrian Civil War'. The short-lived uprising by the socialist paramilitary forces, the Schutzbund, was also sparked by arms searches conducted by the Austrian state. Indecision wracked the declining socialist movement, particularly in Vienna, where the leadership was reluctant to pre-empt the state. The February insurrection was thus a desperate, last-gasp reaction by a socialist movement far from the height of its powers.[79] The radical, militant attitudes in the Asturian coalfields appear to have been absent in Austria. Austrian socialists displayed 'verbal maximalism' but their actions were cautious and their demands stopped short of calling for a dictatorship of the proletariat as Largo Caballero did.[80]

In Spain, socialists framed the situation in urgent terms that served to propel radicalization. During a speech in February 1934, González Peña

[74] *Avance*, 3, 4, 5 Apr. 1934; *La Voz de Asturias*, 3, 4 Apr. 1934.

[75] *Avance*, 5, 8 Apr. 1934.

[76] *Avance*, 29 March 1934.

[77] *Avance*, 28 March 1934.

[78] In contrast, his counterpart in Valencia negotiated the end of a general strike (Valero, *Republicanos*, pp. 128–33).

[79] See A. Rabinbach, *The Crisis of Austrian Socialism: from Red Vienna to Civil War, 1927–1934* (Chicago, Ill., 1983) and C. Jeffery, *Social Democracy in the Austrian Provinces, 1918–1934: Beyond Red Vienna* (London, 1995).

[80] Horn, *European socialists*, pp. 21–3.

declared that there were only two ways forward, 'Germany and Italy, or Russia'. The audience rose to its feet, applauded, and many shouted 'viva *la revolución*'.[81] This reduction of political options also drew Asturias into a wider European framework and compounded a sense of urgency. *Avance* cultivated the accusation that the left – and therefore the working class – was under attack, and contributed to stiffening of resolve and a deepening divide between the left and the state through radical, defiant rhetoric. Not only did the authorities 'persecute' the working class by searching 'only the Casas del Pueblo and the centres of the working class', but the searches – described as '*razzia*' in reference to house raids conducted during colonial warfare in North Africa – meant that Asturias found itself in a 'full state of war'.[82] This image of a provocative state persecuting the working class and causing the country to slide towards war would be repeated over the coming months and formed a crucial part of the newspaper's framing of the need for a revolutionary uprising.

Unite, proletarian brothers!

Whether 'red, white, yellow, [or] flesh-coloured', united fronts were on everyone's lips in early 1934, *Región* observed.[83] Less than two months after this remark, delegates of the Asturian socialist and anarchist movements signed an agreement founding a Workers' Alliance in the back room of a bar in Gijón. The short public announcement in *Avance* expressed the alliance's intention to combat fascism and war, but in private the agreement declared the aim of working towards 'the triumph of social revolution in Spain'.[84] Disguising the revolutionary intent enabled the alliance to work 'freely, without raising the authorities' suspicions'.[85]

Nazism's ascension to power and the destruction of the German left placed renewed impetus on bridging deep divisions on the left. Co-operation was nonetheless difficult and progress tortuous in Spain, as it was elsewhere. Collaboration between socialists and Communists in Germany and Austria was only achieved once the movements were forced underground by

81 *Avance*, 4 Feb. 1934.

82 *Avance*, 24, 27 March 1934.

83 *Región*, 3 Feb. 1934.

84 For the pact, see V. Alba, *La Alianza Obrera: historia y análisis de una táctica de unidad en España* (Madrid, 1978), pp. 205–6 and the announcement in *Avance*, 1 Apr. 1934.

85 'Informe del Comité Regional de la CNT de Asturias sobre su actuación y la de la Alianza Obrera Regional Revolucionaria en los sucesos revolucionarios ocurridos en la provincia de marzo a octubre de 1934' [undated], CDMH, PS Gijón, J series, box 12, file 2, pp. 12–3.

dictatorships. In France, the socialist and Communist rank and file had demonstrated together on 12 February 1934 in opposition to right-wing leagues, but it was nearly six months before the parties signed an antifascist unity pact. The road to the French Popular Front agreed in July 1935 would be lengthy and winding.[86]

Discussions of left-wing unity in Spain usually centre on the Catalan dissident communist Joaquin Maurín.[87] Previously a CNT and PCE activist, Maurín was a sophisticated Marxist thinker and anti-Stalinist who had co-founded the dissident communist BOC.[88] The BOC founded the first 'Workers' Alliance against Fascism' together with two other minority leftist organizations (the Catalan Socialist Union and the *treintista* Libertarian Syndicalist Federation) in Barcelona in March 1933. The Alliance broadened after the November elections to include the Catalan socialists, although the most powerful and numerous working class organization in Catalonia, the CNT, continued to refuse to participate.[89] From this Catalan kernel, the Workers' Alliance seeded through Spain, reaching its apogee a year later in the Asturian Workers' Alliance, which was one of a patchwork of alliances across the country.[90] Yet this genealogy of left-wing unity initiatives only goes so far in explaining the emergence of the Asturian Alliance. Equally important is both renewed agitation among the rank and file for an alliance or united front in Asturias, and a shift in the Asturian anarchist movement. Asturian anarchist leaders jailed after the failed anarchist rising of December 1933 penned a joint appeal to the regional CNT to think afresh about collaborating with the socialists. Although opposed by the national CNT, the Asturian anarchists nevertheless pursued an alliance over the following months.

A renewed wave of grassroots unity initiatives revealed rank-and-file collaboration at the local level. Such initiatives had emerged in other

[86] Horn, *European socialists*, pp. 63–6, 138–42, 149–50. For a detailed analysis of the French case, see J. Jackson, *The Popular Front in France: Defending Democracy, 1934–38* (Cambridge, 1988), ch. 1.

[87] E.g. R. Navarro Comas, 'El Frente Único, las Alianzas Obreras y el Frente Popular: la evolución teórica de los anarquistas ante la colaboración obrera', *Mélanges de la Casa de Velázquez*, xli (2011), 103–20.

[88] For a summary of his thought, see P. Heywood, *Marxism and the Failure of Organised Socialism in Spain, 1879–1936* (Cambridge, 1990), pp. 142–3.

[89] T. Corkett, 'Interactions between the Confederación Nacional del Trabajo and the Unión General de Trabajadores in Spain and Catalonia, 1931–1936' (Unpublished University of Glasgow PhD thesis, 2011), pp. 45–6. See also A. Durgan, *BOC 1930–1936: el Bloque Obrero y Campesino* (Barcelona, 1996), chs 3 and 4.

[90] Durgan, *BOC*, pp. 243–8; Alba, *Alianza*, pp. 96–7.

contexts, like the Ruhr, France and Portugal.[91] Most prominent in the coalfields was the Langrean Pro-United Front Committee, which was similar to the CPUT of 1933. The Committee was a cross-union alliance and 'revolutionary bloc' against fascism at the local level that tapped into rank-and-file enthusiasm. Rallies of 'extraordinary importance' attended by up to 6,000 leftists were 'one of the most transcendental events for the future of workers' and the initiative quickly sparked discussion in other union sections and even applications to join the Langrean Front.[92] The Langrean Front featured individuals of prominent standing to a greater degree than the CPUT; socialists included a candidate in the 1933 elections who was a member of the National Federation of the JS, and the son of the SOMA founder. Unity initiatives beyond the Langrean Front included joint strike and boycott committees and a candidacy to head the Ateneo in Mieres, all of which consisted of varying combinations of socialists, Communists and anarchists.[93]

The socialist leadership's response to these initiatives was initial silence followed by scolding criticism. *Avance*'s reaction was woolly: unity 'need not emerge ... from any private or local initiatives' as unity was apparently 'already ... a reality'.[94] Commenting on the Langrean Front, Amador Fernández criticized 'spectacles that leave a lot to be desired', labelling committees formed on local terms 'unacceptable'.[95] Strategic considerations belonged to the leadership. Largo Caballero's position was ambiguous. In public he welcomed alliances, but in private he was more interested in strengthening the socialist movement than reaching out to Communists or anarchists. He favoured an Alliance in Catalonia due to socialist weakness in the region. Elsewhere they were 'tolerated'.[96] Such a position was consistent with Largo Caballero's commitment to positioning the socialist movement as the sole representative of the working class.

[91] A. Zukas, 'Explaining unemployed protest in the Ruhr at the end of the Weimar Republic', in *Unemployment and Protest: New Perspectives on Two Centuries of Contention*, ed. M. Reiss and M. Perry (Oxford, 2011), p. 165.

[92] *Avance*, 6 Feb. 1934. For positive reactions, see *Avance*, 2, 16 Feb. 1934; *El Noroeste*, 6 Feb. 1934.

[93] *Avance*, 21 Jan., 9, 14 March 1934; Á. Mato Díaz, *La Atenas del norte: ateneos, sociedades culturales y bibliotecas populares en Asturias (1876–1937)* (Oviedo, 2008), p. 97.

[94] *Avance*, 7 Jan. 1934. The PCE Central Committee also condemned the Pro-United Front Committee (P. Miller, 'Un movimiento de oposición radical: el PCE en Asturias, 1931–1934', *Estudios de Historia Social*, xxxi (1984), 131–7, at p. 135).

[95] *Avance*, 7 Feb. 1934.

[96] F. Largo Caballero, *Escritos sobre la República: notas históricas de la guerra en España (1917–1940)* (Madrid, 1985), p. 141.

It is commonplace to state that the PCE rejected Alliances and maintained its preference for a united front from below until September, when their position changed. The Asturian Communists joined the Workers' Alliance on the cusp of the insurrection.[97] Yet this version of events overlooks the frequent collaboration across the left in the coalfields throughout 1934, including in boycotts, strikes, committees against war and fascism, and during 1 May celebrations, despite Communist criticism of the Alliance.[98] BOC leader Maurín even shared a stage with PCE members at the May Day rally in Mieres.[99] Asturias does not appear to have been unique, as there were cases of grassroots co-operation involving the PCE. In Ourense, near Portugal, and in Cádiz, socialists, anarchists and Communists signed a Workers' Alliance in February and co-organized the festivities on 1 May respectively.[100] If the Communist position was complex, so was that of the Asturian anarchists. Despite anarchist signatures to the Asturian Workers' Alliance, many were far from convinced by the initiative, particularly in the coalfields. The agreement came under attack from anarchists in La Felguera, where the more radical FAI was influential. Dissident voices grew in strength over the summer of 1934 and the Workers' Alliance was only ratified by four votes at the regional CNT conference in mid September. Most anarchist mining unions voted against it.[101]

The Alliance did not greatly affect the day-to-day life of left-wing activists in the coalfields. The central committee organized some initial rallies, designated local representatives, intervened in a couple of strikes and discussed some military considerations regarding a possible revolutionary movement. But in August, for example, 'nothing worth mentioning occurred in the Alliance Committee'.[102] Rather than working towards actual revolution – its stated goal – the Alliance was an umbrella under which separate unions developed their own projects.[103] Planning

[97] E.g. Souto Kustrín, *Y ¿Madrid?*, p. 82.

[98] E.g. *Avance*, 8, 29 July, 19 Aug. 1934; *El Noroeste*, 25 Aug. 1934.

[99] *Avance*, 3, 5 May 1934,

[100] J. Prada Rodríguez, *De la agitación republicana a la represión franquista (Ourense 1934–1939)* (Barcelona, 2006), p. 37–8; Macarro Vera, *Socialismo*, p. 314.

[101] 'Informe del Comité Regional de Asturias de la CNT elevado al Pleno Regional de sindicatos sobre los acontecimientos de octubre de 1934 y otro informe de la Comisión de la Alianza Obrera Regional Revolucionaria remitido al Comité citado', 10 Apr. 1936, CDMH, PS Gijón, J Series, box 12, file 3, pp. 11, 30–1; Á. Barrio Alonso, *Anarquismo y anarcosindicalismo en Asturias (1890–1936)* (Madrid, 1988), p. 401; *El Noroeste*, 20 Sept. 1934.

[102] See 'Informe del Comité Regional de Asturias de la CNT elevado al Pleno Regional', pp. 11–14.

[103] Bizcarrondo shares this view in *Octubre del 1934: reflexiones sobre una revolución* (Madrid,

the revolutionary movement was a socialist affair and they refused to share the arms they were smuggling into the province with anarchists.[104] Rather than the Alliance embedding itself in the everyday functioning of union politics, it was a banner that provided a sense of dynamism and confidence in future victory.

Towards the cliff edge

The Asturian socialists' decision to put their signatures to the Asturian Workers' Alliance could be interpreted as crowning the process of radicalization by bringing the leadership into line with the rank and file. In reality, fractiousness continued between the two. The socialist hierarchy wanted to limit strike action, but they could not prevent it. Thousands joined a PCE-organized strike in April despite SOMA opposition and in May, a conflict at the Sotón mine soon revealed the fragility of the leadership's influence over the rank and file. A workforce-organized wildcat strike in protest at a mining deputy escalated into a lockout, the deployment of security forces to guard the pit, solidarity strikes along the Nalón valley, shootouts between strikers and civil guards and the use of physical force against jeering female demonstrators.[105] The SOMA managed to end the strike only for 15,000 to down tools two weeks later when the same mining deputy was transferred to a different mine. A self-designated 'Alliance committee' emerged to lead the strike, although the anarchist SUM and the SOMA both distanced themselves from it.[106]

The SOMA admonished the rank and file in a manner that recalled earlier criticism. For the SOMA, the strike was short-sighted and showed a lack of maturity. It aimed at 'nothing more than to provoke an encounter with the security forces to justify revolutionary attitudes in which those who start them are never those who end up worse off'.[107] As Antuña warned the JS in July, what was needed, 'now more than ever, [was] discipline'.[108] This emphasis on self-control and limiting strike action is usually portrayed as an attempt to protect the socialist movement ahead of a revolutionary movement, yet it was also the continuation of the existing socialist strategy of trying to keep the rank and file on a short leash.

1977), p. 40.

[104] Souto Kustrín, *Y ¿Madrid?*, p. 93.

[105] Shubert, *Road*, p. 152; P. I. Taibo II, *Asturias, octubre 1934* (Barcelona, 2013), pp. 50–1.

[106] *El Noroeste*, 17 June 1934.

[107] *Avance*, 26 June 1934; *El Noroeste*, 27 June 1934.

[108] *Avance*, 29 July 1934.

Meanwhile, a major strike in agriculture had been incubating in the south of Spain since the winter, due to the work of the new leadership of the socialist landworkers' union, the FNTT. When the government announced the derogation of the law of municipal boundaries, the FNTT declared it would strike. The strike did not enjoy the unanimous support of the socialist leadership, which feared for the repercussions it might have on socialist organizations. The fears turned out to be well founded. The government made an early attempt at negotiating a solution, but then moved to crush the strike. On 29 May, the harvest was declared a 'public service', rendering the strike illegal. The strike began on 5 June and while it mobilized 200,000 across central, southern and eastern Spain, strikes took place in less than a third of the municipalities where they had been announced. The press was censored, workers' centres were closed down and the parliamentary immunity of socialist deputies was violated. The authorities arrested 7,000 strikers – though in areas like Valencia, most were released soon after the conflict ended – and the government replaced municipal councils with steering committees.[109] The disarticulation of left-wing organizations in these areas meant they were too weak to participate in the October revolutionary insurrection.

On the northern coast, *Avance* continued its duel with the authorities. As the emblem of socialist radicalism, it had become a target for the authorities. The civil governor ordered the sequestration of the newspaper on ninety-four days out of 186 in 1934, fined it 25,000 pesetas and jailed the editor on three occasions. Such moves only confirmed *Avance*'s message that the state was sliding towards authoritarianism.[110] As the newspaper battled the authorities in what it described as a 'war of extermination' on the 'working class press', it strengthened its ties with its readers, who contributed small donations to pay the fines. The newspaper printed long lists of its benefactors.[111] Mineworkers in Barredos went on strike when a sequestered edition did not arrive.[112] The jailed editor Javier Bueno received well-publicized visits from fellow socialists, including children, photographs of whom were published in *Avance*. Such visits to Bueno in prison imitated, consciously or otherwise, the Communist strategy of sending delegations

[109] F. Cobo Romero, *Revolución campesina y contrarrevolución franquista en Andalucía: conflictividad social, violencia política y represión franquista en el mundo rural andaluz, 1931–1950* (Granada, 2004), pp. 104–14; for Valencia, see Valero, *Republicanos*, p. 143. For arrests, see González Calleja, *Cifras*, p. 217.

[110] Shubert, *Road*, p. 151.

[111] *Avance*, 27 March, 21 July 1934.

[112] *Avance*, 11 July 1934.

to visit imprisoned German Communist leader Ernst Thälmann in 1934 in order to publicize his plight.[113]

Outside the walls of Oviedo's Model Prison, red-shirted members of the Socialist Youth paraded in a show of collective strength and support for Bueno in a manner that revealed their increasing penchant for the trappings of paramilitarism. This martial style – in dress, gestures and actions – had spread through interwar European youth politics. The raised fist salute, which was first used by German Communists in the 1920s, emerged in Spain in 1934 and was performed during demonstrations and by uniformed JS members attending the funeral of Juanita Rico – who died at the hands of Falangists in Madrid – in June.[114] The Socialist Youth propagated martial politics through publishing extracts from the Comintern 'handbook for revolution', *Armed Insurrection*, and a 'Decalogue of the Young Socialist', which called on JS members to arm themselves and form militias.[115] This was politics defined by 'action', in which ideological debates became secondary to actively fighting one's opponents.[116] Even so, while JS members undertook training in preparation for a revolutionary movement, their emphasis was on occupying public space and showing collective strength, rather than pursuing pitched battles, much as the German Social Democrats' Iron Front in the early 1930s was a form of militant posturing rather than a serious street-fighting force.[117] While skirmishes between youths occurred in Madrid, there is little evidence of such encounters in the streets of Oviedo.[118]

The Socialist Youth formed the backbone of the militias who were training for the future revolutionary movement. The organization of the movement fell to a Liaison Committee with members drawn from the PSOE, UGT and JS. Largo Caballero and the Federation of the Socialist Youth (FJS) issued directives to the militias.[119] In February, just before

[113] See Rabinbach, 'Freedom', p. 34.

[114] See photographs in *Mundo Gráfico*, 27 June 1934 and *Avance*, 4 Sept. 1934.

[115] S. Souto Kustrín, 'Taking the street: workers' youth organizations and political conflict in the Spanish Second Republic', *European History Quarterly*, xxxiv (2004), 131–56, at p. 143; *Renovación*, 17 Feb. 1934; A. Neuberg, *Armed Insurrection* (London, 1970 [1928]).

[116] For politics as action, see M. Vincent, 'Political violence and mass society: a European civil war?', in *The Oxford Handbook of European history, 1914–1945*, ed. N. Doumanis (Oxford, 2016), particularly at p. 400.

[117] For the Iron Front, see D. Harsch, *German Social Democracy and the Rise of Nazism* (Chapel Hill, N.C., 1993), ch. 7.

[118] H. García, 'De los soviets a las Cortes: los comunistas ante la República', in Rey, *Palabras*, pp. 136, 139; González Calleja, *Contrarrevolucionarios*, p. 228.

[119] Largo Caballero, *Escritos*, pp. 93–102; S. Souto Kustrín, 'De la paramilitación al fracaso: las insurrecciones socialistas de 1934 en Viena y Madrid', *Pasado y memoria*, ii (2003), 204–5.

Renovación published the 'Decalogue of the Young Socialist', the FJS issued a circular urging JS sections to organize armed militias. Thirty-eight replied that they were undertaking this task or had done so already, six of which were Asturian. The fifth Congress of the Socialist Youth dictated that these militias be organized in a military manner, with a clear hierarchy and the formation of special technical groups.[120] Evidence is thin as to the extent of training activists received. Even in Madrid – the heartland of the radicalized Caballerista youth – the organization of the JS militias was not completed prior to October.[121] Hints in *Avance* provide possible indicators of paramilitary training through reference to 'excursionists'. A group from Pola de Lena formed in May only carried out their first trip into the mountains in late August.[122]

In addition to training militias, socialists engaged in gunrunning and the stockpiling of arms. Arms arrived from a variety of different sources, including Portuguese revolutionaries, a police chief in Madrid, the Alfa sewing machine and small arms factory in Eibar just outside Bilbao, and the arms factory in Oviedo, from which they were smuggled out piece by piece.[123] Local socialist and anarchist groups fundraised for small arms purchases and organized creative means of smuggling weapons into the province, which meant they obtained a motley collection of weapons.[124] The arms caches were insufficient for the needs of an insurrection, but the trafficking did perform another function. The transportation and hiding of weapons involved a large number of individuals and creative strategies. Engaging in these conspiratorial, illicit activities was empowering, fostered in-group bonds and bolstered the crystallization of anti-government feeling through encouraging an adversarial, besieged attitude.[125]

How to deal with fractious, violent, uniformed street politics was a question many European governments faced in the interwar period. In the wake of violence at a British Union of Fascists rally in London in June 1934,

For the financing of the insurrection, see A. del Rosal, *1934: el movimiento revolucionario de octubre* (Madrid, 1984), pp. 229–33.

[120] See Souto Kustrín's piecing together of evidence of preparations in Madrid in *Y ¿Madrid?*, pp. 177–9.

[121] Souto Kustrín, 'De la paramilitarización al fracaso', p. 204.

[122] *Avance*, 26 Aug. 1934.

[123] Rosal, *Octubre*, pp. 234–40.

[124] Taibo, *Asturias*, pp. 80–5.

[125] D. Siemens emphasizes the empowering nature of paramilitary activities for German men in the context of Nazi Stormtroopers in *Stormtroopers: a New History of Hitler's Brownshirts* (New Haven, Conn., 2017), e.g. p. 322.

the British parliament discussed restrictions on the trappings of paramilitary style. In Spain, the government banned – at least in theory – political salutes in March, flags in June and excursions by uniformed individuals at the end of July.[126] The government understood paramilitarism as the cause rather than the effect – or affected style – of radicalism. As arrests for wearing uniforms started taking place, the Asturian JS was defiant, declaring that there was no

> legal precept which prevents us from dressing in the colour that we choose and therefore this Executive Commission recommends all young socialists wear [their] red shirts, on Sundays and holidays at least, and when going to bars, theatres and festivals [*romerías*], etc., thereby fulfilling your duty.[127]

Arrests for wearing paramilitary uniforms continued through August. At the end of the month the government introduced new restrictions on the political participation of those aged under twenty-three, which Salazar Alonso later admitted had been 'designed to circumscribe the left'.[128] The JS accused the government of offering them as a 'sacrifice' to 'capitalist fascism' in 'another of the fascist measures dictated by the monarchizing [*sic*] conglomerate'.[129] Decrying the law as fascist went beyond a rhetorical flourish; rather it formed part of the wider framing of Spain's perceived onward march towards authoritarianism.

The perceived threat of the government as a possible midwife to fascism contrasted with the alternative revolutionary future depicted by *Avance*. A bellicose state was pushing the working classes to act. In mid August, *Avance* warned that 'the country, [was] on a war footing' because of the mobilization of the army and rejected the idea that the Republic could return to its 'primitive position'.[130] The working class no longer desired the Republic of 1931, but rather envisaged a better future through revolution.[131] As the newspaper reiterated:

> Capitalism does not tolerate infiltration. Liberal democracy is a miserable fiction. The enormous working class mass which, with different nuances in its nuclei and people, had placed its confidence [in it], has lost even the shadow of its confidence. For the transformation of the property regime in

[126] González Calleja, *En nombre*, p. 240; *Región*, 29 July 1934.

[127] *Avance*, 1 Aug. 1934.

[128] *Avance*, 14 Aug. 1934; Townson, *Crisis*, p. 263.

[129] S. Souto Kustrín, *Paso a la juventud: movilización democrática, estalinismo y revolución en la república española* (Valencia, 2013), p. 67; *Avance*, 26, 29 Aug. 1934.

[130] *Avance*, 15 Aug. 1934.

[131] *Avance*, 19 Aug. 1934.

> a socialist direction, there is only one path, without pauses or hesitation: the Revolution.[132]

Fatalistically, *Avance* declared that 'the only disastrous revolution would be that which is not attempted'. Comparing Spain to Austria and Germany, it concluded that 'the case of Spain is, essentially, the same'. The decision had to be made between 'declining rapidly towards disappearance and trying to save either everything with victory or a great deal through the fortitude of the action'.[133]

September opened with a flashpoint in Sama that revealed the continuing difficult coexistence of the security forces and the working-class left, and the growing fracture between the local community and the wider state. Security forces had gathered in the town ahead of a demonstration against war and fascism announced by the Women's Socialist Group and which appears to have been unauthorized.[134] The march in the evening was peaceful and headed by women carrying banners. As it neared the town hall, the security forces intervened to disperse it by force. A shot was fired in unclear circumstances, which injured a security guard, and the security forces responded with a round of firing. Demonstrators and bystanders fled as doors closed and shutters slammed down. Three men and three women were injured, and a bystander was killed by a shot to the heart.[135] *Avance*'s depiction of the aftermath of the shooting was thick with rage and resentment:

> [e]veryone with their arms raised. Seven- and ten-year-old children too. Everyone with their backs to the security forces, walking in the direction that the latter want ... It seems as though we are in the middle of a war. In truth it is an invasion. In truth it is the army of a power foreign to the community which is corralling, flogging and shooting at it.[136]

Not only did the security forces humiliate local inhabitants and treat children inhumanely, but they were an occupying force that was incompatible with the coalfields.

Avance's rhetoric was matched by a breakdown in the channels of communication between the different layers of the state. The civil governor refused to speak via telephone to the mayor of Sama or Matilde de la Torre, a socialist deputy who was in Sama at the time. *Avance* often engaged in

[132] *Avance*, 30 Aug. 1934.

[133] *Avance*, 4 Sept. 1934.

[134] This was announced in *Avance* (1 Sept. 1934).

[135] This account is drawn from *Avance*, 2 Sept. 1934; *El Noroeste*, 2 Sept. 1934; *El Sol*, 2 Sept. 1934.

[136] *Avance*, 2 Sept. 1934.

demagogic provocative remarks about the authorities, but in this case, its comments were judicious: 'On other occasions, [the mayor's] intervention was requested by governors to prevent things which were about to happen, which were about to turn into tragedies like yesterday. And the tragedy was avoided'.[137] The governor showed a similar lack of desire for dialogue during a conflict days later at the Fondón mine when the sacking of five mineworkers for demanding a minimum wage led to a sit-down strike at the coalface with two mining deputies taken hostage. The governor responded by sending assault and civil guards, banned the SOMA from intervening and avowed that his authority would be maintained at all costs: the 'intolerable rebellion' would be 'punished as it deserve[d]'.[138]

The growing gulf between the coalfield left and the security forces was not limited to *Avance*'s rhetoric. For the funeral of the bystander killed in the demonstration in Sama – Saturnino Fernández, a JS member – the mayor requested the withdrawal of the state security forces and the day passed peacefully. But the security forces returned to the streets the following day and started frisking citizens, to which socialists, anarchists and Communists responded by striking. The strike committee even asked people to leave Sama to avoid bloodshed.[139] The ability of the municipal authorities and their supporters to maintain order – *their* order – by themselves contrasted with the impossibility of leftists and the security forces coexisting in the streets. The organizing committee of a joint Socialist and Communist Youth rally in Oviedo echoed this sentiment. In rejecting the presence of the police they aimed to give a 'day of peace to the gravedigger, jailer and hospital staff''.[140]

The socialist and Communist rally was to protest against a JAP rally at the symbolic Asturian site of Covadonga, in the west of the province. Covadonga was mythologized as the eighth-century birthplace of the 'Reconquest' of Spain and was a site of Marian pilgrimage.[141] Both supporters and opponents understood the long-planned rally as a barometer of support for each side in the province. While a successful rally for the JAP would show Asturias to be the heartland of true Catholic Spain and a repository of disciplined martial virtue, if it were sabotaged by the Workers' Alliance, the

137 *Avance*, 2 Sept. 1934.

138 *Región*, 8 Sept. 1934.

139 *Avance*, 4 Sept. 1934.

140 *Avance*, 6 Sept. 1934.

141 The politics and memory of Covadonga are analysed in C. Boyd, 'The second battle of Covadonga: the politics of commemoration in modern Spain', *History and Memory*, xiv (2002), 37–64.

left's ability to shut down the province would reveal the strength and unity of the Asturian working class.

The rally took place on 9 September, the day after the feast day of Our Lady of Covadonga. Unsurprisingly, both sides claimed victory. *Región* asserted that 'nothing [had] impeded the gathering of ten thousand people', even as it denounced 'coercion' that prevented sympathizers from attending the 'outstanding' event. In an image with powerful religious undertones, the newspaper explained that one AP member had walked to Covadonga due to the transportation problems caused by the strike.[142] Meanwhile *Avance* proudly described the strike as 'absolute'. Strikers sabotaged train lines, blocked roads with stones and tree trunks, scattered tacks across roads, burned copies of *El Debate* and *ABC* and fired on cars, although no one was injured.[143] The strike was a victory over the right and the state; it was a 'demonstration of unity, the effects of which the concentration of police forces from five provinces could not weaken'. Unity provided the energy and instilled confidence in victory: 'United we will always triumph whenever we try. United we will be able to introduce a society of justice, of workers emancipated from the capitalist yoke'. The 'bloc' that was forming was 'indestructible', even if 'hours of rough struggle' lay ahead.[144]

Preparations for the socialist revolutionary movement continued. Coinciding with the JAP rally, socialists botched a sea-borne arms shipment of 329 boxes of arms and munitions on a boat called the *Turquesa*. The Civil Guard interrupted the landing of the supplies and only ninety-eight made it into the hands of Asturian socialists. Nearly half remained on the boat. High-ranking socialists were implicated. Indalecio Prieto, who had been present during the operation, managed to escape to Bilbao and only parliamentary immunity saved Amador Fernández and Ramón González Peña from arrest.[145] Twenty-three were detained, including councillor and leading Langrean socialist Belarmino Tomás, and the civil governor replaced Asturian socialist mayors with his delegates or else stripped them of their responsibility for public order.[146]

Searches increased in Asturias and across Spain from mid September. In the coalfields, security forces entered socialist, anarchist and Communist centres, the town hall in Mieres and the socialist-owned San Vicente mine,

[142] *Región*, 11 Sept. 1934.

[143] *Avance*, 11 Sept. 1934; *El Sol*, 11 Sept. 1934; *ABC*, 11 Sept. 1934; Salazar Alonso, *Bajo*, pp. 293–5.

[144] *Avance*, 11 Sept. 1934.

[145] *El Noroeste*, 12 Sept. 1934. For a detailed account, see Taibo, *Asturias*, pp. 111–20.

[146] *Avance*, 12, 13 Sept. 1934.

but emerged empty handed, except for a few pistols and, in Turón, a few bombs.[147] The minister of the interior decreed the state of alarm and there was a return to mass searches in the streets. A wave of localized strikes in the coalfields revealed the fractious and tense situation, although these were expressions of local dissidence rather than revolutionary preparation. Socialist policy preferred to avoid a government clampdown and waste of resources. The civil governor complained that 'many strikes are being declared on one pretext one day and on a different one the next' and declared them illegal.[148] In the midst of rising tensions and as local feast days approached, there was a return to targeting religious buildings, including a shrine, chapel and a rectory, with fire and explosives.[149]

The political tensions not only manifested themselves in such attacks and tussles between left-wing militants and the state. They were also embedded in the dynamics of everyday encounters and reveal the sharpness of political divisions at the local level. In the early hours of 1 September, Casimiro D. was stabbed outside a bar in El Entrego (San Martín del Rey Aurelio). He had been accused of planning to attend the JAP rally and of intending to sign-up to the Assault Guard – and therefore betraying the working-class community – which he vigorously denied.[150] Two weeks later a further violent encounter occurred in the same area. Jaime C., a forty-four-year-old businessman and well-known rightist, recounted that he was on a train bound for the rally in Covadonga when Herminio V., a shop assistant and *Avance* contributor, boarded the train and ordered Jaime to alight. This policing of behaviour was backed by the threat of violence: when Jaime refused to leave the train, Herminio drew a pistol, to which Jaime responded by brandishing his own. The train lurched into motion, shots were fired and Herminio and his companions jumped off the train. Herminio's account of the afternoon differed markedly. He denied the accusations and claimed he had been in a bar all afternoon, which several others corroborated.[151]

By the end of September, repeated tussles with state security forces had hardened militant attitudes and created a perceptible fissure between local society and the broader state. *Avance*'s rhetoric had traced a narrative of the descent of the Republic towards fascism, which fed off the identification

[147] *El Noroeste*, 22 Sept. 1934.

[148] *El Noroeste*, 19, 26 Sept. 1934; *Región*, 28 Sept. 1934; *Avance*, 28 Sept. 1934.

[149] *Región*, 15 Sept. 1934; S. Noval Suárez, *Langreo Rojo: historia del martirio y persecución de los sacerdotes en el Arciprestazgo de Langreo durante los sucesos revolucionarios del año 1934* (La Felguera, 1935), p. 99.

[150] AHPA, AP, box 78436, file 257 (1934).

[151] AHPA, AP, box 79435, file 280 (1934).

of fascism in towns and villages across the coalfields. The dark horizon of fascism was juxtaposed with the bright future of revolution, a prospect *Avance* continued to promote. As searches intensified in late September, the newspaper depicted the security forces as a foreign occupying force and warned that armies caused wars.[152] The state was provoking the working class into an inevitable confrontation, while the latter 'consider[ed] Spain to be at the door of a proletarian revolution with a very good chance of triumphing'.[153]

However militant the politics at the local level, they did not amount to a crisis of the state. Nor did the crisis of government that marked the beginning of October, when the CEDA withdrew its support for Prime Minister Samper's government and he resigned. Socialist leaders Besteiro and de los Ríos advised the president to call fresh elections, but Alcalá Zamora turned to Lerroux and asked him to form a government with CEDA ministers.[154] Largo Caballero had been confident that the CEDA's dubious Republican credentials would dissuade Alcalá Zamora from doing so, but he miscalculated. Having repeatedly threatened that the socialists would respond if the CEDA entered government, Largo Caballero was left with little choice when the new ministers were announced on 4 October. The Spanish October ran to a stricter and more public timetable than other episodes of leftist rebelliousness across Europe in 1934.

France's February days and the Austrian Civil War responded to long-term processes and the specificities of each national context, yet they were also respective sudden mass eruptions of militancy within a broader context of leftist flux and reconfiguration between 1933 and 1935 as fascism and right-wing authoritarianism continued to spread across the continent. While fascism has often been depicted as the broad contextual frame for the events of October 1934 in Asturias, the effects of the perceived threat of fascism extended further than this and reached down into the everyday, local level of politics in the Asturian coalfields. Fascism, as a new, hidden, conspiratorial threat, moulded conflicts and how politics was interpreted in the coalfields and how the trajectory of national politics was imagined. The actions of state security forces compounded fears of a slide towards authoritarianism, as did the new development of the encroachment of the Assault and Civil Guard into spaces of left-wing and working-class control, whether homes or political centres. The left fiercely resisted this encroachment, which resulted in a spiralling cycle of protest and repression. Assertive policing alienated

[152] *Avance*, 22 Sept. 1934.

[153] *Avance*, 25 Sept. 1934.

[154] Preston, *Coming of the Spanish Civil War*, pp. 123–4.

the communities of the coalfields from the Republic, even as revolutionary preparations and *Avance*'s radical rhetoric framed the only possible solution to decline as a leap forwards to revolution.

5. Revolution

Like many other fellow journalists, Manuel Chaves Nogales rushed to Asturias to report on the revolutionary insurrection. Chaves Nogales, a liberal Republican and the deputy editor of *Ahora* who was famed for his reports from Soviet Russia, criticized the revolutionary violence which he claimed 'ha[d] nothing to envy, in terms of cruelty, the triumphant Bolshevik revolution'. Yet he was also careful to note that 'a great mass' of Asturian revolutionaries had 'halt[ed] on the threshold of bestiality'. He was critical of the unproven lurid reports of revolutionary brutality that circulated in the right-wing press, and informed his readers that even fascists from the coalfields were indignant at the fabrications.[1] Chaves Nogales was one of the few voices to venture a more nuanced interpretation of the Asturian October. His reports grappled with the contradictions and limits of the realization and destructiveness of the revolution. Such concerns lie at the heart of this chapter's focus on the struggles to define and construct the revolution.

The extent to which the insurrection was revolutionary has long been debated and is usually framed in terms of whether the movement was 'offensive' or 'defensive' towards the Republic.[2] Yet reducing October 1934 to a single adjective does little to convey the reality of a complex and heterogeneous event, in which there were different ideas and objectives of what the movement should be. The socialist hierarchy in Madrid had not planned a social revolution. They had ordered a 'general strike', as Belarmino Tomás, socialist councillor in Langreo and a revolutionary leader, later admitted to the French press.[3] For all Largo Caballero's revolutionary rhetoric, it is likely that he envisaged a combination of general strikes and armed actions by socialist militias that together would paralyse the country. This would precipitate a political crisis in order to prevent CEDA's accession to government, sparking the fall of the government or even ending the

[1] *Ahora*, 24, 26 Oct. 1934.

[2] See, e.g., contrasting views in D. Ruiz, *Insurrección defensiva y revolución obrera: el octubre español de 1934* (Barcelona, 1988) and J. Avilés Farré, 'Los socialistas y la insurrección de octubre de 1934', *Espacio, tiempo y forma, serie v, Historia contemporánea*, xx (2008), 152–3.

[3] *Le Populaire*, 5 Jan. 1935. See also J. Aróstegui, *Largo Caballero: el tesón y la quimera* (Barcelona, 2013), p. 363 and P. I. Taibo II, *Asturias, octubre 1934* (Barcelona, 2013), p. 172.

legislature itself. The limited aims of such a 'revolution', in which strikes and insurrections were an auxiliary strategy, would have resembled the failed Republican-socialist plot of December 1930 that had sought to bring down the monarchy, rather than an attempt to establish a socialist regime. In contrast, Asturian Young Socialists complained in 1936 that they had believed the 1934 revolution 'totalitarian' in its pretensions. They had expected a profound change in Spanish political, social and economic life akin to a social revolution.[4] Instead of adopting a retrospective or macro-level approach to the insurrection, it is more useful to examine the revolutionary process from the perspective of the committees and militias as the situation unfolded before them.[5] The process was necessarily ambiguous, contested and improvised, as militants struggled to define what a revolution was, who was to be included, the fate of those excluded and how a revolutionary should act.

Revolutions are often described as having a 'Janus' face in that the dream of forging a new emancipated society is undercut by a darker side – that of revolutionary violence.[6] But there is a further way of understanding the Janus-faced nature of revolution: in this case, namely, as a liminal moment caught between looking to the future and the past. The Asturian October was a time of flux and transition (though not an 'interregnum'), as revolutionaries attempted to delineate the limits of a new revolutionary 'community' in the midst of a situation in which there were 'radical processes of dissolution and reconstruction, and where guiding symbols and previous markers of certainty are crushed and reconstituted'.[7] The revolutionaries confronted what Hannah Arendt described as the problem of 'beginning' as they decreed a rupture in historical time and tried to conjure a revolutionary future into being in

[4] *La Tarde*, 24, 27 Apr. 1936.

[5] This emphasis on process is influenced by the work of G. Lawson, e.g., 'Within and beyond the "fourth generation" of revolutionary theory', *Sociological Theory*, xxxiv (2016), 106–27.

[6] E.g. A. J. Mayer, *The Furies: Violence and Terror in the French and Russian Revolutions* (Princeton, N.J., 2000). Some recent approaches have emphasized that violence is a 'variable' in revolution, not an intrinsic characteristic (e.g. R. Gerwarth and M. Conway, 'Revolution and counterrevolution', in *Political Violence in Twentieth-Century Europe*, ed. D. Bloxham and R. Gerwarth (Cambridge, 2011), p. 142). It is difficult to see how the societal reconstruction promised by the ideologies in the first half of the twentieth century would allow for a peaceful destruction and reconfiguration of political and social power.

[7] C. F. Roman, 'Liminality, the execution of Louis XVI and the rise of terror during the French Revolution', in *Breaking Boundaries: Varieties of Liminality*, ed. A. Horvath, B. Thomassen and H. Wydra (New York, 2015), p. 148. Revolution as 'interregnum' in J. C. Scott, 'Foreword', in *Everyday Forms of State Formation: Revolution and the Negotiation of Rule in Modern Mexico*, ed. G. M. Joseph and D. Nugent (Durham, N.C., 1994), ix.

the present.[8] Yet even as the revolution opened up a horizon of possibilities, revolutionaries also desired to preserve existing social links and an idea of community. As an insurrection October 1934 failed, and as a revolution it was caught between past and future, preservation and creative destruction.

Taking control

On 4 October 1934, the announcement of the CEDA's entry into government prompted the socialist leadership in Madrid to issue the order for the revolutionary movement to begin. The Spanish socialist leadership had laid preparations for a national revolutionary movement, and strikes and skirmishes occurred across Spain. The Basque Country was the scene of the fiercest clashes outside of Asturias, particularly in industrial areas. Militants in most city neighbourhoods and towns in Vizcaya and Guipúzcoa joined a week-long general strike, punctuated by shootouts with the police, widespread sabotage of the railway network and some requisitioning and redistribution of foodstuffs.[9] The strike was successful in shutting down Madrid, but failed to develop into an insurrection. Strikes also occurred in the south, including in Badajoz, Malaga, Jaén and Cáceres.[10] Events in Barcelona responded to a different dynamic. Lluís Companys, leader of the Catalan government, proclaimed a Catalan state within a federal republic on the evening of 6 October, although this barely lasted twelve hours before Companys and his government were arrested.[11]

Only in Asturias did the events take the form of a sustained insurrection. Teodomiro Menéndez, the envoy destined for Asturias, transported the coded message tucked into his hatband to Oviedo by train. The offices of *Avance* dispatched the order to local socialist sections, which were already on the alert and, in Sama at least, undertaking guard duties.[12] The sound of dynamite exploding in the coal valleys in the early hours of 5 October signalled the beginning of the revolt. On hearing the explosions, anarchists

[8] H. Arendt, *On Revolution* (Harmondsworth, 1973 [1963]), pp. 20ff.

[9] J. P. Fusi, *El País Vasco: autonomía, revolución, guerra civil* (Madrid, 2002), pp. 175–201. See J. R. Garai, J. Gutiérrez and J. Chueca, *Octubre de 1934 en Euskal Herria* (Oñati, 2014) for a detailed account.

[10] For a brief survey, see S. Souto Kustrín, 'Octubre de 1934: historia, mito y memoria', *Hispania Nova. Revista de Historia Contemporánea*, xi (2013), 477–81. For Madrid, see S. Souto Kustrín, *'Y ¿Madrid? ¿Qué hace Madrid?': movimento revolucionario y acción colectiva (1933–1936)* (Madrid, 2004), ch. 3; for Ourense, see J. Prada Rodríguez, *De la agitación republicana a la represión franquista (Ourense 1934–1939)* (Barcelona, 2006), pp. 37–51.

[11] For Catalonia, see *6 d'octubre: la desfeta de la revolució catalanista de 1934*, ed. A. Gonzàlez i Vilalta, M. López Esteve and E. Ucelay-Da Cal (Barcelona, 2014).

[12] Taibo, *Asturias*, pp. 169–70, 179–80; I. Lavilla, *Los hombres de octubre* (Gijón, 2004), p. 41.

in La Felguera sent a delegate across the river to Sama to investigate and decided subsequently to join the insurrection.[13] Stockpiled arms were unearthed, and attention turned to ensuring military control of the coal valleys by defeating the state security forces.

Preparations for the movement were nevertheless incomplete. Despite the gunrunning over the previous months, the revolutionaries were not well armed. Only half of the socialist militias had weapons.[14] Not every member of the socialist ranks had been drilled in preparation for the insurrection. Arturo Vázquez, a socialist, later recounted that although he expected 10,000 participants from Mieres, only 1,300 reliable individuals had been entrusted with training and knowledge of the future rising. Trained militants in Langreo and San Martín del Rey Aurelio numbered approximately 400 and 500 respectively.[15] Even so, the socialist paramilitary organizations were much more developed than that of the Communists, whose MAOC (Antifascist Workers' and Peasants' Militias) had only started to organize shortly before the insurrection.[16] When Communists in Sama were invited to join the movement, they admitted to not possessing weapons.[17] Anarchist groups in Gijón had repeatedly requested the socialists share their stockpiles of weapons over the previous months, but the socialists had stalled, meaning that revolutionaries in the port city were poorly armed.[18] The lack of arms would never be resolved satisfactorily despite the capture of arms factories in Trubia and Oviedo and the improvisation of a rudimentary armaments industry in the coalfields. To remedy the shortfall, revolutionaries employed dynamite, whose destructive power became an emblem of the insurrection.

The trained militias were a small proportion of the working-class left, yet they vastly outnumbered the state security forces in the coalfields. The revolutionaries' first objective was to attack Civil Guard posts and garrisons. In most areas, the battle was relatively short, but in Sama the guards resisted for thirty-six hours, which slowed the revolutionaries' advance.[19]

[13] XXX [*sic*], *Lo que yo he visto: La Felguera en la revolución asturiana* (New York, 1935), pp. 9–10; M. Villar, *El anarquismo en la insurrección de Asturias: la CNT y la FAI en octubre de 1934* (Madrid, 1994 [1935]), p. 119.

[14] J. Rodríguez Muñoz, *La revolución de Octubre de 1934 en Asturias: orígenes, desarrollo y consecuencias* (Oviedo, 2010), p. 236.

[15] Lavilla, *Los hombres*, pp. 30, 52.

[16] In Madrid, the MAOC dated from 1933, at least notionally (see M. Tagüeña Lacorte, *Testimonio de dos guerras* (Barcelona, 1978), p. 38).

[17] Lavilla, *Los hombres*, p. 41.

[18] 'Informe del Comité Regional de la CNT de Asturias sobre su actuación', pp. 36–41.

[19] B. Díaz Nosty, *La comuna asturiana: revolución de octubre de 1934* (Bilbao, 1974), p. 172.

In Aller, SCOM members barricaded themselves in their union centre in the only armed resistance to the revolutionaries undertaken by fellow civilians. Several died or were captured, while others managed to escape.[20] After the revolutionaries secured the coalfields, attention turned to Oviedo. The failure to sabotage the power supply – the signal to revolt – meant the uprising had failed to materialize on 5 October as planned. Instead, the streets were deserted and the atmosphere was tense, due to a general strike.[21] The following day militia columns entered the provincial capital and managed to gain control of most of the city. Over the next few days fighting raged in the city centre, but the revolutionaries were unable to dislodge government forces from key buildings, including the Santa Clara barracks and the cathedral.

The uprising resulted in a sizeable amount of Asturian territory coming under the revolutionaries' control. The insurrection reached beyond the coal valleys and Oviedo to Cangas de Onís in the east and Grado in the west, to the coast to the north and south to the border with the province of León. The revolutionaries held the upper hand for the first six days of the revolt, but during the final week, the momentum shifted to the military reinforcements that had arrived by sea and land. The army slowly eroded the area under revolutionary control until only the coalfields were left.

The armed forces were under the command of General Eduardo López Ochoa, a liberal and freemason who had been appointed as commander-in-chief of the 15,000-strong armed forces after Prime Minister Lerroux rejected Minister of Defence Diego Hidalgo's preferred candidate, General Francisco Franco. Franco was instead assigned an advisory role. General López Ochoa led a regiment of infantry, which descended on Asturias from the west; Colonel José Solchaga approached from the east; and General Carlos Bosch (later replaced by General Amadeo Balmes) advanced north from León, but soon became bogged down by revolutionary resistance in the mountain passes. Lieutenant Colonel Juan Yagüe led a detachment of the battle-hardened Army of Africa formed by units of the Foreign Legion and indigenous Moroccan troops – the *Regulares*. The air force provided aerial support through bombing, which was a particularly terrifying experience for residents of the coalfields.[22]

[20] See Taibo, *Asturias*, pp. 196–8; D. Ruiz, *Octubre de 1934: revolución en la República española* (Madrid, 2008), pp. 292–3.

[21] J. A. Cabezas, *Morir en Oviedo: historia en directo (vivencias de un periodista)* (Madrid, 1984), pp. 56–63.

[22] S. Balfour, *Deadly Embrace: Morocco and the Road to the Spanish Civil War* (Oxford, 2002), pp. 251–2; for López Ochoa's account, see *Campaña militar de Asturias en octubre de 1934 (narración táctica-episódica)* (Madrid, 1936). See also J. E. Álvarez, 'The Spanish Foreign

Government troops reached the outskirts of Oviedo on 11 October, which constituted a turning point. The army had already retaken Gijón and the insurrectionists in Oviedo had lost momentum. A final push to seize the arms factory had not remedied the lack of weapons and it had become increasingly clear that the Asturians were on their own, although the provincial revolutionary committee felt the need to send someone across the lines and all the way to León to read newspapers in order to confirm it.[23] Regarding the situation to be hopeless, the provincial revolutionary committee ordered a retreat on 11 October and distributed 14 million pesetas stolen from a bank vault to aid the flight of leading revolutionaries.[24] Even as town and village revolutionary committees fled, the militias did not disintegrate. A second provincial committee, formed by younger and more radical activists, took the place of the first. This second committee lasted a day at most before the revolutionaries regrouped under the leadership of a third wave of committees.[25] Fighting continued for a further week until the government troops entered the coal valleys on 19 October.

Revolutionary authority was articulated through a network of committees. The provincial revolutionary committee functioned as a figurehead, but the real dynamism behind revolutionary action lay in the committees that managed the revolutionary process at the local level. These committees formed in towns or villages, which constituted the logical geographical unit for the organization of the insurrection and the locus of community-based networks. The composition of the committees reflected these solidarities and embodied both the spirit of the Workers' Alliance and previous strike and unity committees. Members of the committees were not just prominent local socialists, but also anarchists and communists of different stripes. There was a careful commitment to plurality. Political groups and unions were allotted proportionately greater influence on the committees than their numerical strength to ensure representation for all left-wing voices. In 'eminently socialist' Mieres, the committee included two

Legion during the Asturian uprising of October 1934', *War in History*, xviii (2011), 200–24. Bombing is mentioned in several accounts, e.g., N. Molins i Fábrega, *UHP: la insurrección proletaria en Asturias* (Gijón, 1977 [1935]), pp. 128–9; M. Grossi, *La insurrección de Asturias* (Madrid, 1978 [1935]), pp. 173–5.

[23] Taibo, *Asturias*, p. 390.

[24] On the fate of the money, see Taibo, *Asturias*, pp. 583–7.

[25] According to the socialist account, the second committee lasted eight hours. Benavides increases this to ten, while Shubert declares it lasted a day (Lavilla, *Los hombres*, p. 139; M. Benavides, *La revolución fue así (octubre rojo y negro)* (Barcelona, 1935), p. 360; A. Shubert, *The Road to Revolution in Spain: the Coal Miners of Asturias, 1860–1934* (Urbana, Ill., 1987), p. 8); see also Taibo, *Asturias*, p. 428.

representatives each from the socialists, anarchists and official Communist Party, and one from the dissident communist BOC.[26] While there were some internal frictions, particularly between dissident communists and the PCE, the overall tendency during the insurrection was towards local-level co-operation rather than conflict.[27]

Between re-empowerment and revolution

The seizing of power was depicted as a moment of cathartic release. It alleviated the anger and frustration at the harassment of the working class caused by the security forces over the previous months. Disarming the security forces and occupying the streets asserted left-wing hegemony and expressed a particular conception of the social order; the working class was now back in control. Carlos Vega, in his report to the PCE, remarked that 'reactionary elements' in Oviedo hid, while 'workers and women' appeared in the streets and raised their voices to say 'now it's our time' and 'come out, let's see your faces'.[28] A sentimental description of militias departing Pola de Laviana enthused that they left 'the capital of their municipality, the whole municipality, in the hands of the representatives of the revolution, in many of whom they had placed their confidence and mandate of popular revolutionary will through their votes' in the municipal elections of 1931.[29] The revolution thereby signified the re-empowerment of the left at local level. In a similar way, rather than destroying the local seat of political power, the new revolutionary committees simply assumed political and administrative direction of towns and villages. Militants burned some official documents, but did not torch town halls. The local revolutionary committee wrapped itself in the cloak of existing authority, to the extent that municipal seals were used to validate committee-issued vouchers.[30]

The relative normality of life – 'much more normal than many hastily written accounts have suggested' – similarly reveals a certain continuity in the coalfields during the insurrection under the reasserted power of the local

[26] Ruiz, *Insurrección*, p. 131; Lavilla, *Los hombres*, the quotation at p. 33.

[27] Grossi, a BOC member, unsurprisingly, pointed the finger at the PCE as the focal point for 'disagreements' (Grossi, *La insurrección*, pp. 27–8, 45, 48).

[28] C. Vega, 'Copia de un informe remitido al Comité Central del PCE por Carlos Vega relativo a los sucesos revolucionarios de octubre de 1934', CDMH, PS Madrid, box 721, file 3, p. 8.

[29] Lavilla, *Los hombres*, p. 75.

[30] A. de Llano Roza de Ampudia, *Pequeños anales de quince días: revolución en Asturias octubre de 1934* (Oviedo, 1935), p. 181; *El Noroeste*, 17 Oct. 1934.

left.[31] In Mieres, as elsewhere, 'normal life carried on as always [except] a bit disturbed by the fear of the aeroplanes'.[32] Revolutionaries had no desire for the destruction of the economic foundations of coalfield society. Foremen were charged with conserving the mines and metalworkers made sure to keep the blast furnaces functioning so that they did not cool and crack.[33] Even as goods and cash were pilfered from shops in Siero and Bimenes, there was little physical damage to the establishments themselves and in areas like Laviana and Allande 'losses [we]re not worth mentioning'.[34] The relative normality of life in the coalfields contrasted with that in Oviedo, for the capital constituted the frontline. Looting and destruction were more common.[35] Alfredo Mendizábal, a professor at the University of Oviedo, described his ordeal in the midst of the fighting in Oviedo as consisting of 'nine interminable days, with their terrible nights. We could only hear gunfire … and the incessant thunder of dynamite', although he only had 'praise' for the miners who risked their lives to look after them.[36]

The case of Laviana provides insight into how revolutionaries sought to reconcile the competing aims of preserving social cohesion and re-founding the social and economic order in the name of revolution. As in other areas under revolutionary control, the use of money was prohibited, but the revolutionary authorities developed a novel system that circumvented their own ban: the socialist mayor and his deputy organized a monetary collection for local shopkeepers. The measure intended to compensate businesses – albeit indirectly – for their goods 'so that small business owners [did] not suffer losses' and the funds continued to grow even after the insurrection.[37] The improvised system attempted to preserve the fragile bonds of community and safeguard the livelihoods of local members of the petty bourgeoisie. The initiative in Laviana was unique. Food distribution in Pola de Lena had a much sharper revolutionary edge for it divided society

31 Díaz Nosty, *La comuna*, p. 174.

32 F. Solano Palacio, *La revolución de octubre: quince días de comunismo libertario* (Madrid, 1994 [1936]), p. 52; *El Noroeste*, 23 Oct. 1934; Llano, *Pequeños anales*, p. 150.

33 *El Noroeste*, 29 Nov. 1934; Villar, *El anarquismo*, p. 125. See also *La Veu de Catalunya*, 28 Oct. 1934.

34 Asociación Mercantil Española SA, 'Segunda Relación de los Comerciantes de Asturias que han sufrido quebranto con motive de la huelga revolucionaria', Barcelona, 5 Nov. 1934, CDMH, PS Madrid, J series, box 50, file 3.

35 Grossi, *La insurrección*, pp. 28, 41–2; Solano Palacio, *La revolución*, p. 48. See also *Región*, 15, 18 Dec. 1934 and *El Noroeste*, 15 Nov. 1934.

36 *Cruz y raya: revista de afirmación y negación*, Nov. 1934.

37 Lavilla, *Los hombres*, p. 75. See also Llano, *Pequeños anales*, pp. 158–9. *El Noroeste*, 23 Oct. 1934.

along class lines: the working classes could use vouchers to obtain food while the middle class had to pay with money.[38]

Replacing money with a voucher system aimed at more than a return to the status quo before 5 October or even the elections of November 1933. By abolishing money, revolutionaries aimed to strike a blow against the socioeconomic underpinnings of society itself. Inhabitants of Oviedo took vouchers to shops where staff were forbidden from accepting money, while in Mieres a sophisticated system was organized with each family-assigned cards allotting them a daily allowance of food. This quota was nevertheless calculated using monetary values.[39] A similar system was introduced in La Felguera after the committee blamed the 'few scruples of some people' for the need to reorganize the allocation of foodstuffs halfway through the insurrection. The value of food allowances was calculated in pesetas.[40] What mattered for revolutionaries was banning the circulation of money as the physical symbol and tangible manifestation of capitalism in the daily lives of coalfield residents.

Banning the use of money was the clearest example of a revolutionary measure undertaken during the insurrection. In doing so, the revolutionaries acted according to what they believed to be the revolutionary script for social revolutions, as defined by previous examples of revolution, the teachings of political doctrine and their fantasies of revolutionary utopia.[41] Requisitioning foodstuffs, clothing and transport and reorganizing their distribution for the needs of the local population and the insurrectionary forces was less clear-cut.[42] The measures blended left-wing revolutionary dreams with the exigencies of waging war on the state. Reorganizing healthcare and controlling the food supply fused radical left ideas with the urgent need for committees to pursue greater control over local resources in what was developing into a mini civil war.

The language that framed the measures was much less ambiguous. The proclamations produced by revolutionary committees and pasted up on walls or read out by revolutionary patrols declared that a new world was dawning. In separate proclamations issued in Sama and La Felguera,

38 Grossi, *La insurrección*, p. 75.

39 Llano, *Pequeños anales*, pp. 67, 177–8; Grossi, *La insurrección*, p. 77. Solano Palacio claims money was banned everywhere, except in Sama (La *revolución*, p. 72).

40 Villar, *El anarquismo*, pp. 123–4.

41 See *Scripting Revolution: a Historical Approach to the Comparative Study of Revolutions*, ed. K. M. Baker and D. Edelstein (Stanford, Calif., 2015).

42 See Ruiz, *Insurrección*, p. 126; Villar, *El anarquismo*, pp. 114–15; for Sotrondio, see *El Noroeste*, 23 Oct. 1934.

the 'revolutionary movement' and 'social revolution' were announced to have 'triumphed'.[43] An eloquent proclamation attributed to libertarian influences from the market town of Grado framed the moment slightly differently. It declared that a 'new society' was emerging from the death of the old in a process governed by 'natural laws'. With power in the hands of revolutionaries, the revolution had succeeded, but the fruits of victory remained just beyond their grasp: 'a few hours – no longer – and there will be more bread on every table and joy in every heart'.[44]

The proclamations announced the revolution as a rupture in historical time that constituted a new beginning. Yet the imagined re-founding of the social, economic and political order was nevertheless tied to the community as the source of legitimacy. In Sama, the revolution was 'triumphant' thanks to 'the community [*pueblo*]'; in Mieres, the committee was the 'interpreter of the popular will'; and in Valdesoto (Siero) money was banned by 'agreement of the assembled community [*pueblo reunido*]'.[45] The committee in Grado imagined itself to be channelling the community's desires and called on the community to 'feel intense satisfaction at seeing their ideal realized'.[46]

The revolutionary enthusiasm, the falsehoods they peddled and their unclear authorship mean that historians have been critical of the proclamations.[47] Certainly the proclamations cannot be read as representative of all revolutionaries, still less the communities under their control. Yet the proclamations are the only surviving documents produced in the heat of the revolutionary process and served to articulate the revolution,

[43] For the proclamation issued by the Sama Revolutionary Committee, see Molins i Fábrega, *UHP*, pp. 88–9; for the proclamation issued by the La Felguera Revolutionary Committee, 6 Oct. 1934, see Llano, *Pequeños anales*, p. 161.

[44] For the proclamation issued by the Grado Revolutionary Committee, undated, see Villar, *El anarquismo*, pp. 90–2.

[45] For the proclamation issued by the Sama Revolutionary Committee, see Molins i Fábrega, *UHP*, pp. 88–9; for the proclamation issued by the Mieres Revolutionary Committee, see D. Ruiz, *Asturias contemporánea (1808–1936)* (Madrid, 1975), pp. 104–5; for the proclamation issued by the Valdesoto Revolutionary Committee, see Villar, *El anarquismo*, p. 121.

[46] For the proclamation issued by the Grado Revolutionary Committee, undated, see Villar, *El anarquismo*, pp. 90–2.

[47] E.g. Taibo, *Asturias*, pp. 454–5; Ruiz, *Insurrección*, p. 127. Alejandro Valdés, a Communist, claimed authorship of one of the *bandos* (F. Erice, 'El octubre asturiano. Entre el mito y la interpretación histórica', in *De un octubre a otro: revolución y fascismo en el periodo de entreguerras, 1919–1934*, ed. A. Andreassi and J. L. Martín Ramos (Madrid, 2010), p. 204).

announce a radical rupture and open up 'the realm of the possible'.[48] The documents framed the situation as revolutionary and individual actors as revolutionaries. The socialist Alberto Fernández recognized forty years after the events that the propaganda produced was 'absurd', yet it was 'effective in accordance with the enthusiasm of the moment'.[49] The proclamations were not a reflection of reality, but an attempt to call a new revolutionary reality into being by encouraging local residents to perceive themselves as experiencing a revolutionary beginning.

The proclamations and measures pursued by the committees were one way of trying to give shape to the revolution. Another means of defining the revolution was through violence. Behind the frontline, the violence that accompanied the birth of the new order overwhelmingly targeted the Church. As part of the initial wave of violence, church buildings and religious images were destroyed across the coalfields.[50] As on previous occasions, such as the 'Tragic Week' of 1909 when convents and churches were burned in Barcelona, and as would occur during the Civil War, the Church was the institution singled out to 'bear the sins of the old order'.[51] During the Asturian October, to detain the priest and wreak destruction in the parish church formed part of the revolutionary ritual – it was 'to do something revolutionary'.[52] In Tuilla, images were publicly burned and vestments worn in the street in a public expunging of religion from the community.[53] Not only was Catholicism the most visible and widespread symbol that could be identified with the right, but anticlericalism was also an important way of showing one's radical mettle.

The revolution would therefore be anticlerical and the majority of the victims of the revolutionary 'furies' were religious personnel. Thirty-three priests, seminarians and religious were killed during the insurrection. Either they were murdered, or they died in unclear circumstances, while many

[48] E. Selbin, *Revolution, Rebellion, Resistance: the Power of Story* (London, 2010), p. 24.

[49] See Taibo, *Asturias*, p. 455.

[50] *El Noroeste*, 23 Oct. 1934; *Región*, 11 Nov. 1934.

[51] M. Vincent, '"The keys of the kingdom": religious violence in the Spanish civil war, July–August 1936', in *The Splintering of Spain: Cultural History and the Spanish Civil War, 1936–1939*, ed. C. Ealham and M. Richards (Cambridge, 2005), p. 72. On Tragic Week, the classic study is J. C. Ullman, *Tragic Week: a Study of Anticlericalism in Spain* (Cambridge, Mass., 1968).

[52] J. Canel [J. Díaz Fernández], *Octubre rojo en Asturias* (Barcelona, 1984 [1935]), pp. 145–6.

[53] S. Noval Suárez, *Langreo Rojo: historia del martirio y persecución de los sacerdotes en el Arciprestazgo de Langreo durante los sucesos revolucionarios del año 1934* (La Felguera, 1935), pp. 125–30.

more were arrested and imprisoned. The victims were male. Just as female religious would suffer much less violence during the Civil War, in 1934, female religious were not only spared the furies, but also escorted away from danger in Oviedo. This reflected the 'taboo' of killing nuns and a chauvinistic attitude that women were not a threat to the revolutionary process, which extended to female religious even being asked to provide food and medical care.[54] A further eleven civilians including well-known rightists, company bosses, a magistrate, and a student, also died at the hands of revolutionaries, as well as ten civil and assault guards who died or were killed away from the frontline.[55] Revolutionary violence targeted those identified as political enemies of the working class left.

These killings cannot be reduced to a simple logic, chronology or geographical area, but there was a degree of patterning to the violence. Several fatalities occurred in an initial settling of scores as revolutionaries seized control of the coalfields. In this context, revolutionary violence could either subsume or offer a veneer of justification for the extrajudicial exaction of popular justice or personal vendettas. The parish priest of Valdecuna (Mieres) and Rafael Rodríguez Arango, director of the Carbones La Nueva mining company, were both killed on the first day of the insurrection in separate incidents. The latter, who had previously been attacked in September 1934, was targeted in a case of revenge over a labour dispute.[56] Adolfo Suárez, a magistrate, was shot by a militiaman in Oviedo after being implicated in the Sanjurjo coup.[57] The lethal use of violence was not just a demonstration of proletarian power and the righting of perceived past wrongs. One explanation for the murder of the director of the Manjoya dynamite factory posits that the attack was an attempt by someone to ingratiate himself with the revolutionary militias.[58] In this case, the lethal performance of class hatred served to bind the individual to the revolutionary community with blood.

Score-settling was curbed by the rapid assertion of revolutionary authority. Once an area was under the control of the committees or militias such instances were less common. The most infamous killings

[54] See Llano, *Pequeños anales*, pp. 17, 26, 35, 50, 61–2, 81–2. For medical care and food preparation, see Noval Suárez, *Langreo rojo*, pp. 33, 107; ACNP, *Asturias Roja*, p. 76. For the 'taboo', see Vincent, '"Keys"', p. 86.

[55] Díaz Nosty, *La comuna*, pp. 338–40.

[56] M. Castejón Rodríguez, 'La patronal hullera asturiana en la Segunda República' (unpublished UNED PhD thesis, 2009), pp. 404, 415.

[57] Canel, *Octubre*, p. 137.

[58] Taibo, *Asturias*, p. 272.

occurred in two separate episodes in Turón that stand out for taking place in an area firmly under revolutionary control, rather than on the fringes of revolutionary authority or at the beginning of the insurrection. Eight de la Salle brothers who worked at the school owned by Hulleras del Turón, their Passionist confessor and two *carabineros* (customs guards) were taken from their prison on the night of 8–9 October and executed in the cemetery. The local parish priest and coadjutor shared their prison but were spared this fate. Probing into why they survived may shed light on the deaths of their former fellow prisoners. The coadjutor later explained that the two of them were saved because 'only eleven prisoners could fit' in the lorry.[59] According to a martyrological account, when the revolutionaries came to collect the religious brothers, they questioned the parish priest and coadjutor about 'the amount of time they had been imprisoned, their names, etc.', before deciding they could stay.[60] Any explanation of the deaths is necessarily speculative, but in saving the parish clergy while sending the de la Salle brothers and a Passionist confessor to their deaths, the revolutionaries singled out the individuals with fewer established links to the local community. The de la Salle brothers taught children from the valley, but they were outsiders: none was Asturian, they lived a life relatively isolated from the community and several had only recently arrived in Turón. The confessor was only in the valley to confess the children. The de la Salle brothers worked in a school funded by Hulleras del Turón and they could have symbolized the local structures of capitalism.

The brothers were not the only figures connected to Hulleras del Turón to be killed. Rafael del Riego, director of Hulleras del Turón, and two others figures linked to the company and the local political right were also murdered days later. Different explanations have been offered, including revenge for blacklisting during labour conflicts or for the killings of civilians on the outskirts of Oviedo by government forces, or a desire to silence Riego because of what he could later testify about the revolutionaries.[61] While the latter is much less plausible, citizens in Mieres and Sama did clamour for reprisals against prisoners in response to reports of killings by government forces, and guard duties had to be increased. At the time of the second wave of murders in Turón, the revolution was on the retreat, and

[59] Á. Garralda García, *La persecución religiosa del clero en Asturias 1934, 1936 y 1937: martirios y odiseas* (Avilés, 2009 [1977]), pp. 506–8.

[60] *Los mártires de Turón: notas biográficas y reseña del martirio de los religiosos bárbaramente asesinados por los revolucionarios en Turón (Asturias) el 9 de octubre de 1934* (Madrid/Barcelona, 1934), p. 68.

[61] Taibo, *Asturias*, p. 447; Ruiz, *Octubre*, p. 289.

bombing by government forces was taking its toll. It is possible that killing Riego and two other representatives of the political right in Turón was a vengeful, symbolic act of revolutionary justice. Similar reprisals would also be seen after air raids during the Spanish Civil War.[62]

The overall tally of approximately fifty deaths, while significant, is remarkably low – and much lower than revolutionary violence in the central and eastern European soviets at the end of the First World War, which itself paled in comparison to the brutality of the wave of counter-revolutionary revenge.[63] The proliferation of arms, increasing disillusionment during the last days of the Asturian insurrection and strain of fighting the army, along with a population of tens of thousands under their control begs the question as to why vengeful revolutionary violence did not claim more victims. Scholars of other revolutionary contexts have underlined that areas experiencing a power vacuum or disputes between rival groups for control of a given area often see a greater prevalence of violence.[64] There was no real interregnum or power vacuum in the coalfields, nor were there warring revolutionary factions. Revolutionary authority was constituted quickly and generally curtailed the use of violence, with the notable exception of the killings in Turón. Militias respected the authority and decisions of the committees rather than operating independently as marauding bands. Those arrested were taken straight to the local revolutionary committee. In the case of two Jesuits murdered at the roadside in Mieres, the two clerics had first been arrested and taken before the revolutionary committee in Mieres. Their captors only executed them when the committee refused to take charge of them.[65]

Revolutionaries in Mieres and Sama protected civil guards from the 'mob' and refused to cede to a popular desire for cathartic violence. When the hiding place of the leader of FE-JONS in Mieres was discovered, revolutionaries protected him and Belarmino Tomás is said to have sworn 'bloody hell, I'll strangle whoever shoots. They belong to the revolution; they're not yours or mine' as he shepherded a civil guard through a crowd in Sama.[66] Tomás distinguished between just and illegitimate uses of violence

[62] Grossi, *La insurrección*, pp. 106–8; G. Ranzato, 'The Spanish Civil War in the context of total war', in '*If You Tolerate This … ': the Spanish Civil War in the Age of Total War*, ed. M. Baumeister and S. Schüler-Springorum (Frankfurt, 2008), p. 240.

[63] R. Gerwarth, 'The central European counter-revolution: paramilitary violence in Germany, Austria and Hungary after the Great War', *Past & Present*, cc (2008), 175–209.

[64] Gerwarth and Conway, 'Revolution', p. 144.

[65] F. Martínez, *Dos jesuitas mártires en Asturias* (Burgos, 1936), pp. 43–55.

[66] *El Noroeste*, 19 Sept. 1935; Taibo, *Asturias*, p. 220.

for revolutionary ends. The violence of the revolution was envisaged as grander and nobler than the murdering of prisoners. For the revolution's supporters, delineating the boundaries of violence served to define the limits of the revolution itself. Young women interceded on behalf of a priest, shouting 'blood, no. Blood, no. Revolution, only revolution', when some wanted to kill him.[67] Revolution was distinguished from bloodletting. Even though professing anticlericalism was an important marker of left-wing identity, there was not universal approval of the use of violence against the Church. Socialists on the provincial revolutionary committee firmly opposed using dynamite against the cathedral, whose tower was an important strategic position for the government forces. Militiamen ignored their opposition and destroyed an ancient chapel in an attempt to breach the cathedral walls.[68]

The fate of the vast majority of the perceived enemies or threats to the revolution was to be remanded in prison. The arrest of engineers, business owners and members of clergy were widespread, and other detainees included a judge and pharmacists.[69] The bosses at Duro-Felguera, despite having engaged in a long and bitter dispute with the CNT in 1933, were kept confined in the company offices for their own safety. They were denied freedom, but were not physically harmed.[70] Preventative arrests of those perceived as potential enemies merged with taking advantage of the insurrection to settle political scores. Given that revolutionaries drew on their own experiences in the towns and villages when making arrests, the two were virtually consubstantial. A later account of the events in Olloniego attributed many of the arrests to the fractious relationship between the PRLD and the socialists.[71] Unsurprisingly, those arrested were often defined as fascists, whether they were members of the Catholic Youth, CEDA or priests.[72] The term was used flexibly to designate enemies of the revolution.

Even as the patrols made dozens of arrests, many rightists remained free or in hiding. If the voting figures from the 1933 elections were an indication of political leanings, to arrest all rightists would have been impossible.

[67] Asociación Católica Nacional de Propagandistas de Oviedo, *Asturias roja (octubre de 1934): sacerdotes y religiosos perseguidos y martirizados* (Oviedo, n.d. [1935]), p. 75.

[68] This occurred as the first committee discussed the withdrawal of the revolutionaries (Díaz Nosty, *La comuna*, pp. 204–5).

[69] For reports on Olloniego, Mieres and Sotrondio, see *El Noroeste*, 20, 23 Oct., 15 Nov. 1934.

[70] Noval Suárez, *Langreo rojo*, pp. 101–5.

[71] *El Noroeste*, 15 Nov. 1934.

[72] See ACNP, *Asturias roja*, pp. 60, 199; *Los mártires de Turón*, p. 58; Canel, *Octubre*, p. 137.

When conducting arrests, revolutionaries targeted significant representative figures of the right and middle class in an attempt to intimidate right-leaning citizens. Arrests were thus a symbolic move that underlined the forging of a new revolutionary society, while also serving as a warning to opponents. The symbolic nature of revolutionary justice extended to the revolutionaries' own ranks. In Oviedo, Teodomiro Menéndez, the veteran Asturian socialist leader and a reluctant revolutionary, was responsible for those detained by revolutionary patrols in Oviedo. He imprisoned some of those brought before him, but released many more. Although some younger revolutionaries criticized him, in general there was satisfaction that he was going through the motions of implementing revolutionary justice.[73] The performance of authority was sufficient to satisfy the militias. Just as arresting the priest and abolishing the use of money was a fundamental part of the revolutionary process, so was hauling the detainees before a committee or improvised tribunal in order to enact a new form of justice. Implicit in reshaping the social order was the understanding that the principles underpinning justice had changed.

Would-be revolutionaries turned to reference points from their political culture in order to orientate and understand their actions. They fell back on revolutionary 'scripts' by invoking or imitating pre-existing models, though through their own interpretation. Unsurprisingly, Asturian revolutionaries turned in part to the example set by the most recent reference point: the Bolshevik Revolution. The intention of creating a 'Red Army' is the clearest example of seeking to emulate the Russian revolutionary 'script' and indeed it followed, intentionally or otherwise, the advice in the Comintern-produced handbook for revolutionaries, *Armed Insurrection*.[74] Militias dubbed 'Red Guards' already policed the rear-guard of the revolution through patrols that stopped and questioned residents, conducted arrests and read out proclamations.[75] The Red Army, meanwhile, would exhibit 'iron discipline' and impose severe punishments for desertion and disobedience.[76] Not all agreed with the prospect of a Red Army, particularly the anarchists, although a wall poster in an anarchist district of Gijón that spoke of a 'Red Army' reveals the issue to be more complicated than the clear-cut distinctions made by accounts in

[73] Cabezas, *Morir*, p. 102; Díaz Nosty, *La comuna*, p. 279.

[74] A. Neuberg, *Armed Insurrection* (London, 1970 [1928]), p. 186.

[75] Molins i Fábrega, *UHP*, p. 136.

[76] For the proclamation issued by the Sama Revolutionary Committee, 7 Oct. 1934, see Molins i Fábrega, *UHP*, p. 125.

the aftermath of the insurrection.[77] The Red Army did not materialize; instead, it remained limited to a desire printed on the proclamations. But even as a rhetorical device, declaring that a Red Army was the missing ingredient for a 'total triumph' indicates that the revolutionary process was understood and measured according to the Russian precedent.[78] As the militias retreated from the advancing army, forming a ruthless, disciplined Red Army would be the way to success.

Referencing Russia in the proclamations also elevated the Asturian insurrection into a longer narrative of epic revolutionary struggles, both geographically and temporally. Invoking the Red Army and the Bastille in the revolutionary proclamations staked the Asturians' claim to the importance of the insurrection. They were heirs to a longer tradition of European revolutions and now the 'world [was] watching' them. The revolutionaries had to fulfil their historical duty and the expectations of the workers of the world, although they could rely on the assistance of the 'fatherland of the proletariat' to help them construct 'the solid Marxist edifice on the ashes of all that is rotten'.[79] Fernando Solano Palacio, an anarchist, reported that 'Bolsheviks' even spread rumours that there were Soviet warships located off the Spanish coast poised to come to the Asturians' aid.[80]

More common than international references was the publication of domestic 'news' in the proclamations. Proclamations reported on alleged victories by columns of left-wing militias across Spain, from the capturing of provincial capitals to the arrest of leading politicians. The news was a complete fabrication. The news – or propaganda – functioned on one level to encourage local citizens to contribute to the revolutionaries' war effort and increase collective confidence in victory. On another, the fake news was a means of constructing revolutionary authority and legitimacy. The authors employed relatively sophisticated techniques to convince local inhabitants of the veracity of the reports. A proclamation issued in Grado presented news via a list consisting of two curt, informative sentences per province, which evoked the style of telegrams and lent it an air of authenticity.[81] In

[77] El Llano Revolutionary Committee, 'Parte del día de hoy', undated, in Llano, *Pequeños anales*, p. 132.

[78] Sama Revolutionary Committee, 'Noticias de Madrid', 7 Oct. 1934, in Molins i Fábrega, *UHP*, p. 138.

[79] For the proclamation issued by the Provincial Revolutionary Committee, 16 Oct. 1934, see Molins i Fábrega, *UHP*, pp. 130–1.

[80] Solano Palacio, *La revolución*, p. 51.

[81] El Llano Revolutionary Committee, 'Parte del día de hoy', and Grado Revolutionary Committee, 'Noticias oficiales de la revolución', 13 Oct. 1934, in Llano, *Pequeños anales*, pp. 132, 150–1.

Turón, the committee had taken control of a radio station and broadcasted to the local population using loudspeakers. Revolutionary programming included 'imaginary talks' in French between the Asturian aristocrat Pedro Pidal and the French president, at least according to the right-wing journalist Luis Bolín.[82]

Stress, uncertainty and rumour abounded, and so these reports preyed on a local population hungry for reliable information.[83] Residents of the coalfields could only access the revolutionaries' version of events or the newspapers and flyers dropped by the Spanish air force that encouraged the insurrectionaries to surrender. The government-produced flyers denied there was any upheaval in Asturias, which residents in the grip of the insurrection could see was a patent lie. One revolutionary proclamation played on the evident untruth to cast doubt on the government's claim that the rest of Spain was calm.[84] Few revolutionaries believed the reports that did filter through. A captured mineworker told government forces that the revolutionaries thought the radio reports were lies.[85]

The news reports were also an expression of exuberant revolutionary creativity. Revolutionaries imagined and projected possible, plausible futures. Ceferino Álvarez later wrote that 'we kept people informed about everything that was going on, of how we arrived in Oviedo, of how things were going' and 'we were always objective and limited ourselves to what was really happening, to what was true and to what we were hoping for'.[86] He allowed for a creative interpretation of reality. This revolutionary creativity was also patent in expressions of revolutionary identity across walls and vehicles, in what was one of the most striking features of the coal valleys noted by journalists who visited in the aftermath. Journalists observed that 'all of the armour-plated vehicles had big red letters which read: "¡viva *la revolución*!" [and] "Asturias is under our control. UHP!"' and that there were 'no walls in Asturias in which there is not a viva to Russia scrawled or inscriptions like "Let's save Russia!"'.[87] The Belgian Mathieu Corman,

[82] L. Bolín, *Spain: the Vital Years* (London, 1967), p. 132.

[83] This is a common theme in M. Álvarez Suárez, *Sangre de octubre: U.H.P. Episodios de la revolución en Asturias* (Madrid, 1936), e.g. pp. 58–9.

[84] For the proclamation issued by the Provincial Revolutionary Committee, 11 Oct. 1934, see Ruiz, *Asturias contemporánea*, p. 106.

[85] Canel, *Octubre*, p. 107.

[86] C. Fontalbat and C. Álvarez, *Ceferino Álvarez Rey: historia de un minero de Asturias (1907–2009)* (Oviedo, 2010), p. 85.

[87] Cabezas, *Morir*, p. 94; *La Veu de Catalunya*, 28 Oct. 1934. See also Solano Palacio, *La revolución*, p. 81.

who made a detour on his motorcycle journey to the region for some revolutionary tourism, saw a road sign that read 'Gijón 60km' and under which someone had scrawled, 'Moscow, just a step away'.[88]

A revolutionary community

The awkward synthesis of restoring perceived lost left hegemony and the revolutionary re-founding of the social order was also evident in how a revolutionary community was mobilized. This collective subject was constructed partly through violence, which served to cement the brotherhood of militiamen and exclude those identified as enemies, but also through the symbols and strategies to regulate access to the revolutionary community. The requirements of armed struggle meant the mobilization of local society and provided an opportunity for people to be protagonists in armed struggle and actively participate in reshaping the local social, political and economic order.

The insurrection provided a particular opportunity for young people, who played a key role in the militias and the wider revolutionary insurrection. The author of a later account of the insurrection in Olloniego was scandalized at the involvement of the 'maddened youth' who were the protagonists of the revolt: 'sixteen-year-old rascals armed with dynamite and a rifle slung over their shoulders'.[89] Female protagonism in the insurrection scandalized some commentators. There are some limited vignettes of women's participation in the insurrection as fighters. According to the authorities, eighteen year-old Dolores Vázquez dressed as a man and carried two pistols on the frontline.[90] But in general, fighting remained a male preserve, reflecting patterns of political violence in wider interwar Europe.[91] Grossi, a committee member in Mieres, claimed that women did fight, yet provides no further evidence, while a socialist recounted that women in Mieres were refused arms and had to accompany the militias as nurses.[92]

Although opportunities for frontline militia service were limited, young women did take advantage of the situation provided by the insurrection to play an active role in the revolutionary process, even if they were obliged to adopt roles less challenging of traditional gender norms. Women's active

[88] M. Corman, *Incendiarios de ídolos: un viaje por la revolución de Asturias*, trans. C. García Velasco (Oviedo, 2009 [1935]), p. 65.

[89] *El Noroeste*, 15 Nov. 1934.

[90] *El Noroeste*, 9 Dec. 1934.

[91] M. Vincent, 'Political violence and mass society: a European civil war?', in *The Oxford Handbook of European History, 1914–1945*, ed. N. Doumanis (Oxford, 2016), p. 400.

[92] Grossi, *La insurrección*, pp. 37, 58; Lavilla, *Los hombres*, p. 39.

participation in the insurrection tended to be in similar auxiliary tasks, such as medical care or food preparation, as was common during the Civil War.[93] In September 1935, a female member of the Communist Youth was arrested near Madrid. She confessed to having participated in the insurrection as a stretcher-bearer and by transporting dynamite, before hiding in the mountains.[94] The parents of a young woman arrested in the mountains after the insurrection lamented their 'double disgrace' in that she had besmirched her family's honour by participating in the revolution and accompanying a man to whom she was not married.[95] Even Aida Lafuente, the most celebrated female revolutionary martyr who is represented as dying with a machine gun in her hands, had spent her time working in food preparation, or as a messenger or a nurse before Oviedo came under attack.[96] Women's participation in violence was much easier to eulogize retrospectively.

The revolutionary community adapted existing symbols and created new ones to help forge a sense of collective identity and cohesion. *The Internationale* was no longer simply a song of 'hope' expressing a desire for emancipation; it was now linked to armed action and victory.[97] It was sung after defeating the civil guards in Olloniego, as militias departed for the front and when the arms factory in Trubia was captured.[98] Singing *The Internationale* was a conscious collective performance of the working class as a revolutionary subject. The raised clenched fist became the ubiquitous revolutionary gesture. It had originated in the German Communist Party in the 1920s and would be the quintessential symbol of antifascism during Spanish Civil War.[99] When individuals or groups met in the street, they raised their clenched fists and uttered the passwords of '*salud*, comrade' or 'UHP'.[100] Requisitioned vehicles with 'UHP' daubed in red on their

[93] M. A. Mateos, *¡Salud, compañeras! Mujeres socialistas en Asturias (1900–1937)* (Oviedo, 2007), p. 180. See also *El Noroeste*, 20 Oct. 1934; Taibo, *Asturias*, p. 313. On the Civil War, see M. Nash, *Defying Male Civilization: Women in the Spanish Civil War* (Denver, Colo., 1995), particularly at pp. 105–9.

[94] *El Noroeste*, 20 Sept. 1935.

[95] *El Noroeste*, 9 Dec. 1934.

[96] Taibo, *Asturias*, pp. 415–17.

[97] Grossi, *La insurrección*, p. 29.

[98] *El Noroeste*, 15 Nov. 1934; Solano Palacio, *La revolución*, p. 54; Díaz Nosty, *La comuna*, p. 219. See also Benavides, *La revolución*, p. 228.

[99] For background, see H. García, 'Was there an antifascist culture in 1930s Spain?', in *Rethinking Antifascism: History, Memory and Politics, 1922 to the Present*, ed. H. García, M. Yusta, X. Tabet and C. Clímaco (New York, 2016), p. 101.

[100] There are reports of other passwords: 'PP' ('proletarian power'), '*Trabajadores rojos salud*' ('*salud*, red workers'), 'FAI', 'Pablo Iglesias' and '*Hermanos proletarios, salud*' ('*salud*,

windscreens sounded their horns three times, once for each letter of the password.[101]

These symbols and gestures were not simply public performances of revolutionary fraternity and support for the insurrection. The gesture and password were also a key mechanism for managing the local population. They served to regulate access to the revolutionary community. As Vega later explained, '[e]verywhere the password UHP was demanded'; without it, an individual would be 'arrested and identified straightaway'.[102] Yet other evidence suggests that militias and committees were not always so zealous in excluding those who were not revolutionaries. They did not always detain those unfamiliar with the new code of behaviour; rather, at times they adopted an instructional role in order to manage the local population. In Oviedo, a priest greeted revolutionaries with a fascist salute and '*salud*, comrades'. Rather than assaulting or arresting him, the militiamen showed him the correct salutation.[103] In a similar case in Aller, the revolutionary committee instructed a Passionist brother in the correct performance of the raised fist salute.[104] Revolutionaries were conscious that local society was not starkly delineated between friend and foe. Those in the grey zone between the two could be incorporated into the revolutionary process.

Such incorporation could be conducted through coercion. Later reports maintain that some were forced to 'do guard duty or go to the frontline'.[105] Witness statements from an investigation into an assault in September 1935 include the allegation that the accused and his brother had been coerced into participating in the insurrection by undertaking guard duties. He singled out the victim of the assault as the revolutionary responsible.[106] Some rightists and members of the clergy attempted to evade arrest or persecution by volunteering their labour in the makeshift hospitals. They could justify this ostensible support for the insurrection on humanitarian grounds. Despite the intimacy of the coalfield communities, others managed to disguise

proletarian brothers'). Nevertheless, UHP was the main password (Cabezas, *Morir*, p. 114; Ruiz, *Insurrección*, p. 98, n. 1; Álvarez Suárez, *Sangre*, p. 188).

[101] Suárez Álvarez, *Sangre*, p. 104.

[102] Vega, 'Copia', p. 13. See also C. Vega, 'Notas complementarias al informe elevado al Comité Central del PCE', CDMH, PS Madrid, box 721, file 3, p. 14.

[103] ACNP, *Asturias roja*, p. 73.

[104] *Episodios de la revolución en Asturias: los pasionistas de Mieres (Asturias) y la revolución de octubre de 1934. Episodios narrados por los mismos protagonistas* (Santander, 1935), pp. 67–8.

[105] *El Noroeste*, 15 Nov. 1934; Taibo, *Asturias*, p. 457.

[106] AHPA, AP, box 78437, file 178 (1935).

themselves as a way of surviving the insurrection.[107] The revolutionary community was thus formed of a combination of willing volunteers and those who understood its new codes and symbols, as well as those co-opted into participating in the revolutionary process. Proclamations threatening those who looted or disseminated false news reveal the fragility of the community that the revolutionaries were attempting to construct and the codes of revolutionary honour that underpinned it.

Defeat

The revolutionary utopia proclaimed as triumphant at the beginning of the insurrection slowly slipped out of reach during the second week of the fighting. The final proclamations accepted that defeat was inevitable and began to historicize the insurrection. The third provincial revolutionary committee – headed by Belarmino Tomás and based in Sama – framed the end of the revolution as 'a stop on the way, a parenthesis, a restorative rest' and a 'truce in the struggle'; the insurrection was no longer a historical terminus, but part of the onward march towards the inevitable revolution.[108] The anarchist committee in La Felguera echoed these sentiments. The revolution now belonged to the future, not the present: 'When it will be we do not know, but we will participate [in it], because our ideas inspire us, they make our impulses vibrate and accelerate the pace of our revolutionary train'.[109]

Despite the fragility of revolutionary authority during the final days of the insurrection, it did not splinter and collapse. The insurrection ended with a remarkable negotiated surrender. Belarmino Tomás crossed the lines and parleyed with General López Ochoa. Tomás, prompted by reports of murder, rape and looting by government troops on the outskirts of Oviedo, had two conditions of surrender: there would be no reprisals and the Moroccan troops would remain at the rear.[110] According to the agreement, the army would enter the coalfields on 19 October. The transfer of authority from the committees to the army was relatively orderly. In Mieres, the committee released its prisoners and established a transitional authority.[111]

[107] See M. Kerry, 'Painted tonsures and potato-sellers: priests, passing and survival in the Asturian Revolution', *Cultural & Social History*, xiv (2017), 237–55.

[108] For the proclamation issued by the Provincial Revolutionary Committee, 18 Oct. 1934, see Ruiz, *Asturias contemporánea*, p. 107.

[109] For the proclamation issued by the La Felguera Revolutionary Committee, 18 Oct. 1934, see Villar, *El anarquismo*, pp. 136–7.

[110] See the interview with Tomás in *Le Populaire*, 5, 6 Jan. 1935.

[111] Grossi, *La insurrección*, pp. 128–9.

Meanwhile, revolutionary leaders and militias fled into the mountains. Some would go into exile and not return until 1936.

With the defeat of the revolutionary insurrection, the Asturian October – or 'commune' – entered the pantheon of failed left-wing attempts at revolution. Without wider support, it was doomed to fail. The Asturian revolutionaries did not envisage that they would be on their own. Their confidence in success is evident in the enthusiastic reception given to the first planes seen overhead during the insurrection. Before the bombs began to fall, the planes were recognized as 'emissaries' of revolution rather than a reconnaissance mission. A landing strip was even cleared in Laviana and shouts of 'they are ours!' greeted the first planes that flew over Olloniego, where 'it seemed logical not to suppose anything different … and it was even said that a pilot saluted with a raised fist'.[112] Revolutionaries wanted to see themselves reflected in the pilots. Even as a failed revolution, the Asturian insurrection was lived as a revolutionary process. The proclamations attempted to call into being a revolutionary future, even if this did not actually occur.

The fate of the insurrection depended on external, national factors. The context was far less propitious than the situation in central and eastern Europe at the end of the First World War, where defeat, demobilization, hunger and the dissolution of traditional political authority offered a window for a potential radical left seizure of power. The situation was very different in Spain in 1934. There was no crisis of the state, in either its legitimacy or capacity to act. Crucially, the military was willing to defend the government, though the Army of Africa was drafted in to crush the insurrection, as it was believed to be more trustworthy and less tainted by domestic politics than the forces on the mainland.[113] The critical role played by the military is clear when compared to 1931 and 1936. Whereas the army refused to stand by King Alfonso XIII in 1931, it was divided in 1936, with significant sectors willing to follow conspirators in rebelling against the government.

The insurrection was not just an event; it was also a process. It is necessary to take the words and ideas of the participants seriously, as they provide a window onto the world that they tried to outline and create, even if the visions were nothing more than the ink on proclamations pasted on walls in public places. As in any revolution, the insurrectionaries had to work out how to recast the social, political and economic order, and it is not surprising that they swayed between reasserting left-wing hegemony – a

[112] Llano, *Pequeños anales*, p. 159; Lavilla, *Los hombres*, p. 26.

[113] Balfour, *Deadly Embrace*, p. 251.

situation they were familiar with – and attempts to destroy the existing order. The revolution was a liminal moment caught between the reassertion of the old and the construction of the new. It was a contested process that was understood and defined by participants, whether militias or committees, in different ways. The violence and the symbols used to define the revolutionary community – who belonged and who did not – went to the very core of the struggle to define what the revolution was.

It is not clear how many died in the Asturian October. In his detailed quantitative study of political violence in the Second Republic, González Calleja is unable to provide a definitive figure. The blurring of fighting into the repression as well as mass burials and the burning of corpses make any figure an approximation. The circumstances of death are only known for 200 revolutionaries, at best a quarter of the final figure. The official death toll stands at 855 civilians – which includes revolutionaries, victims of the repression and others who died behind the lines – and 229 members of the security forces and army in Asturias, which ascends to 1,051 civilians and 284 soldiers and police for Spain as a whole.[114] Most believe these figures too low for Asturias and 'civilian deaths', which include the militias, are generally thought to number around 1,100, to which between 300 and 350 members of the armed and security forces can be added.[115]

One of the victims of the repression was the journalist Luis Higón Rosell, better known by his penname Luis Sirval. Like Chaves Nogales, he travelled to Asturias to report on the insurrection. His investigation into the reprisals by the army brought him to the attention of the authorities and he was arrested. Three legionaries, worried about what Sirval had uncovered, visited him and demanded that he reveal his sources. When he refused, they shot him in the courtyard.[116] Denunciation of deaths like Sirval's and amnesty for the thousands imprisoned after October served to be a powerful rallying cry for the left, for the repression of the Asturian revolutionary insurrection was wide-ranging, bitter and decisive in moulding the fractious and polarized nature of politics in the time leading up to the Civil War.

[114] E. González Calleja, *Cifras cruentas: las víctimas mortales de la violencia sociopolítica en la Segunda República española (1931–1936)* (Granada, 2015), pp. 11, 176, 232.

[115] For similar figures, see Rodríguez Muñoz, *La revolución*, pp. 825–6; Taibo, *Asturias*, p. 476; Díaz Nosty, *La comuna*, pp. 337–8. See also E. González Calleja, *En nombre de la autoridad: la defensa del orden público durante la Segunda República española (1931–1936)* (Granada, 2014), pp. 228–40.

[116] Balfour, *Deadly Embrace*, p. 255; Taibo, *Asturias*, pp. 504–10.

6. Repression and the redefinition of politics during the long 1935

On 16 February 1935, Julio C. S. appeared in court charged with the illegal possession of a weapon. Julio admitted the pistol was his and testified that the Assault Guard had instructed him to find a firearm – an easy task, they said, as 'guns even gr[e]w on trees' – for they demanded one in exchange for a work permit. Julio did indeed claim to have found the pistol under a tree. Implausible though his testimony may appear, witnesses, including a priest and a foreman, corroborated his statement and the court absolved him. Julio fared better than thousands of others who suffered the repression of the revolutionary insurrection. Nevertheless, despite his 'good standing' and non-participation in the events of October, Julio was also caught up in the repression and its contradictions: all industrial workers were sacked and a gun was required for a work permit, but presenting a weapon appeared to indicate that its bearer was a revolutionary.[1]

The defeat of the October movement led to the arrest of thousands of leftists and restrictions on left-wing political activities across Spain. Yet it was in Asturias, where the insurrection was defeated in a military campaign, that the repression hit the hardest and radically reshaped political, social and cultural life in the coalfields in what is labelled here the 'long 1935', stretching from late October 1934 to the elections of February 1936. Thousands were rounded up – many of whom were tortured – and spent months in prison as the authorities opened hundreds of investigations into their participation in the insurrection. New municipal authorities were appointed who purged their workforces. Left-wing institutions were closed down and their press silenced. Politics was reduced to 'order' – the reassertion of the traditional social order and a strong emphasis on respect for authority.

The revolutionary insurrection was not the only leftist movement to be quashed with extreme violence in the interwar period. From the Freikorps' crushing of the Spartakists in Berlin and the brutal suppression of the Hungarian Soviet in 1919, to fascist violence against leftist activists during the Italian *biennio rosso*, the revolutionary moments at the end of

[1] AHPA, AP, box 79458, file 138 (1935).

the First World War saw the transplantation of the violent strategies from the war to domestic political problems.[2] The construction of right-wing dictatorships in the 1930s was accompanied by different tactics. In Austria Dollfuss pursued a 'salami' strategy of slowly slicing away at the social democrats while the inauguration of Hitler's rule in Germany saw restraints on Nazi violence lifted and a period of 'structured chaos' that disarticulated the left.[3] Yet Spain in 1934 was not emerging from a war, nor had the formal mechanisms of democratic rule been strangled. The repression of the Asturian insurrection was different insofar as it was conducted by a democratic regime, although elections and a future return to power of the left appeared remote in late 1934. A democratic framework did not preclude a repression that prefigured some aspects of the Francoist repression during and after the Spanish Civil War. Relying on exclusion and the presence of the army was ultimately unsustainable, particularly in the context of the Asturian coalfields, and only increased polarization, fashioned a crisis of community at the local level and set the foundations for a wave of fragile left-wing radicalism in 1936.

Repression, hot and cold

Faces peered fearfully from behind windows and doors as government forces 18,000-strong entered the mining valleys on 19 October 1934.[4] Many revolutionaries had already fled into the mountains, hiding their weapons or leaving them behind in schools or other buildings for collection by the army, as agreed by Belarmino Tomás and General López Ochoa.[5] On entering the coal valleys, the government forces looted and burned Casas del Pueblo and some homes, including Tomás's house, where they grabbed everything from watches to a kilogram of fruit jelly.[6] These terrorization strategies had been employed during the capture of Oviedo, when government troops murdered patients in the hospital and between twenty-

[2] On this period, see e.g., R. Gerwarth, *The Vanquished: Why the First World War Failed to End* (London, 2016).

[3] T. Kirk, *Nazism and the Working Class in Austria: Industrial Unrest and Political Dissent in the 'National Community'* (Cambridge, 1996), the quotation at p. 41; R. Bessel, *Political Violence and the Rise of Nazism: the Storm Troopers in Eastern Germany, 1925–1934* (New Haven, Conn., 1984), pp. 98–105; D. Schumann, *Political Violence in the Weimar Republic, 1918–1933: Fight for the Streets and Fear of Civil War* (New York, 2012), p. 270.

[4] E. López Ochoa, *Campaña militar de Asturias en octubre de 1934 (narración táctica-episódica)* (Madrid, 1936), pp. 163, 171.

[5] See P. I. Taibo II, *Asturias, octubre 1934* (Barcelona, 2013), p. 474.

[6] For the ransacking of Tomás's home, see M. Nelken, *Por qué hicimos la revolución* (Barcelona, 1936), p. 164.

five and fifty prisoners in the Pelayo barracks. They also engaged in murder, rape and looting in the peripheral districts of the city. The techniques drew on Spanish experiences of conducting a decades-long colonial war in North Africa, and for Franco, appointed military advisor by the minister of defence, Asturias was a frontier war.[7] Soldiers sold watches and other pilfered goods in improvised markets, just as they would during the Civil War.[8] Not all approved of the soldiers' behaviour and some officers attempted to restrain the actions of their troops.[9]

The hot repression was soon replaced by the round-up and prosecution of suspected revolutionaries in a vast campaign that continued throughout 1935. Nearly fifty provisional prisons had been created within two days of the end of the insurrection and summary military trials began immediately.[10] At least 15,000 Asturians are calculated to have passed through the prison system as a result of the revolutionary insurrection and 2,587 were still incarcerated in 1936.[11] The state of war – proclaimed in the whole of Spain on 6 October – was eventually replaced in Asturias, as in regions like Barcelona, Madrid and Vizcaya, with the state of alarm, which dictated censorship of the press and restrictions on civil liberties and the right of association. It remained in place until January 1936.[12] Troops continued to be stationed in the coalfields even after the state of war was lifted and throughout 1935 they gave the impression that the valleys were subject to military occupation. Foreign observers also remarked on the omnipresence of khaki uniforms and restrictions on groups in public spaces in Oviedo. British Labour MP Leah Manning reported in late 1934 that security forces 'hustle[d] workers wherever they could find two or three of them together' and nine months later Argentinian journalist Roberto Arlt wrote that Oviedo felt like the 'inside of a prison' as 'three

[7] S. Balfour, *Deadly Embrace: Morocco and the Road to the Spanish Civil War* (Oxford, 2002), pp. 253–4. See also P. Preston, *The Spanish Holocaust: Inquisition and Extermination in Twentieth-Century Spain* (London, 2012), p. 82; M. R. de Madariaga, *Los moros que trajo Franco* (Barcelona, 2006), pp. 139–43. For comments on the figures, see E. González Calleja, *Cifras cruentas: las víctimas mortales de la violencia sociopolítica en la Segunda República española (1931–1936)* (Granada, 2015), p. 229.

[8] Taibo, *Asturias*, p. 475; M. Seidman, *The Victorious Counterrevolution: the Nationalist Effort in the Spanish Civil War* (Madison, Wis., 2011), p. 43.

[9] Balfour, *Deadly Embrace*, p. 254.

[10] Preston, *Spanish Holocaust*, p. 84; Taibo, *Asturias*, pp. 475, 513.

[11] Taibo, *Asturias*, p. 542.

[12] For a chronology of the states of exception, see E. González Calleja, *En nombre de la autoridad: la defensa del orden público durante la Segunda República española (1931–1936)* (Granada, 2014), pp. 329–31.

out of five' people on the streets were dressed in military uniform. It was 'impossible to talk without armed witnesses'.[13]

The cold repression encompassed the beatings and torture that accompanied the authorities' search for fugitive revolutionaries and firearms. Even if killings were not the order of the day, non-lethal physical violence was central to the daily experience of real or suspected revolutionaries in prisons and coalfield towns and was the main mechanism for terrorizing the Asturian left. Manuel García recalled that every day a lorry of assault guards arrived in Olloniego and beat everyone in sight.[14] In prisons and detention centres methods of torture included the 'tri-motor' (suspending the victim from their wrists, which were bound behind their back), the 'laughter pipe' (running a gauntlet of guards) and the 'water bath' (submerging the prisoner in freezing water before beating them). The degrading abuse also included the use of hammers on knees and hands and twisting or applying heat to sexual organs.[15] A former councillor in Oviedo was subjected to a half-hour beating followed by six-and-a-half hours spent standing facing the wall under the threat of death if he moved. Others were beaten and left for days without food or drink, or, in a particularly degrading move, forced to lick toilet bowls. In Turón, civilians, including women dressed in mourning, were present and participated in torture sessions. Two Falangists whose fathers had been killed by the revolutionaries beat an imprisoned socialist councillor to death.[16]

Such was the treatment to which prisoners were subject before they were formally charged or put on trial. The beatings were not usually intended to be lethal, although the number of suicides and deaths in detention – along with the numbers incapacitated for future work – indicates a lack of regard for the welfare of prisoners at the very least. Prisoners committed

[13] L. Manning, *What I Saw in Spain* (London, 1935), p. 86; R. Arlt, *Aguafuertes (andaluzas, marroquíes, gallegas asturianas, vascas y madrileñas)* (Paracuellos de Jarama, 2015), pp. 272–3.

[14] Cited in Taibo, *Asturias*, p. 500.

[15] The denunciations included detailed reports on the repression and were distributed as pamphlets (Los presos de Asturias, *¡Acusamos!* ... (n.p., 1935)) and reproduced in other accounts (e.g. Nelken, *Por qué*). For digital versions of the denunciations by Félix Gordón Ordás, Fernando de los Ríos, Julio Álvarez del Vayo and Vicente Marco Miranda, see <http://www.asturiasrepublicana.com/crirep.asp> [accessed 6 Nov. 2018]. See also Ignotus [M. Villar], *La represión de octubre* (Barcelona, 1936). For English versions, see Manning, *What*. In 1936 the newspaper *Ayuda* published a series of testimonies of torture and *La Libertad* reproduced a letter and the signatures of women attesting to its veracity on 4 Feb. 1936.

[16] *¡Acusamos!*, pp. 17–18. F. Gordón Ordás, 'Por la salud del régimen. La represión en las provincias de Asturias, León y Palencia', 11 Jan. 1935, available at <http://www.asturiasrepublicana.com/criticagordon3.html> [accessed 6 Nov. 2018].

or attempted suicide by cutting or stabbing themselves, and one man (allegedly) threw himself into the Nalón river and drowned when in the hands of civil guards.[17] Such deaths were the result of prisoners' desperation or an attempt by the authorities to disguise a death in custody.[18]

Lisardo Doval, the 'Jackal', was a key figure in the use of torture. Doval, a major in the civil guards, was appointed 'special delegate of the minister of war for public order' and given carte blanche in his task of combing the region for revolutionaries. He was familiar with Asturias, for he had commanded the Civil Guard in the province in the 1920s. For six weeks in November and December 1934, the security forces under his orders ranged through Asturias and León undertaking mass arrests. Two thousand individuals passed through his headquarters – the Adoratrices convent in Oviedo – where torture was systematic. An outcry over Doval's actions and his 'relish for brutality' led to an investigation and he was sent back to Spanish Morocco in December, a decision that disappointed the mining bosses.[19] Despite Doval's removal from the region, he was only one of the '"specialists" in anti-subversive struggle' and torture continued after he left.[20]

The most infamous episode from the repression occurred in the early hours of 25 October. In revenge for the death of twenty-five soldiers in a truck explosion, twenty-four prisoners were bundled into a lorry and taken to Carbayín, where they were shot or hacked to death and their bodies secretly buried. Such nocturnal '*sacas* [removals]' would be a preferred method of extrajudicial killing during the Spanish Civil War.[21] Rumours soon circulated as to the fate of the men taken to Carbayín. Their relatives investigated the whereabouts of the missing men and discovered the cadavers. The military authorities handed over just one body (the others being interred in a common grave), which only fuelled rumours and horror stories of how the prisoners had been treated.[22]

The killings in Carbayín were exceptional, yet only hindsight provided this relative comfort. At the time, they appeared to be further evidence of a

[17] *Región*, 2 Dec. 1934; AHPA, AP, box 79450, file 24 (1935); *El Noroeste*, 17 Feb. 1935. For a similar alleged suicide by drowning, see *El Noroeste*, 19 Dec. 1934. For further cases, including Teodomiro Menéndez, see Taibo, *Asturias*, pp. 551–2, 562.

[18] *El Noroeste*, 19 Feb. 1935.

[19] Preston, *Spanish Holocaust*, pp. 87–8; M. Castejón Rodríguez, 'La patronal hullera asturiana en la Segunda República' (unpublished UNED PhD thesis, 2009), pp. 420–1.

[20] González Calleja, *En nombre*, p. 234.

[21] Gordón Ordás, 'Por la salud'.

[22] Taibo, *Asturias*, pp. 484–6.

blanket, indiscriminate terrorization that encompassed the intentional use of lethal violence. Of the twenty-four victims in Carbayín, not all were revolutionaries. One was a CEDA-supporting teacher, while another had been arrested for a traffic offence.[23] The military authorities had threatened fugitive revolutionaries with the death penalty. López Ochoa issued a proclamation on 20 October dictating that 'all those who are found to possess weapons or explosives [over the next twenty-four hours] will undergo summary trial and be shot if found guilty'.[24] His pronouncements fleshed out into policy the justifications for lethal violence that had been voiced by politicians and could be read in the press. The cabinet itself approved death sentences for military officials involved in the rebellion in Catalonia, although these were later commuted.[25] Even though only two death sentences were carried out of the many handed out to revolutionaries who had participated in the Asturian insurrection, it was not clear at the time that sentences would be commuted and that extrajudicial killing would be rare. The repression was not a finely tuned instrument. Fugitive and captured revolutionaries and their families were under no illusions as to the fate that could await them. Women, fearful that the Carbayín executions would be repeated, held nocturnal vigils outside the improvised prison in Sama to impede further *sacas*.[26]

Military campaigns against left-wing militias and the unchecked use of violence in repressing left-wing revolutionary movements occurred in other areas of Europe in the interwar period. But the repression of the 1934 revolutionary movement operated in a different manner to other European states. The repression did not occur in a power vacuum or in the fragile situation of unconsolidated state power after the First World War in central Europe. Here the 'mobilizing power of defeat', backstabbing myths, the dissolution of borders and traditional political authority, and frustrated imperial and national dreams shaped the white terrorization of radical left political movements, including the Munich and Hungarian Soviets in 1919.[27] Nor was the repression akin to the shockwave of violence

[23] Taibo, *Asturias*, pp. 484–6.

[24] González Calleja, *En nombre*, p. 234; F. Aguado Sánchez, *La revolución de octubre de 1934* (Madrid, 1972), p. 304; J. Rodríguez Muñoz, *La revolución de Octubre de 1934 en Asturias: orígenes, desarrollo y consecuencias* (Oviedo, 2010), p. 714.

[25] N. Townson, *The Crisis of Democracy in Spain: Centrist Politics under the Spanish Second Republic* (Brighton, 2000), pp. 273–4. See also B. Díaz Nosty, *La comuna asturiana: revolución de octubre de 1934* (Bilbao, 1974), p. 350.

[26] M. Benavides, *La revolución fue así (octubre rojo y negro)* (Barcelona, 1935), p. 460.

[27] For a summary, see Gerwarth, *Vanquished*, ch. 9. For Germany, see M. Jones, *Founding Weimar: Violence and the German Revolution, 1918–19* (Cambridge, 2016).

that followed Nazism's ascent to power, which disoriented and crushed the German left in 1933. In March and April, groups of Stormtroopers broke into and destroyed Social Democratic Party property, raised Nazi flags, and tortured socialists, as the police either looked on or colluded in the acts.[28] In Asturias, even as the violence and occupation of socialist centres sent out a clear message about which authority held sway in the coalfields, the Spanish army did not seek to cement a new political project. The distinctiveness of the repression of the Asturian October lies in the mass use of state violence by a democratic regime rather than a nation-state suffering the fallout of war or constructing a dictatorship.

For residents of the coalfields, the widespread use of violence and indiscriminate arrests were a shocking exhibition of state power, but even those members of the working class untouched by violence struggled to avoid the purges of the workforce. Factories and mines closed their doors and cancelled all contracts. Testament to the scale and blanket nature of the dismissals is the number of files opened in 1936 to investigate the sackings. Within five months, 7,000 individual files had been opened.[29] When mines began to reopen in mid December 1934, it took weeks for the workforce to be replenished. By February 1935, only 531 were back at work at Fábrica de Mieres, which constituted a fifth of the former mining workforce, to say nothing of those employed in steel production.[30]

All industrial workers were forced to reapply for their jobs in a carefully controlled process that assumed workers were guilty until proven innocent. This process was closely managed by the mining and steel companies and security forces – and, at SHE mines, by the SCOM.[31] It provided an opportunity for companies to reassert their authority after the experience of the first biennium of the Republic, by selecting those they wanted to admit as workers. Workers soliciting employment at Duro-Felguera had to file past a civil guard who had survived the revolution. He alone could determine whether they were readmitted to employment.[32] The authorities introduced a new identity card that was required in order to work. Mining companies supplied the cards and four photographs of the worker: one for the card, one for the company and two for the local police forces.[33] The

[28] Bessel, *Political Violence*, pp. 102–3; D. Siemens, *Stormtroopers: a New History of Hitler's Brownshirts* (New Haven, Conn., 2017), pp. 333–4.

[29] *Avance*, 3 July 1936.

[30] *Región*, 3 Feb. 1935.

[31] Taibo, *Asturias*, p. 482.

[32] *El Noroeste*, 15 Nov. 1934.

[33] *Boletín oficial de la provincia de Oviedo*, 5 Dec. 1934.

withholding of identity cards over the following months prevented many from working and was another tool for disciplining the workforce.[34] The process of obtaining a job was complicated further by the security forces' requirement of a firearm in exchange for work: those who handed in a weapon would not be prosecuted as long as they were not leaders or had not committed blood crimes.[35] Yet individuals risked being charged with illegal possession of a firearm, as happened to Julio C. S.

The mining companies took advantage of the favourable context provided by the defeat of the insurrection to remove benefits that mineworkers had gained. The right to free coal was withdrawn, workers were evicted from company housing and companies stopped paying pensions and subsidies, which violated the agreements reached with the SOMA in 1933.[36] The situation in the coalfields was a radicalized version of what was occurring across the country as employers lowered wages and increased working hours in what constituted a 'drastic worsening' of working conditions.[37] In Valencia, where the Workers' Alliance was second in strength to Asturias, union centres closed for months, working hours were extended, wages were lowered and union membership fell. In rural areas, the 'combination of the legacy of disunity, repression and recession [left them] demoralized and their unions eviscerated'.[38]

Sackings also occurred at municipal councils. More than 2,000 councils were removed across Spain and replaced with councillors from the governing parties, which in the coalfields led to districts managed by the Radical Party, CEDA and PRLD.[39] The new municipal steering committees dismissed whole corps of municipal workers. Several units were dissolved in Oviedo, including butchers and tax collectors, who had to reapply for their jobs.[40] The municipal authorities in Laviana agreed to suspend all municipal teachers on 31 October, while in Langreo 'suspicious' teachers

[34] E.g. *Región*, 25 Apr., 4 May 1935; *La Tarde*, 24 June 1935.

[35] López Ochoa, *Campaña*, pp. 175–6.

[36] Taibo, *Asturias*, p. 482; *Región*, 13 Dec. 1934; *El Noroeste*, 25 Dec. 1934.

[37] F. Rey, *Paisanos en lucha: exclusión política y violencia en la Segunda República española* (Madrid, 2008), p. 439; J. M. Macarro Vera, *Socialismo, República y revolución en Andalucía (1931–1936)* (Seville, 2000), pp. 373–4.

[38] R. Purkiss, *Democracy, Trade Unions and Political Violence in Spain: the Valencian Anarchist Movement, 1918–1936* (Brighton, 2011), pp. 322–4. For Galicia, see J. Prada Rodríguez, *De la agitación republicana a la represión franquista (Ourense 1934–1939)* (Barcelona, 2006), p. 63.

[39] Townson, *Crisis*, p. 279.

[40] C. Benito del Pozo, *El ayuntamiento republicano de Oviedo, 1931–1936* (Oviedo, 1989), p. 110.

were removed.[41] The provincial deputation revealed a zealous desire to purge undesirable workers by sacking hospital staff for a variety of reasons – not simply for undocumented absences during the insurrection, but also for previous suspensions.[42] The purges were thus an opportunity to reconfigure the workforce according to the new authorities' image. In other parts of Spain, the authorities also seized the chance to assert a different political and economic order.[43] Teachers in Valencia were sacked.[44] The government decreed a new category of 'abusive strike' which allowed contracts to be cancelled when a strike was called for reasons unrelated to work or which did not adhere to the timetables set out in labour law.[45]

The atmosphere was oppressive in the Asturian coalfields as curfews, safe conducts and restrictions on meetings constrained the activities of citizens. Many classrooms were turned into army billets and in some cases remained so until the end of 1935.[46] Casas del Pueblo, co-operatives and cultural centres were looted, burned and closed, or turned into prisons, as occurred to the Casa del Pueblo in Sama, which an anarchist described as a 'den of torment'.[47] The SOMA was suspended at the request of the civil governor, although in fact he wanted the union dissolved.[48] With centres ransacked or closed, the institutional heart of local communities for many was removed, profoundly reshaping previous patterns of sociability.

Journalists painted a sombre image of the coal valleys during the long 1935. In the absence of work, misery quickly gripped households in late 1934. In Mieres, women and children begged for leftovers from the soldiers' mess and the town was 'submerged in a sea of tears and sorrow'.[49] La Felguera was a 'picture of misery' and there was a 'tragic silence' in miners' houses in Ujo where 'at the windows and balconies, squalid and barefoot children [could] be seen, along with poverty-stricken women with brick-coloured

[41] L. Borque López, *El magisterio primario en Asturias (1923–1937): sociedad y educación* (Oviedo, 1991), pp. 206, 209.

[42] AHPA, Actas de la comisión de la Diputación Provincial, 19 Sept. 1933 to 17 Sept. 1935, ff. 308–12.

[43] E.g. for Andalusia, Macarro Vera, *Socialismo*, p. 371.

[44] S. Valero, *Republicanos con la monarquía, socialistas con la República: la Federación Socialista Valenciana durante la II República y la Guerra Civil (1931–1939)* (Valencia, 2015), p. 150.

[45] *Gaceta de Madrid*, 3 Nov. 1934.

[46] For updates, see *Región*, 24 Feb. 1935; *El Noroeste*, 27 Feb., 17 Apr., 22 Oct. 1935.

[47] Taibo, *Asturias*, pp. 474–5; Ignotus [M. Villar], *La represión de octubre*, p. 244.

[48] *Región*, 30 Nov. 1934; *El Noroeste*, 30 Nov. 1934.

[49] *El Noroeste*, 6, 15 Nov. 1934.

skin, thin, sickly and threadbare'.[50] The absence of male workers due to death, exile or imprisonment often left families without principal wage earners. Women bore the burden of providing for both their families and imprisoned male relatives.[51] The effects of the vast police–military operation on local society would become clearer in 1936, but appeared to have already engendered a deepening distrust of the authorities, particularly the security forces. Rumours that diphtheria vaccines were designed to damage the mental development of children led to them refusing to attend school and running from the Civil Guard.[52] The authorities were sufficiently frustrated to declare publicly that the rumours were 'absurd'.[53]

The repression trapped communities in a social half-life that continued through 1935. Unemployment was a significant problem for Mieres as the annual fiestas neared while in Sama the celebrations took place 'with the liveliness that is feasible in these moments'.[54] The opening of cinemas and some cultural centres did little to alleviate the sombreness and in any case, restrictions remained. The Ateneo Obrero in La Felguera reopened at the end of November, but there were to be no meetings, and it had to close at nine o'clock in the evening. In a measure that confirmed the stasis and isolation of the coal valleys from Spanish political life, only existing stocks of newspapers and books could be read. Only bars remained as a space where unrepentant revolutionaries could discuss their ideas and dissect current affairs in hushed voices.[55]

Yet conversing in the tavern was dangerous. The security forces also went to bars to glean information on fugitives and arrested those who criticized the repression.[56] Relying on eavesdropping and disguising policemen as 'cart drivers' or 'villagers' suggests that town and village communities offered little help in pursuing revolutionaries and that the police had to resort to subterfuge.[57] But the dynamics of repression cannot be reduced to a binary of external military forces oppressing the population of the coalfields. The underground left continued to wield a certain amount of power and exert pressure on residents. At the same time, the authorities relied

[50] *El Noroeste*, 11 Dec. 1934; A. Camín, *El valle negro* (México, 1938), p. 104.

[51] See the testimony of Á. Flórez Peón in *Memorias de Ángeles Flórez Peón "Maricuela"* (Oviedo, 2009), p. 36.

[52] *El Noroeste*, 21, 30 March 1935.

[53] *El Noroeste*, 10, 22 March 1935.

[54] *El Noroeste*, 26 June, 28, 30 July 1935.

[55] *El Noroeste*, 15, 30 Nov. 1934.

[56] *Región*, 20 Nov. 1934; *El Noroeste*, 9 Apr. 1935.

[57] *Región*, 20 Nov. 1934.

on denunciation and collaboration from citizens to police the population – half a million pesetas was found in Sotrondio thanks to the work of informers.[58] Surviving letters from the archive and testimonies drawn from court records do not provide a comprehensive picture of denunciation and collaboration, but they do reveal how the insurrection and its repression intensified political and personal rivalries that divided communities in the coalfields.

Citizens sent many hand- and type-written letters to the authorities denouncing their neighbours for participating in the insurrection and providing information to aid the repression. One letter alleged 150 revolutionaries had retreated to a cave with three to four thousand guns, dynamite and food for six weeks. Only those who knew the password could gain access. Another embellished an accusation that SOMA leader Graciano Antuña had handed out fistfuls of banknotes with the writer's own theorization of the origins of the insurrection. A handwritten note in Asturian dialect provided a long list of alleged revolutionaries. The brief descriptions, such as 'the son of one who used to be a butcher…' and 'Belarmino, son of one from Ronzón who has a wooden leg and was president of the communist centre', could only be deciphered by someone familiar with the community.[59]

Collaborating with the authorities as an informer could confer a degree of power in the reconfigured political context. Yet influence did not equate to impunity despite some appearing to confuse the two. Jesús P. R., a mineworker and informer for the Civil Guard, was drinking in a bar in Turón one evening when he publicly announced that he had enemies locally because he was an informer and therefore enjoyed 'influence'. He asked a man present, Francisco G. G., how he would react to provocation, to which Francisco said he would do nothing. Jesús – emboldened by his status and state of inebriation – illustrated his point by assaulting Francisco and then the bar owner. Despite the influence he claimed to enjoy, the Civil Guard arrested him and he was prosecuted.[60]

[58] For denunciation, see *Accusatory Practices: Denunciation in Modern European History, 1789–1989* (Chicago, Ill., 1997), ed. S. Fitzpatrick and R. Gellately. For Spain, see P. Anderson, *The Francoist Military Trials: Terror and Complicity, 1939–1945* (New York, 2010). For the money, see *El Noroeste*, 2 Jan. 1936.

[59] Confidential note, Madrid, 14 Nov. 1934, CDMH, PS Gijón, J series, box 50, file 1; letter to Commander Doval from a worker from Santa Ana, 12 Nov., 1934, CDMH, PS Gijón, J series, box 50, file 1; untitled, undated, handwritten note [statement by Pilar Bernaldo de Quirós], CDMH, PS Gijón, J series, box 50, file 1.

[60] AHPA, AP, box 78442, file 15 (1935).

Informing could confer power and influence with the authorities, but it was not without risk. Participants and those who supported the insurrection still walked the streets, even if they could not express their politics openly, and some were willing to avenge or protect themselves from 'miserable informers' with violence if necessary.[61] When Belarmino G. C., a day labourer, was arrested for shooting a miner at midnight in mid August 1935, he claimed that he was the real victim in this particular case as the town was 'harassing him to death' for passing information to the Civil Guard.[62] In the case of the death of Manuel G., *Región* reported that there were several explanations circulating, 'but the most widespread … is that Manuel is accused of having denounced several individuals who had taken part in the revolutionary events'.[63]

True or not, claiming harassment by fugitive revolutionaries aligned the individual with the side of the law and presented himself – the cases invariably involve male protagonists – as an upstanding member of the community. It was a logical line of defence. Belarmino G. G., when questioned regarding an assault of which his brother stood accused, blamed the victim for the attack:

> everything that has now happened is because two days after the revolution was declared Salvador [the victim of the attack] went to the house under investigation and, armed with a rifle, he forced them to hand over the shotgun they had ... to the Revolutionary Committee ... at the same time they forced them [*sic*] to do guard duty, which they refused to ...

Belarmino embellished his account by accusing Salvador of possessing looted money, which he based on hearsay and Salvador's alleged expansive spending in bars.[64]

The statements to the police paint a clear picture of a society divided between revolutionaries and upstanding citizens enduring unbearable oppression that continued even after the military defeat of the insurrection, but denunciations provide a more differentiated image of their communities. Framed as personal appeals to Doval, they made pointed criticism of the authorities and their own communities. They alleged, for example, that a corporal had accepted a bribe to remove socialists from prison and that rightists were colluding with revolutionaries in order to save themselves.[65]

[61] *El Noroeste*, 17 Nov. 1934.

[62] AHPA, AP, box 78438, file 158 (1935).

[63] *Región*, 25 July 1935.

[64] AHPA, AP, box 78437, file 178 (1935).

[65] Letter to Commander Doval from El Entrego, 24 Nov. 1934, CDMH, PS Gijón, J series, box 50, file 1.

One criticized the 'rich' for saving revolutionaries in a gesture of gratitude for having survived the insurrection, while another warned Doval that parish priests 'go around intervening on everyone's behalf and you should not listen to them'.[66] Certainly three priests claimed after the Civil War that treating former revolutionaries well during the long 1935 saved them from the wave of anticlerical violence at the beginning of the conflict, although it is unlikely that more than a handful did this.[67] In indicating their frustration that justice lacked the required zeal, the letters' authors reveal that individuals proactively tried to shape the repression in the coalfields, as occurred in other contexts of denunciation in which the repression meant 'the state [was put] at the disposal of its citizens'; the latter could draw upon the resources of the former.[68]

Beneath the imagined clean dividing lines of politics, the repression was complicated by the entanglement of personal and professional relationships. In the case of a murder of a company guard by his subordinate at the entrance to the Fondón mine, the accused, Avelino C. G., argued that he had acted in self-defence. The deceased had repeatedly threatened him, as Avelino had reported the guard's sons for participating in the insurrection. While he foregrounded the insurrection and aligned himself with the law, witnesses suggested that their differences lay in work matters that predated October 1934.[69] The repression intensified the fragmentation of society as personal affairs became public and politicized once refracted through the lens of the revolution.[70]

A province under quarantine

Less than a month after the end of the insurrection, an international delegation arrived in Oviedo for what turned out to be a 'brief and tempestuous' visit.

[66] Letter to Commander Doval from a worker from Santa Ana, 12 Nov. 1934 and untitled, undated, handwritten note [statement by Pilar Bernaldo de Quirós], CDMH, PS Gijón, J series, box 50, file 1.

[67] Á. Garralda García, *La persecución religiosa del clero en Asturias 1934, 1936 y 1937: martirios y odiseas* (Avilés, 2009 [1977]), pp. 405–7, 463, 546.

[68] P. Anderson, 'Singling out victims: denunciation and collusion in the post-Civil War Francoist repression in Spain, 1939–1945', *European History Quarterly*, xxxix (2009), 7–26, at p. 12. For these themes in the context of the Second World War, see also J. Gross, *Revolution from Abroad: the Soviet Conquest of Poland's Western Ukraine and Western Belorussia* (Princeton, N.J., 2002).

[69] AHPA, AP, box 78437, file 167 (1935).

[70] As Kalyvas warned, it is important not to assume that the master cleavage maps onto local cleavages in civil wars (S. Kalyvas, 'The ontology of "political violence": action and identity in civil wars', *Perspectives on Politics*, i (2003), 475–94).

The British Labour Party activist and former MP Ellen Wilkinson, who had visited Spain the previous year to seek support for the International Relief Committee for the Victims of German Fascism, journeyed to the province alongside Labour Party peer Lord Listowel and Bourthoumieux, a lawyer from the Association Juridique Internationale, after visiting Prime Minister Lerroux and an imprisoned Largo Caballero in Madrid. On arrival in Oviedo, a 'hostile crowd' gathered outside the café where they dined, and followed them to a meeting at the Provincial Deputation with Doval. He quickly expelled the delegation from the province.[71] The Asturian right-wing daily *Región* revelled in their expulsion and praised the protestors for giving Listowel, Wilkinson and Bourthoumieux the reception they 'deserved'. The newspaper accused them of only showing interest in the treatment of prisoners and neglecting the destruction of Oviedo.[72]

Región's delight in the expulsion of the overseas visitors was rooted in a wider desire to control the narrative of the insurrection and the repression. Right-wing publications presented the revolutionaries as a barbarous, ungodly horde beholden to foreign ideologies. Theirs was a vision of a 'nation under siege … with only the sword of the army and the shield of Catholic faith to protect Spain'.[73] The Manichean depiction was central to the election campaign of February 1936 and would underpin Francoist and Republican narratives during the Civil War.[74] The portrayal of the insurrection was also heavily gendered, from an emphasis on gruesome atrocities, which were not usually true, to highlighting female participation. As the female body was also the repository and guarantor of national honour, the nation was under threat, while women's activities during the insurrection were brandished as evidence of the breakdown of the social order.[75]

The Asturian press added an additional angle to this portrayal of the insurrection. For *Región*, Asturias had been martyred in a criminal rebellion by the revolutionaries, whose betrayal of their *patria* meant they had forfeited their right to call themselves Asturians. *Región* propagated a

[71] M. Perry, *'Red Ellen' Wilkinson: Her Ideas, Movements and World* (Manchester, 2015), pp. 302–7, the quotations at p. 305.

[72] *Región*, 16 Nov. 1934. See also protests by business leaders and the JAP (*El Noroeste*, 16, 17 Nov. 1934). For their reception in Britain, see H. García, *The Truth About Spain! Mobilizing British Public Opinion, 1936–1939* (Brighton, 2010), p. 26.

[73] B. D. Bunk, *Ghosts of Passion: Martyrdom, Gender, and the origins of the Spanish Civil War* (Durham, N.C., 2007), p. 51.

[74] For these discourses during the Civil War, particularly the nationalistic component, see X. M. Núñez Seixas, *¡Fuera el invasor! nacionalismos y movilización bélica durante la guerra civil española (1936–1939)* (Madrid, 2006).

[75] For a discussion of the gendered readings of the insurrection, see Bunk, *Ghosts*, ch. 4.

rigid narrative in which the province had to atone for its sins on its own. Asturias, an extrapolation of 'martyred' Oviedo, was a victim of 'Marxism' that had 'suffered for Spain' and could only heal itself sealed off from the rest of the world, in what constituted a performance of autarchic penance.[76] Reconstruction now fell to the 'people of order'. Silencing the left and restricting political options reduced politics in the long 1935 to a narrow understanding of politics as order.

Región was zealous in policing this narrative and attacking those who criticized the repression. It labelled calls to investigate the treatment of revolutionaries a 'farce' and 'an insult to the Spanish Army, to Asturias and to Spain'; it was '*Región* and Asturias against the 'anti-*patria*'.[77] The newspaper was not alone in attempting to control the portrayal of Asturias. The Oviedo city council proposed a ban on the sale of newspapers which deviated from the right's narrative and agreed to appoint a committee of 'paladins of truth' to combat the 'calumnies' spread in the press in a move of chest-thumping regional pride.[78] Six months after the expulsion of Wilkinson, Bourthoumieux and Listowel, the governor general of Asturias, ejected French observers from the trial of those committing murders in Turón during the insurrection. He accused them of meddling in Spanish affairs that were no business of theirs.[79]

Censorship and the ban on left-wing organizations in Asturias meant that the right-wing newspapers had no competition in the dissemination of their narrative of events. Yet investigations by deputies protected by parliamentary immunity and reports published abroad raised awareness of the atrocities committed during the defeat of the revolutionaries and the torture of those imprisoned. By early 1935, the government was forced to acknowledge international criticism directed at the repression in Asturias and published its own version of the insurrection.[80] Luis Bolín, the London correspondent for the conservative daily *ABC*, led a campaign by Spanish monarchists that included 'talks on the BBC and … articles for the *Morning Post*' to counter reports of torture. Such reports encompassed the pamphlet *Spain, October 1934* with a foreword by the French writer Henri Barbusse and produced by International Red Aid (SRI) – a Communist organization – and an article in *Foreign Affairs* penned by Luis Araquistáin, a leading

[76] *Región*, 11 Nov. 1934.

[77] *Región*, 12, 30 Nov. 1934.

[78] The council sent a telegram to the minister of the interior in protest (*Región*, 3 Nov. 1934; AO, Actas, 16 June 1933 to 16 June 1934, ff. 71–2, f. 119).

[79] *Región*, 19 June 1935.

[80] Townson, *Crisis*, p. 284.

Caballerista.[81] In Spain, there was greater freedom to publish outside of Asturias. *Heraldo de Madrid* and Bilbao's *El Liberal* published accounts of the insurrection. The Asturian socialist newspapers that were permitted in 1935 avoided reporting on the insurrection and the repression to prevent the wrath of the authorities, focusing instead on internal doctrinal and strategic matters.

The struggle over reporting on the insurrection and the repression formed part of the 'invention' of October, which was a central battleground of Spanish politics during the long 1935.[82] This invention emerged through newsprint and a flurry of pamphlets and books with contrasting interpretations of the insurrection. There were martyrological accounts from clerical victims and right-wing commentators, eyewitness accounts from those who had lived through the insurrection, such as Aurelio de Llano, and leftist accounts, including the novelized version penned by José Díaz Fernández and published in *Diario de Madrid*.[83] *Región* was outspoken in its criticism of the serialized publication of Díaz Fernández's heroic depiction of the revolutionaries, which it labelled a 'pile of pages full of lazy and deplorable writing', and appealed to all Asturians to protest to the editor of *Diario de Madrid*.[84]

For *Región*, the military was the sole bulwark against the return of revolution. It was the 'little soldiers' who had brought 'tranquillity on the night of 20 October' and peace depended on their presence.[85] The perceived threat posed by the dangerous revolutionary other was revealed in an anxious motion presented at a council meeting in Oviedo:

> It is no secret for anyone that one of the main causes of the helpless situation of our city was its insufficient garrison. Oviedo is surrounded by an important industrial and mining zone ... there is military industry and explosives production which are of national importance. Related to this is the patriotic need that the garrison be increased.[86]

[81] García, *Truth*, pp. 26–7; for Bolín's account, see L. Bolín, *Spain: the Vital Years* (London, 1967), pp. 135–6. Reports included *Spain, October 1934* (Paris, 1935); L. Araquistáin, 'The October Revolution in Spain', *Foreign Affairs*, xiii (1935), 247–61.

[82] R. Cruz, *En el nombre del pueblo: república, rebelión y guerra en la España de 1936* (Madrid, 2006), pp. 70ff.

[83] E.g. *Los mártires de Turón*; Llano, *Pequeños anales*; Molins i Fábrega, *UHP*; Díaz Fernández published his account under the pseudonym José Canel, see J. Canel [J. Díaz Fernández], *Octubre rojo en Asturias* (Barcelona, 1984 [1935]).

[84] *Región*, 2, 3, 4, 7 Aug. 1935.

[85] *Región*, 21 March 1935.

[86] AO, Actas, 22 June 1934 to 10 Jan. 1936, f. 140. See also *Región*, 31 Jan. 1935.

The only solution was to bolster the defences of the city, which appeared under siege by a working class synonymous with revolution. In emphasizing the importance of the military to safeguarding the social order, *Región* did not openly appeal for military intervention in politics – as would occur in July 1936 – nor was it especially vocal in defending the army as a repository of Spanish identity and tradition. Rather, the army simply guaranteed security. Repeated troop manoeuvres and exercises in 1935 were thus a reassuring spectacle for the 'people of order'.[87] In July, CEDA leader and minister of war, José María Gil Robles, oversaw manoeuvres in the coalfields involving 3,000 troops using live ammunition, and a military parade in Oviedo, which recalled scenes from after the insurrection.[88]

The difficulty in relying on the presence of the military to safeguard social peace was the repeated invocation of the spectre of revolution, which served to inculcate anxiety. As *Región* warned its readers, '[t]he working masses retain their arms because they want to repeat the attack'.[89] On several occasions in 1934 and 1935, rumours spread through the province of planned strikes, arms caches and the return of revolution, playing on existing anxieties that were fed by the press. The far right fanned them further in accordance with their desire to undermine the political order. Frustrated at the destabilizing effect of rumours, the governor fined those responsible, including a leading Falangist and his wife.[90]

For those who did not identify with the narrative propagated of the insurrection and the reduction of politics to 'order', the political atmosphere – choked by censorship and restrictions on the freedom of association – was stifling. One individual, describing himself as an 'honourable worker who loves work and culture', wrote an open letter to the civil governor in July 1935 asking 'publicly if it is possible for one to be a Communist, socialist, "leftist Republican" or simply a liberal' as 'it actually appears to be the opposite'. The author hid his name and location as there was 'a serious threat ... hanging over me if I disclose the daily harassment of which I am the object because I am a socialist'. He ended by questioning, 'are we allowed to think?'[91]

Relying on censorship and the presence of the military was ultimately unsustainable. Neither could absolute control be wielded over the narrative

87 *Región*, 15, 17, 18, 25 May 1935; *El Noroeste*, 25 Sept., 8 Nov. 1935.

88 *El Noroeste*, 23 July 1935.

89 *Región*, 27 Nov. 1934.

90 For example, *El Noroeste*, 27 Dec. 1934, 30 Apr., 7 June 1935; *Región*, 18 Sept. 1935. For the authorities' response, see *El Noroeste*, 2 Apr. 1935; *Región*, 20 Sept. 1935; J. M. García de Tuñón Aza, *Apuntes para una historia de la Falange asturiana* (Oviedo, 2001), p. 39.

91 *La Tarde*, 8 July 1935.

of events, nor Asturias remain under quarantine indefinitely. In the midst of the national election campaign in early 1936, the state of alarm was lifted in the province and the Asturian left was finally able to discuss the insurrection and repression in the public sphere. *Región* could not hide its rage:

> The leftist newspapers, now free of the gag, have thrown themselves into the most shameless campaign in which the central theme is the repression by the security forces of the horrors of the red October in Asturias. Photomontages, fiddled statistics [and] articles drool calumnies over the Civil Guard and Army.[92]

An opportunity

The long 1935 provided the right with an unprecedented opportunity to redirect the Republic. The banning of unions and left-wing political parties in Asturias, the 'gag' on their press and the imprisonment and exile of activists afforded right-wing groups the unchallenged freedom to paint an alternative vision of the Republic. New municipal councils and steering committees across the country meant municipal resources could be redirected at the local level and previous agreements overturned. Religious orders returned to provincial welfare institutions and councils in Langreo and Aller paid the food and cleaning bills of the armed forces in their districts.[93] Sensitive to the change in political winds, parish priests requested that municipal authorities return parish cemeteries that previous councils had seized using Republican legislation. Councillors were sympathetic but reluctant to relinquish their hold on burial grounds. They were more open to overturning bans on funeral processions with the raised cross.[94]

Yet little was achieved by these administrations, which were more content with balancing budgets after the alleged profligacy of the previous administration rather than rechannelling the Republic at the local level. There was also little effort made to alleviate the social problems caused by the repression. Welfare initiatives introduced by the newly appointed councils were ad-hoc, precarious affairs that relied on volunteers – often young women – and donations, and owed much to traditional private forms of charity. The meagre resources struggled to deal with the sheer number of those who required aid; in Langreo alone, over 500 families received 35,000

[92] *Región*, 11 Jan. 1936.

[93] For a similar return of religious personnel in Andalusia, see Macarro Vera, *Socialismo*, p. 371.

[94] See the decision to consult lawyers on the cemetery in Langreo, while the ban on Catholic funeral processions was revoked in San Martín del Rey Aurelio (AL, Actas, 23 June 1934 to 12 Sept. 1935, f. 79; *Región*, 2 Jan., 23 March 1935).

pesetas in cash hand-outs.[95] After an initial wave of activity, these initiatives fizzled out. The canteen for children in Turón closed in mid April due to a lack of funds despite repeated appeals for donations.[96] The authorities showed little interest in providing widespread, systematic welfare assistance.

A more sustained attempt at aid may have facilitated more support for the new municipal authorities. As regards trade unions, there was also little to attract former members of the SOMA or the SUM to the SCOM in terms of the latter's achievements. As the only legal mining trade union, the SCOM was ideally placed to assert itself as an effective voice for mineworkers, but the mining companies preferred to ignore it. When SHE refused mineworkers the paid holidays they were legally owed, the SCOM's protests fell on deaf ears. This obliged the SCOM to overturn its strategy of co-operation with the company, and it threatened a strike. Finally, the authorities intervened to force the SHE to bow to the legislation. Despite this victory, there is no evidence it aided the union.[97] The SHE's reticence reflected the companies' contentment with repression as a means of controlling the demands of the workforce, rather than improving living or working conditions. They were content with 'cutting off a few heads [and] punishing the rebels', as the social Catholic canon, Maximiliano Arboleya, complained.[98] When the mining bosses finally turned to Arboleya in February 1936 to find a way of making their workforce more sympathetic to them, it proved too late for any effective action to be undertaken.[99]

The political right was unable to capitalize on the opportunity to expand offered by the absence of a public left-wing challenge in Asturias. Popular Action, which claimed over 50,000 members in the province in 1935, did not experience a surge in membership.[100] Right-wing organizations in the coalfields were fragile. JAP rallies in the coalfields relied on orators from Gijón, the women's section of AP in Sama acknowledged it was struggling and the Catholic Youth had a small membership.[101] There was an attempt at the national level to attract workers to the right via a National Labour

95 *Región*, 28 March 1935; *El Noroeste*, 5, 27 Apr. 1935.

96 At the time, it was feeding 220 children (*El Noroeste*, 14 Apr. 1935). For earlier appeals, see *El Noroeste*, 21 Feb., 6 Apr. 1935.

97 Castejón Rodríguez, 'La patronal', pp. 427–8.

98 Arboleya's letter is cited in D. Benavides, *El fracaso social del catolicismo español: Arboleya Martínez, 1870–1951* (Barcelona, 1973), p. 555.

99 Benavides, *El fracaso*, pp. 618–19, 627, 629–32.

100 J. R. Montero, *La CEDA: el catolicismo social y político en la II República* (2 vols, Madrid, 1977), i. 374.

101 *Acción*, 28 Dec. 1935; *Región*, 24 July, 13 Oct. 1935.

Front, which was financed by Catholic Action and aimed to bring together independent unions in an organization that could constitute an 'alternative to the UGT', but it was 'extremely weak' in practice.[102] Its Asturian branch brought together the SCOM and independent unions from Avilés and Gijón, yet did not spark a revival of the SCOM's fortunes. Nor did appeals for new independent, 'apolitical' unions have much effect.[103]

The right blamed their failure to expand on a 'hostile' environment, including the social pressures of *qué dirán* ('what will the neighbours say?'), which deterred local residents from visible support of the right.[104] There is evidence that political divisions were sufficiently cemented to prevent mass changes of allegiance across the left–right divide. A new Catholic school in La Argañosa – a left-wing stronghold in Oviedo – had only managed to recruit forty students two months after opening.[105] The left continued to exhibit strength despite being unable to mobilize publicly. Despite the restrictions, there were a small number of strikes in 1934. The authorities came down hard on any stoppage. Those who downed tools during the trial of revolutionaries from Turón were sacked and then subjected to a two-week lockout.[106] A UGT-CNT construction strike in July revealed a resilient left undeterred by the robust response from the governor. Despite a ban on assemblies, violence against strikers and the use of blackleg workers, the strike lasted for two months and was successful: those sacked were readmitted and the demand for a forty-four-hour working week was achieved. The governor tied himself in knots in an attempt to deny that there was a strike. Admitting it would have meant holding his hands up to a failure in his management of provincial affairs.[107] The strike indicated both the strength of the left (even when it had to work underground), and the inability of the authorities to offer any solution except force to what they perceived as threats to public order (rather than the expression of economic discontent).

If the overall picture was one of stagnation and paralysis in the coalfields, it did not differ markedly from the spectacle offered by national politics. While the Radicals and CEDA shared government office, they did not see eye to eye. The revolutionary insurrection was a point of contention that made co-operation difficult. The Radicals did not share CEDA's attitude to

[102] Montero, *CEDA*, ii. 576–80.

[103] *Región*, 13, 28 Dec. 1934, 20 July 1935; *El Noroeste*, 14 Feb. 1935.

[104] *Región*, 24 July 1935.

[105] *Región*, 6 Oct., 10 Dec. 1935.

[106] On strikes in 1935, see Castejón Rodríguez, 'La patronal', pp. 421–2, 427, 429.

[107] Taibo, *Asturias*, pp. 578–80.

death penalties for former revolutionaries. Two CEDA ministers resigned in April after they refused to sign the commutation of the death sentences of Ramón González Peña and Teodomiro Menéndez, which provoked a governmental crisis. The subsequent government formed solely of Radicals and the small PRLD lasted a month before it collapsed. CEDA's strategy of slowly inching towards control of the government appeared to be working. The centre-right Republicans ceded the majority of ministries in the following administration to CEDA and Agrarian Party deputies, including Gil Robles as minister of war. As the CEDA consolidated its position, it hardened its political line. Filiberto Villalobos, the PRLD minister of education, was vilified and forced to resign due to the lack of support for his education reforms. Manuel Giménez Fernández, the social Catholic CEDA minister of agriculture, saw his agrarian reform watered down to inefficacy through amendments.[108] The combination of political differences between the Radicals and the CEDA, the weakness of the former and the lack of interest in government-led reform of the latter, meant that the long 1935 was a year of a political half-life in which little was achieved.[109]

The return of the left

In the post-insurrectionary context of hunger and misery, left-wing organizations tried to introduce their own initiatives to assist supporters and family members, but their efforts were hampered by the repression and having to operate covertly or else under the protection afforded by parliamentary immunity. The initial priority was to extract fugitive revolutionaries from Asturias, which began in late December.[110] According to Taibo, 200–300 went into exile, although the figure seems low given that 121 alone went to the USSR and the main nucleus was located in France and Belgium.[111] Help for those imprisoned in Asturias took longer to organize, and incarcerated socialists were frustrated at the lack of immediate assistance. Legal aid arrived in the form of socialist lawyer Mariano Moreno Mateos, who was quickly overwhelmed by the volume of investigations. Communist

108 See J. R. Montero, *La CEDA: el catolicismo social y político en la II República* (2 vols, Madrid, 1977), ii. 173–207; J. Tusell, *Historia de la democracia cristiana en España* (2 vols, Madrid, 1974), i. 282–312.

109 E.g. much hand-wringing regarding poverty and unemployment only resulted in a desultory amount spent on public works (Townson, *Crisis*, p. 281).

110 Taibo, *Asturias*, pp. 545–6.

111 Taibo, *Asturias*, pp. 533, 593; *La Tarde*, 4 May 1936. They were looked after by the International Mining Federation (J. S. Vidarte, *El bienio negro y la insurrección de Asturias* (Barcelona, 1978), p. 416).

organizations, including SRI, are regarded as effective in providing aid, but it was not until spring 1935 that SRI initiatives gained a clear organizational form and there was still no SRI committee in Oviedo by mid April 1935.[112] That same month, the SRI founded the National Committee of Aid for the Victims of October, which was backed by socialist, Communist and Republican organizations, and channelled funds to families and prisoners. The Association of Defence Lawyers for Those Indicted for the Events of October was similarly an SRI-funded cross-party organization (although the socialists distanced themselves from it at national level). It provided legal support for prisoners across Spain and was established in Gijón from March.[113]

Legal assistance aside, the suppression of left-wing political parties and unions meant organizing aid was very difficult. Women played a prominent role in facilitating the organization of aid; female parliamentary deputies visited prisoners and transported orphans out of the province, and other politically active women arranged clandestine meetings in the mountains.[114] Protected by parliamentary immunity, the Communist Dolores Ibárruri and socialists Matilde de la Torre, Veneranda Manzano and María Lejárraga supported families through initiatives like the Committee in Aid of Working-Class Children, which raised 50,000 pesetas and evacuated 500 children. The Committee was the new label for the Women Against War and Fascism committee formed in 1934.[115]

Even as activists on the ground occupied themselves with supporting

[112] See the letter from Mariano Moreno Mateos to Juan Simeón Vidarte, 23 Dec. 1934, in Vidarte, *El bienio*, pp. 331–2; L. Branciforte, *El Socorro Rojo Internacional en España (1923–1939): relatos de la solidaridad antifascista* (Madrid, 2009), pp. 160–3; A. Elorza and M. Bizcarrondo, *Queridos camaradas: la Internacional Comunista y España, 1919–1939* (Barcelona, 1999), p. 229; letter to an unnamed 'comrade' from the SRI National Executive Committee, 15 Apr. 1935, in AHPA, AP, box 78446, file 62 (1935).

[113] For the National Committee and SRI, see Branciforte, *El Socorro*. For Asturias, see Letter from Rufino García to SRI Central Committee, 29 March 1935, AHPA, AP, box 78446, file 62 (1935).

[114] M. A. Mateos, *¡Salud, compañeras! Mujeres socialistas en Asturias (1900–1937)* (Oviedo, 2007), p. 181. For the authorities clamping down on the left, see e.g., *El Norooeste*, 20 Aug., 8 Oct. 1935; AHPA, AP, box 78446, file 62 (1935).

[115] See L. Branciforte, 'Legitimando la solidaridad femenina internacional: el Socorro Rojo', *Arenal*, xvi (2009), 27–52, at pp. 43, 45–6; F. Erice, 'Mujeres comunistas: la militancia femenina en el comunismo asturiano, de los orígenes al final del franquismo', in *Los comunistas en Asturias (1920–1982)*, ed. F. Erice (Gijón, 1996), especially p. 322; Mateos, *¡Salud, compañeras!*, p. 181; *Ayuda. Portavoz de la solidaridad*, 27 Feb. 1936. For Ibárruri's versión, see D. Ibárruri, *Memorias de Dolores Ibárruri, Pasionaria: la lucha y la vida* (Barcelona, 1985), pp. 187–90.

prisoners, much of the movement, including those in exile and in prison, was engaged in debating future strategy. The defeat of the revolutionary insurrection and the repression meant that the socialists required a new way forward. Fierce, lengthy discussions took place in prison galleries and through correspondence and newsprint as socialists argued over the future of the movement.[116] The debates and political manoeuvrings led to the definitive crystallization of three factions with contrasting views on alliances with other political parties, and, to a lesser extent, purges and responsibility for the insurrection.[117] The left faction was identified with Largo Caballero, who had been arrested in his nightclothes on 14 October and remained imprisoned in Madrid. Prieto, who maintained a pragmatic, centrist position, had fled across the border to France hidden in the boot of a car. Besteiro headed the smaller, conservative wing of the socialists. With Largo Caballero imprisoned, Juan Simeón Vidarte became the de facto leader of the PSOE. He pursued a strategy of rebuilding an alliance with the left Republicans, which was welcomed by Prieto.[118] Although Largo Caballero had approved Vidarte's initial moves in April, the Caballeristas, which included important sections of the JS, were far from impressed by the attempt to resurrect the Republican–socialist alliance. The frictions between Caballeristas and reformist Prietistas increased from late spring and culminated in the resignation of Largo Caballero over a matter relating to the PSOE's statutes at the end of the year. The internal struggle to control the socialist movement would continue through 1936 and during the Spanish Civil War.[119]

The left Republicans had been immersed in their own process of reorganization in the months prior to discussing a possible alliance with the socialists. Azaña's Republican Action merged with former Radical Socialists

[116] E.g. Prieto's articles were collected in *Documentos socialistas: escritos de Indalecio Prieto, Ramón González Peña, Toribio Echevarría, Amador Fernández, Antonio Llaneza, Alejandro Jaume, Francisco Torquemada, jóvenes presos de Asturias y de Madrid, etc., etc.*, ed. I. Prieto (Madrid, n.d.). For Caballerista criticism, see C. de Baráibar, *Las falsas "posiciones socialistas" de Indalecio Prieto* (Madrid, 1935) and for criticism of Caballero, see G. M. de Coca, *Anti-Caballero: crítica marxista de la bolchevización del partido socialista (1930–1936)* (Madrid, 1975 [1936]).

[117] J. Aróstegui, *Largo Caballero: el tesón y la quimera* (Barcelona, 2013), p. 379.

[118] H. Graham, *Socialism and War: the Spanish Socialist Party in Power and Crisis, 1936–1939* (Cambridge, 1991), p. 20; letter from Prieto to the Executive Commission of the PSOE, 23 March 1935, in Prieto, *Documentos*, pp. 19–26.

[119] This summary of a complicated struggle is based on Aróstegui, *Largo Caballero*, pp. 379–417; Graham, *Socialism*, pp. 20–4. See also S. Juliá, *La izquierda del PSOE (1935–1936)* (Madrid, 1977), pp. 5–28; P. Heywood, *Marxism and the Failure of Organised Socialism in Spain, 1879–1936* (Cambridge, 1990), pp. 164–7.

and a Galician Republican party to form the Republican Left (IR) in April 1934. Five months later, Martínez Barrio's breakaway Radicals merged with another group of Radical Socialists to create the Republican Union (UR). Despite tensions, the IR and UR reached a working relationship by May 1935 and momentum grew behind the left Republicans through the rest of the year. In the middle of November, Azaña, whose rallies attracted crowds of up to 400,000 supportive of an amnesty and a renewed progressive Republican project, sent the socialists a letter proposing an alliance. The Caballerista response was to demand that all of the working-class left, with the exception of the anarchists, be included. In their eyes, Communist involvement would prevent the PCE outflanking the socialists and weaken the reformist Prietistas.

Largo Caballero's demand that the PCE be included in the alliance brought the Communists 'out of the ghetto', but the latter was also facilitated by a change in Comintern policy.[120] At its seventh congress in September 1935, the Comintern endorsed a policy of popular fronts, according to which Communists would collaborate in the defence of bourgeois democracy. This was a significant departure from the 'class against class' policy of the Third Period (1927–34) that had prohibited alliances with other political groups and attacked social democrats as 'social fascists'. The change was due to the rise of fascism and rank-and-file unity initiatives. In France, fears of a bellicose Germany and the continued rise of right-wing leagues stimulated the desire for a broader popular front than the socialist–Communist pact signed in the summer of 1934. The French socialists endorsed the policy of a popular front in June 1935 and the following month socialists, Communists and the middle-class Radical party jointly celebrated Bastille Day.[121] Political positions had shifted, and so had language and symbols. The red flag and *The Internationale* mixed with the French tricolour and the *Marseillaise.* The French Communists switched from invoking the working class to emphasize the 'people'.[122] This nationalization of Communist political language would become evident in Spain in 1936 in the PCE's shift towards speaking in the name of the 'working people' as opposed to the working class.

There was a further bone of contention within the Spanish socialist ranks, which centred on the 'Bolchevization' demanded by sectors of the

[120] Graham, *Socialism*, p. 19.

[121] G.-R. Horn, *European Socialists Respond to Fascism: Ideology, Activism and Contingency in the 1930s* (New York, 1996), pp. 98–101; J. Jackson, *The Popular Front in France: Defending Democracy, 1934–38* (Cambridge, 1988), pp. 22–51.

[122] For this emphasis on the people, see J. Wardhaugh, *In Pursuit of the People: Political Culture in France, 1934–1939* (Basingstoke, 2009), Bastille Day at p. 84.

Socialist Youth. The Caballerista leadership of the JS produced a pamphlet, *Octubre: segunda etapa*, in early 1935 that constituted a withering attack on 'reformism' and 'centrism'. They positioned themselves as the revolutionary vanguard, demanded a purge of the socialist ranks and called for the PSOE to leave the Second International.[123] Demanding 'Bolchevization' may have been a way of 'deflect[ing] public attention from the PSOE left's passivity during October 1934' and letters from Spanish exiles to Largo Caballero calling for the expulsion of those who had not participated in the revolution would have made for uncomfortable reading for him.[124] Members of the Asturian JS rejected *Octubre* in a letter of 5 March. They criticized Soviet Communism, advocated an alliance with the Republicans and remarked that 'there is no other betrayal – recognize it well – than those who have boasted of their exalted revolutionism only to have shown excessive cowardice in practice', in what was a pointed criticism of the Madrid JS for their relative inaction during October 1934.[125] The 'Bolchevization' matter was closely bound up with frictions within the socialist movement. The letter was widely circulated and in various versions adulterated to be strongly censorious of Largo Caballero, who believed the letter a Prietista strategy to undermine his position.[126]

Asturias is often cited as a bastion of Prietista reformism and the aforementioned letter from young members appears to confirm this. The reality was more complex and the position of Asturian socialists was far from homogeneous. Gonzalez Peña and Antuña expressed support for Prieto and Largo Caballero respectively in March 1935.[127] A fawning letter of support for Largo Caballero from Moscow in early 1936 feted October 1934 as a 'glorious' struggle against fascism that had united workers. The signatories, which included a dozen Asturian socialists, demanded 'Bolchevization' via a struggle against 'odious reformism and centrism' and to learn from the

[123] For the full text of *Octubre: segunda etapa*, see C. Ramírez, *Balance de una ruptura: los socialistas en el gobierno, en la guerra y en la revolución* (Madrid, 2012), pp. 277–328.

[124] For the quotation, see Graham, *Socialism*, p. 18. Letter from Ruperto García et al to Francisco Largo Caballero, Jan. 1936, CDMH, PS Madrid, box 2371.

[125] For the letter from the socialist prisoners in the model prison of Oviedo to the Executive Commission of the National Federation of the Socialist Youth, see Prieto, *Documentos*, pp. 179–87.

[126] Aróstegui, *Largo Caballero*, p. 388. Prieto in fact claimed to have requested the removal of criticism of Largo Caballero from the letter (letter from Prieto to Negrín, 26 June 1935, in Prieto, *Documentos*, p. 112).

[127] See P. Preston, *The Coming of the Spanish Civil War: Reform, Reaction and Revolution in the Second Republic* (London, 1978), p. 136; letter from Francisco Largo Caballero to Graciano Antuña, 25 Mar. 1935, CDMH, PS Madrid, box 2371.

example set by the USSR.[128] The dispersal of the Asturian socialist movement in prisons, exile and clandestinity contributed to the fragmenting pressures and internal frictions.

As socialist internal debates raged and the left Republicans and socialists moved towards an alliance, the wider political situation was changing. Two scandals rocked the Radicals, precipitated their decline and heralded the prospect of elections. The first was the *Straperlo* affair, which implicated important figures in the Radical Party, including Lerroux. The matter revolved around a fraudulent roulette machine and bribes made in exchange for permits to install it. Lerroux was cleared of wrongdoing, but as the Radical Party struggled with desertions and internal chaos, the Tayá scandal broke. Radical ministers were accused of fraudulently resolving a compensation case over a contract involving shipping in Equatorial Guinea. The CEDA withdrew their support from the government and Prime Minister Chapaprieta resigned on 9 December.[129]

Political momentum had grown behind what would become the Popular Front, but it was Gil Robles who seemed to have achieved his objectives. The implosion of the Radicals left the CEDA poised to control the next government at the perfect moment. The party had demanded revision of the Constitution ever since its approval in December 1931. Now that four years had passed, this could be achieved through a simple majority in the Cortes, rather than requiring the assent of two-thirds of the chamber. Importantly, however, President Alcalá Zamora doubted Gil Robles's Republican credentials and refused to offer him the chance to form a government. Instead, he turned to the Galician Republican Manuel Portela Valladares, who piloted the moribund legislature towards elections in February 1936.[130] Furious, Gil Robles began consulting generals, including Franco, on a coup d'état that would force the president to appoint a CEDA government.[131]

The changing political winds were perceptible in Asturias, and in late 1935, it seemed that the left was poised to return to public life. Rumours circulated that municipal councillors were set to resign and those elected in 1931 would return.[132] The governor reasserted his authority by banning 'the advertisement of newspapers in a coercive or scandalous way' as part of a

[128] Letter from Ruperto García et al. to Francisco Largo Caballero, Jan. 1936, CDMH, PS Madrid, box 2371.

[129] Townson, *Crisis*, pp. 315–29, 332–7.

[130] Preston, *Coming of the Spanish Civil War*, pp. 165–71; Townson, *Crisis*, pp. 336–8.

[131] E. González Calleja, *Contrarrevolucionarios: radicalización violenta de las derechas durante la Segunda República, 1931–1936* (Madrid, 2011), p. 298.

[132] E.g. *Asturias*, 21 Dec. 1935; *El Noroeste*, 21, 29 Dec. 1935.

clampdown on leftist resurgence in Spain more widely.[133] Political meetings were still illegal, unions could not function under the UGT banner and arrests, searches of homes and military trials persisted.[134] Faced with this panorama, those tasked with preparing the groundwork for elections were women. Socialist deputy Matilde de la Torre urged Asturian women – who were 'alone against the enemy' – to engage in political activities, such as checking the electoral register for errors ahead of the elections.[135]

The state of alarm was lifted in Asturias in early January and constitutional guarantees returned across the country. The return of the left was immediately felt, but attempts at restricting political expression and the threat of military power remained. Although 'vivas!' to socialism and revolution and red-shirted activists reappeared on the streets of Oviedo in jubilant expressions of left-wing political identity, the governor quickly banned the public display of political ideas 'through shirts, insignias and gestures'. The measure did not explicitly target the left, but those arrested were left-wing activists.[136] More ominously, military manoeuvres continued in the province even as the election campaign was in full swing. The Foreign Legion marched through the streets of Oviedo accompanied by cries of 'death to the socialists', shooting practice occurred on a daily basis, and military manoeuvres took place overlooking Oviedo.[137] The threat of violence and the assertion of military power were present during the election campaign, even when constitutional guarantees were back in force.

Freed from censorship, a tide of articles in socialist *La Tarde* focused on the use of torture during the repression and paid close attention to the security forces' use of violence during the election campaign.[138] Accompanying this denunciation of the repression and the euphoric public return of the left was the frisking of the opposition for arms. Rather than relying on the authorities, left-wing activists assumed the task of stopping opponents and searching them for weapons. Stripping opponents of weapons was humiliating, an assertion of power and a form of revenge, as well as an attempt to ensure personal safety. But it also revealed a fragility and anxiety that would be at the heart of radicalism during the Popular Front spring of 1936.

[133] *El Noroeste*, 21 Dec. 1935; González Calleja, *En nombre*, p. 240.

[134] *El Noroeste*, 1, 4, 10, 17, 19 Dec. 1935; M. Bizcarrondo, 'Democracia y revolución en la estrategia socialista de la Segunda República', *Estudios de Historia Social*, xvi–xvii (1981), 227–459, at p. 344.

[135] *Asturias*, 23 Nov. 1935; Mateos, *¡Salud, compañeras!*, pp. 184–5.

[136] *Región*, 12, 14, 16, 29 Jan. 1936.

[137] *Región*, 7 Jan., 1 Feb. 1936; *La Tarde*, 13 Jan. 1936; *El Noroeste*, 9, 14 Feb. 1936.

[138] E.g. *La Tarde*, 15 Jan., 5, 10 Feb. 1936.

The long 1935 was a year of political half-life in which little was achieved at the national level or by the administrations in the coalfields. There was little will to provide an alternative vision of the Republic. Mining companies were content with sacking workers and allowing working conditions to deteriorate. Politics as order relied on the exclusion of the left, but also the spectre of revolution. The problem was that the repression was deep and widespread, yet it was not sufficiently protracted to do anything but temporarily disarticulate the Asturian left. This ensured that there would be a backlash in 1936 once the left returned to public political activity and to power after the elections. The insurrection and repression therefore reshaped politics prior to the Civil War. Amnesty was a powerful, popular banner for the Popular Front, while for the right the insurrection made the spectre of revolution very real indeed. But beyond the political campaigns, the insurrection and particularly the repression intensified the fragmentation of society. Personal affairs, refracted through the lens of the revolution, became public and politicized. The repression had politicized society in a particular way, which would become evident in 1936. It had been harshest in Asturias, but Asturias did not see the most widespread eruption of labour conflict or violence in 1936. Instead, the long 1935 configured a particular kind of fragile radicalism, which posed problems for Republican governance prior to the Civil War.

7. A fragile radicalism: the Popular Front spring of 1936

A week of spring rain had not dampened spirits. When Ramón González Peña stepped off the train at Puente de los Fierros on Sunday 1 March 1936, an enthusiastic crowd greeted his return to Asturias with applause. After paying homage to the dead of October 1934 in Mieres, he travelled to Oviedo, which he had to enter on foot due to the number of people on the streets. *La Tarde* hailed his return as the homecoming of the true voice of the Asturian people, while the occupation of the streets of Oviedo by the working class revealed the province to be 'red Asturias'.[1] This image of the working class asserting itself in public spaces is typical of both the French and Spanish popular fronts in 1936. In France, the massive strike wave of June 1936 that greeted the electoral victory of the French Popular Front was a jubilant celebration of working-class strength, identity and visibility, even as the rise of right-wing leagues and street violence posed serious problems for French political life. Yet as hope grew towards an 'apotheosis' in France in July, in Spain the mood was very different.[2] Political and social polarization, violence, strikes and right-wing conspiracies mean that the five months that separate the general elections of February 1936 and the July military coup form one of the most complex periods in Spanish history.

The shadow of the Civil War looms large over the spring of 1936 and debating responsibility for the conflict continues to shape historiographical debate. According to the Francoist narrative, the Popular Front spring was a period of chaos and *desgobierno* (misgovernment or lack of government authority) remedied by a military intervention that saved Spain from Communist revolution. The Communist conspiracy was a fabrication, although substantial levels of protest and violence across the country – labelled by Stanley Payne as the 'most famous civil disturbance in Spanish

[1] *La Tarde*, 2 March 1936; *El Noroeste*, 3 March 1936.

[2] For the jubilation and 'apotheosis', see J. Jackson, *The Popular Front in France: Defending Democracy, 1934–38* (Cambridge, 1988), pp. xii, 10. For more on levels of violence, see B. Jenkins and C. Millington, *France and Fascism: February 1934 and the Dynamics of Political Crisis* (Abingdon, 2015), p. 151.

history' – were not.[3] A particular point of contention is the role of the government. Gabriele Ranzato and Payne depicted the Popular Front governments as fluctuating between impotence, unwillingness to guarantee order and facilitation of a revolutionary process.[4] Eduardo González Calleja criticized this recurrent cliché of Popular Front 'chaos' and 'misgovernment' for neglecting the government's attempts to curb violence.[5]

While there was an increase in political violence (estimates of the number of fatalities range from 270 to 450), the spring of 1936 was not a period of chaos in Asturias, nor did the region see the development of a proto-revolutionary movement.[6] The legacy of the insurrection and the long 1935 conditioned the nature of politics in the province, as it did in Spain more widely. There was a clear crisis of community evident in purges, boycotts and the vigilance of the security forces, which contributed to a renewed radicalism. This radicalism was nevertheless fragile, defensive and inwardly focused, as political groups, trade unions and workplaces tried to rearticulate communities broken by the repression. Leftist militias, distrustful of the state, took the policing of the Republic into their own hands, in defence of the Popular Front and their own understanding of the Republican project.

Elections

On 15 January 1936, the Republican Left (IR), Republican Union (UR), PSOE, communists (the PCE and the POUM) and the Syndicalist Party signed the Popular Front agreement. Hardly radical, the pact was a return to the spirit of freedom and justice that had inspired the Republican–socialist governments of the first biennium. The agreement promised agrarian and education reform and an amnesty for those imprisoned for 'political and social crimes'. In contrast to the first biennium, however, the pact promised only an electoral agreement. The Republicans would occupy government

[3] S. Payne, 'Political violence during the Spanish Second Republic', *Journal of Contemporary History*, xxv (1990), 269–88, at p. 279. For a summary of the historiography, see E. González Calleja, 'La historiografía sobre la violencia política en la Segunda República española', *Hispania Nova: revista de historia contemporánea*, xi (2013) 403–36.

[4] G. Ranzato, 'El peso de la violencia en los orígenes de la guerra civil de 1936–1939', *Espacio, tiempo y forma, serie v, Historia contemporánea*, xx (2008), 159–82; S. Payne, *The Collapse of the Spanish Republic, 1933–1936: the Origins of the Civil War* (New Haven, Conn., 2006), pp. 197–215.

[5] E. González Calleja, *En nombre de la autoridad: la defensa del orden público durante la Segunda República española (1931–1936)* (Granada, 2014), pp. 259–60.

[6] E. González Calleja, 'La necro-lógica de la violencia sociopolítica en la primavera de 1936', *Mélanges de la Casa de Velázquez*, xli (2011) <http://journals.openedition.org/mcv/3825> [accessed 13 Jan. 2019].

office on their own. Accordingly, the Republican parties were assigned a greater number of candidates on the joint election tickets than other parties in order to bolster the stability of a future Republican government.[7]

The right, consisting of the CEDA, the monarchists of Renovación Española, the Carlist Traditionalist Communion and the still-minuscule FE-JONS, was not united by a similar commonly-agreed programme or coalition at a national level. The CEDA, as in 1933, was pragmatic and willing to negotiate with different groups to form provincial-level 'anti-revolutionary fronts' and in Asturias the CEDA repeated the joint candidacy with the PRLD.[8] Backed by huge funds, the CEDA mounted a modern mass propaganda campaign across the country, producing 2.7 million posters and fifty million flyers with forty different designs. The elections were framed as an 'apocalyptic struggle' for the soul of the country.[9] *Región* warned readers they faced a choice of 'death or life' and 'peace or revolution'. The left represented 'freemasonry, separatism, revolution, Marxism, hunger, death', while the CEDA embodied 'religion, national unity, prosperity, social justice, work, peace'.[10] Contrasting the Spanish nation, peace and prosperity with the alleged destruction heralded by 'Marxism', along with insinuating that Moscow controlled the Popular Front, provided some of the ingredients for the future political culture of Francoism forged during the Civil War.[11]

The legacy of the insurrection and the repression was central to the sharply polarized atmosphere during the election campaign. The country was divided between the Popular Front and anti-revolutionary fronts, which squeezed out Prime Minister Portela Valladares's attempt at a centrist electoral slate. The situation was tense, and twenty-five people lost their lives in violent incidents.[12] Despite having been the scene of the insurrection, Asturias was absent from the list of provinces with fatalities, although there

[7] See S. Juliá, *Orígenes del frente popular en España* (Madrid, 1979), pp. 216–21; H. Graham, *Socialism and War: the Spanish Socialist Party in Power and Crisis, 1936–1939* (Cambridge, 1991), ch. 1.

[8] P. Preston, *The Coming of the Spanish Civil War: Reform, Reaction and Revolution in the Second Republic* (London, 1978), p. 169; J. R. Montero, *La CEDA: el catolicismo social y político en la II República*, (2 vols, Madrid, 1977), ii. 312.

[9] Preston, *Coming of the Spanish Civil War*, pp. 171–4. See also Montero, *CEDA*, ii. 317–8.

[10] *Región*, 4, 16 Feb. 1936.

[11] *El Noroeste*, 16 Feb. 1936. See also Montero, *CEDA*, ii. 322–6; R. Cruz, *En el nombre del pueblo: república, rebelión y guerra en la España de 1936* (Madrid, 2006), p. 93. For a similar discourse in Andalusia, see J. M. Macarro Vera, *Socialismo, República y revolución en Andalucía (1931–1936)* (Seville, 2000), pp. 397–8.

[12] Cruz, *En el nombre*, p. 97.

were scuffles and violent encounters between opposing political groups. Activists pasting up CEDA posters exchanged shots with their political opponents while a man in a bar in Pola de Laviana was stabbed for refusing to shout 'death to fascism!'[13] The Catholic Youth in Sama claimed its leaders had received death threats and that one of its members had been attacked.[14]

The ballots held on 16 February delivered a narrow victory for the Popular Front. Neither the Popular Front nor the right polled more than 50 per cent of the votes, but the system, which favoured coalitions, meant that the Popular Front obtained a clear majority in parliament with 265 seats. This grew to 285 in May once elections had been rerun in areas where there had been irregularities. Particularly significant in facilitating the victory of the Popular Front was the CNT. In a marked change from 1933, there had been few anarchist calls for abstention and the promise of amnesty was a powerful call for the supporters and family members of those who had been jailed in the wake of October 1934.[15] The left republicans of IR and UR gained 125 seats between them, followed by the socialists with ninety-nine seats. The PCE experienced a substantial increase in influence by adding fifteen deputies to their existing representative. The parties in government between 1933 and 1935 fared badly. The scandal-ridden Radicals collapsed from over 100 deputies to just five. The CEDA did better, but losing twenty-seven seats and dropping to eighty-eight deputies was a disaster insofar as it did not deliver 'all power to the *jefe*!' as posters had demanded. There was no electoral breakthrough for the fascist party, FE-JONS. Its leader, José Antonio Primo de Rivera, lost his seat (which left the party without representation in the Cortes) and associated parliamentary immunity.[16]

On the announcement of the first results in the early hours of 17 February, Gil Robles visited Prime Minister Portela Valladares to persuade him to declare martial law rather than hand power to the Popular Front. He was joined by the chief of staff, Franco, who attempted to organize a military

[13] *Región*, 7 Jan., 8 Feb. 1936. For conflicts over posters see also Cruz, *En el nombre*, p. 97. Álvarez Tardío noted the relative lack of lethal violence in areas with previously high levels of social conflict, e.g. Barcelona (M. Álvarez Tardío, 'The impact of political violence during the Spanish general election of 1936', *Journal of Contemporary History*, xlviii (2013), 463–85, at p. 475).

[14] *Región*, 13 Feb. 1936.

[15] E.g. C. Ealham, *Class, Culture and Conflict in Barcelona, 1898–1937* (Abingdon, 2005), p. 148; G. Álvarez Chillida, '*Negras tormentas* sobre la República. La intransigencia libertaria', in *Palabras como puños: la intransigencia política en la Segunda República*, ed. F. del Rey (Madrid, 2011), pp. 103–4.

[16] On the elections, see the classic study J. Tusell, *Las elecciones del Frente Popular* (Madrid, 1971).

uprising but failed. Portela Valladares resisted the pressure but had been unsettled enough to transfer power to Azaña's new administration earlier than planned.[17] After this initial threat to Republican democracy, Gil Robles and the CEDA were subdued, for the party was in chaos. Their accidentalist strategy lay in tatters. The results reaffirmed many supporters' 'disgust' with democracy and they started to turn their backs on the CEDA.[18] Support in Salamanca 'evaporated almost overnight' and the party was 'thrown into turmoil'.[19]

In Asturias, the Popular Front achieved a clear victory on a provincial level, with 170,000 votes over 150,000 for the CEDA-PRLD, that was reflected in Oviedo and the coalfields.[20] The exception in the latter was Aller, where the Popular Front fell a thousand votes short of the CEDA-PRLD, although in all municipalities the rightist slate continued to attract a significant minority of voters. While approximately a fifth of the vote went to the CEDA-PRLD in Mieres and Langreo, this rose to over a quarter in San Martín del Rey Aurelio and Laviana and increased further up the valleys in rural areas.[21] Compared to the 150,000 votes for the CEDA-PRLD list, FE-JONS candidates received only a handful of votes.[22] Their supporters lived in Gijón (112 votes) and Oviedo (52), rather than the coalfields: Falangists received nine votes in Mieres, five in Langreo, two in Aller and none in Laviana or San Martín del Rey Aurelio.[23]

Despite the Popular Front victory, the number of right-wing votes was again disconcerting for left-wing activists. As in 1933, they tried to account for the number of CEDA-PRLD votes. Leftists were perplexed that a class-

[17] Preston, *Coming of the Spanish Civil War*, pp. 179–80; E. González Calleja, *Contrarrevolucionarios: radicalización violenta de las derechas durante la Segunda República, 1931–1936* (Madrid, 2011), pp. 302–3.

[18] S. Lowe, *Catholicism, War and the Foundation of Francoism* (Eastbourne, 2010), pp. 109–11.

[19] M. Vincent, *Catholicism in the Second Spanish Republic: Religion and Politics in Salamanca, 1930–1936* (Oxford, 1996), p. 239. For similar remarks on Galicia, see E. Grandío Seoane, *Los orígenes de la derecha gallega: la CEDA en Galicia (1931–1936)* (Sada, 1998), pp. 277–9, 286ff.

[20] *Boletín oficial de la provincia de Oviedo*, 27 Feb. 1936.

[21] For results, see *La Tarde*, 17 Feb. 1936; *Región*, 18 Feb. 1936. It could be argued that voters for the CEDA-PRLD were in fact voting for the PRLD without sharing the values of the CEDA. However, voters still had to stomach the rhetoric of the CEDA and a breakdown of voting in Aller indicates that voters did not favour PRLD candidates over the CEDA on their ballot papers (*Boletín oficial de la provincia de Oviedo*, 29 Feb., 2, 5 March 1936).

[22] *La Voz de Asturias*, 22 Feb. 1936.

[23] M. Suárez Cortina, *El fascismo en Asturias* (Gijón, 1981), pp. 281–2.

based analysis failed to explain the results. In Ciaño-Santa Ana, the 113 votes for the right far exceeded the eight local business owners. Thirty-five votes for the right in Veneros (Langreo) were explained away as men who 'let themselves be beaten by weaknesses', including selling their ballot for a job. Yet in contrast to the reaction to the previous elections, the rhetoric had a harder edge in 1936. Voting for the right was a betrayal of the local community. It was now the responsibility of the town to 'unmask' these 'cowards' and 'traitors'.[24] Violence was absent from the coalfields, but there were incidents of retributive acts accompanying victory across Spain, from stones thrown at buildings to cases of assault.[25]

The dominant tone in the streets – and in the prisons – was nevertheless the exuberant celebration of victory by Popular Front supporters. In the uncertain political interregnum following the elections and before the promised amnesty was decreed, there were riots in some prisons across the country, including in Oviedo, where the newly elected PCE deputy Dolores Ibárruri negotiated the freeing of prisoners on 20 February to diffuse the tense situation.[26] Those released paraded around Oviedo in a joyous and peaceful demonstration of victory. According to *La Voz de Asturias*, there were more people on the streets of the capital the following day than during a holiday. Singing crowds flocked to the station to greet SOMA leader Amador Fernández, who had been in exile in France and Belgium, and in the evening, the municipal band played. It seemed 'for a moment [that] the face of the city had changed completely'.[27] The former prisoners returned to the coalfields to a rapturous welcome from friends and families who deserted mines and workshops to greet them.[28]

The image of joyous, singing crowds celebrating a victory that promised justice via state-led reform appeared to hark back to the first biennium. In addition, the recovery of left-wing political and cultural life seemed to indicate a return to pre-insurrection modes of being. Casas del Pueblo reopened and councillors who had been removed from office due to the insurrection regained their seats. A large audience witnessed the first meetings of the reinstated councils in Langreo and San Martín del Rey Aurelio.[29] Sensitive to the abrupt shift in political winds, mining and steel

[24] *La Tarde*, 24, 28 Feb. 1936.

[25] See Grandío Seoane, *Orígenes*, p. 281; Macarro Vera, *Socialismo*, pp. 402–3.

[26] D. Ibárruri, *Memorias de Dolores Ibárruri, Pasionaria: la lucha y la vida* (Barcelona, 1985), pp. 227–33. See also Cruz, *En el nombre*, p. 109.

[27] *La Voz de Asturias*, 22 Feb. 1936.

[28] *Región*, 22 Feb. 1936; *El Noroeste*, 23 Feb. 1936.

[29] *El Noroeste*, 23 Feb. 1936; *La Tarde*, 28 Feb. 1936.

companies announced the readmission of workers fired after the insurrection before they were required to do so.[30] Municipal councils reinstated former employees and sacked those appointed after October 1934, annulled previous appointments and agreed monetary compensation for workers suspended after the insurrection, which symbolically reversed decisions taken by the local authorities in 1934 and 1935.[31] There was a renewed secularizing impulse across Spain manifest in initiatives like taxes on bell-ringing, a refusal to sponsor town fiestas and the removal of religious personnel from state-run welfare institutions.[32] In short, there appeared to be a return to life prior to October 1934. As Ramón García Montes, who was a child in the Asturian coalfields at the time, recalled, the 'life of our family returned to normal. Everything began to function as it had before the revolution'.[33] Yet the insurrection and repression had fractured communities in the coal valleys. There could be no return to the status quo *ante*.

Fractured communities

The shadow of October 1934 was ever present in 1936. The insurrection formed a key component of Asturian leftist identity on an individual and collective level that was invoked in speeches and in the press. Speaking to the crowd gathered in Oviedo to celebrate 1 May, the civil governor recalled the insurrectionary fallen and claimed their 'martyrdom and death [had] made possible the re-conquest of the Republic'.[34] For activists, the insurrection constituted the central marker not only of their radical credentials, but also of leftist – and by extension working class – identification in 1936. Previously they had reeled off their participation in strikes or boasted of their anticlericalism when defending themselves in the press; now they invoked the insurrection and repression.[35]

[30] M. Castejón Rodríguez, 'La patronal hullera asturiana en la Segunda República' (unpublished UNED PhD thesis, 2009), p. 430; *El Noroeste*, 26, 28 Feb. 1936; *Boletín oficial de la provincia de Oviedo*, 26 Feb. 1936.

[31] AO, Actas, 17 Jan. 1936 to 31 July 1937, ff. 20, 21; AA, Actas, 5 Dec. 1935 to 23 Apr. 1937, ff. 43–4, 67; AHPA, Actas, 24 Sept. 1935 to 20 May 1937, pp. 180–4. See also González Calleja, *En nombre*, pp. 263–4; Macarro Vera, *Socialismo*, pp. 409–10.

[32] AHPA, Actas comisión de la Diputación Provincial, 24 Sept. 1935 to 20 May 1937, pp. 269, 294–7, 349–50; F. Rey, *Paisanos en lucha: exclusión política y violencia en la Segunda República española* (Madrid, 2008), pp. 512–3; G. Collier, *Socialists of Rural Andalusia: Unacknowledged Revolutionaries of the Second Republic* (Stanford, Calif., 1987), p. 143.

[33] R. García Montes, Ángeles *rojos sin alas para volar* (Siero, 2009), p. 33.

[34] *La Tarde*, 4 May 1936.

[35] For October 1934 as a yardstick during the Civil War, see Graham, *Socialism*, pp. 19ff.

Political parties, trade unions and workforces conducted investigations and internal purges which probed conduct during the insurrection and the long 1935. The PCE cell in Sama met to judge the conduct of 'comrade Damián' for a statement he had signed when interrogated after the insurrection. Recognizing that this was 'a weakness that Bolsheviks must not have', he apologized and insisted that he had not informed on anyone. The cell, after hearing that Damián was a good comrade who had fought well in the insurrection, decided to express its disappointment but not to expel him.[36] Although such 'self-criticism' formed part of Communist techniques for enforcing party discipline and standards of conduct, the purges and investigations were not limited to Communist political culture.[37] Socialist Party and trade union sections organized assemblies to discuss and judge the conduct of members over the previous months and years.[38] Even leaders were scrutinized. The Socialist Group in Oviedo examined the conduct of eminent figures such as Manuel Vigil Montoto (the 'father' of Asturian socialism), Teodomiro Menéndez and Lorenzo López Mulero, the mayor of Oviedo.[39] Mining workforces also met to debate the conduct of their fellow workers during the repression and the election campaign.[40]

The purges could appear to be the result of the appeals by sectors of the JS for the 'Bolchevization' of the socialist movement in 1935. There were certainly increasing ties between the socialists and Communists in the labour and youth movements, although in different ways. Communists recognized the predominance of socialism in trade union organizing and their own failure, by agreeing to dissolve their own unions and join the socialist organizations at the end of the 1935. Communist SUM members affiliated to the SOMA.[41] The JS, meanwhile, had come increasingly under the influence of the Third International. Negotiations between the JS and the JC culminated in the merger of the two organizations in 1936 to form the United Socialist Youth under a decidedly Communist

[36] Actas de la reunión extraordinaria celebrada por la Célula de Barrio no. 1, de Sama para tratar el caso de las críticas al camarada Damián, CDMH, PS Gijón, H Series, box 15, file 16. T. Rees underlined the importance of 'willpower' in the PCE in 'Living up to Lenin: leadership culture and the Spanish Communist Party, 1920–1939', *History*, xcvii (2012), 230–55, at p. 252.

[37] See T. Rees, 'Deviation and discipline: anti-Trotskyism, Bolshevization and the Spanish Communist party, 1924–34', *Historical Research*, lxxxii (2009), 131–56.

[38] E.g. *La Tarde*, 26 Feb., 23 March 1936.

[39] *La Tarde*, 22 Apr., 13 May 1936. For biographies, see the 'Diccionario biográfico del socialismo español'.

[40] E.g. at the Mariana pit (*Región*, 25 March 1936).

[41] S. Juliá, *La izquierda del PSOE (1935–1936)* (Madrid, 1977), pp. 176–81.

line.[42] At the Asturian JS congress in April, reformists received a barrage of criticism.[43] Yet the purges of spring 1936 in the coalfields – whether in trade unions, party sections or at the workplace – overflowed any narrow attempt at 'Bolchevization' tied to particular political objectives. The purges and investigations were instead part of a broader crisis of the left and the community.

The purges were fuelled by allegations about members' and neighbours' conduct that circulated through rumours and whispering campaigns. The JS treasurer in La Moral was accused – falsely, it would later prove – of supplying arms to the security forces during the repression while the secretary of the Socialist Group in Siero declared himself the victim of a 'defamatory campaign', which included accusations of theft.[44] The potential consequences of the whispers were serious and could include expulsion from the union, or social ostracism. A younger mineworker accused of signing a petition in support of death sentences for revolutionaries received threats and contemplated suicide.[45] These whispering campaigns were not a brief flurry after the elections, but continued through the spring and into the summer.

To counter the rumours, the accused frequently turned to the press in order to appeal for public opinion to judge the matter. Frustrated at the allegations and snide comments directed at his wife and children, the secretary of the Socialist Group in Siero called on the 'people of Siero' to judge him.[46] Similarly, a civil guard 'comrade' wrote to *La Tarde* to end rumours about his brother, a municipal policeman, appealing to 'all citizens and comrades' to present evidence so that 'public opinion' could judge his conduct.[47] In these appeals, public opinion was coterminous with the left-wing community, endorsement from which would save the individual from ostracism. As the appeals recognized, investigations into an individual's conduct offered the possibility of absolution or redemption. The assemblies were a mechanism for remaking ties within a particular Socialist Group, trade union section or workforce. Through demonstrating one's innocence to comrades or neighbours, an individual could, in theory at least, absolve

[42] The classic study is R. Viñas, *La formación de las Juventudes Socialistas Unificadas (1934–1936)* (Madrid, 1978).

[43] For reports of the congress, see *La Tarde*, 24, 27 Apr., 4 May 1936.

[44] For La Moral, see *La Tarde*, 11 May 1936; for Siero, see *Avance*, 18 July 1936.

[45] *La Tarde*, 3 Feb. 1936.

[46] *Avance*, 18 July 1936.

[47] *La Tarde*, 4 March 1936. Accusations were often published, e.g., *La Tarde*, 9 March 1936.

him or herself and re-join a political group or be symbolically re-accepted into the community.

One of the difficulties for the accused was the retrospective application of standards of behaviour that did not account for the murky realities and pressures of the long 1935. Many, like Damián, had not lived up to the standards later demanded in 1936, whether due to fear, torture, indiscipline, personal relationships and loyalties, opportunism or even a shift in political outlook. A common self-defence strategy was to claim to have been duped into attending an AP rally or joining a right-wing union in 1935.[48] These assertions were probably a way of backpedalling fast now that the political context had shifted again.

The rumours, vehement public defences and expulsions reveal the profound crisis of community caused by the experience of the insurrection and repression. This crisis was also manifest in forms of public ostracism that revealed how difficult it was for opposing groups to occupy the same social spaces in 1936. SOMA members in Mieres were instructed to leave a bar if mineworkers who had obtained jobs after October 1934 entered and the owner refused to expel them.[49] The retreat of politics to the local sphere in order to grapple with the crisis of community is also evident in other contexts of political crisis. In working-class districts of Berlin, for example, as Swett observed, there was a shift to 'neighbourhood forms of justice', including shunning, as a defensive response to the economic and political crisis of the early 1930s. This retrenchment was a way of asserting power over an arena that activists could control – or at least attempt to do so.[50]

The threat of an economic sanction issued to the bar owner in Mieres carried echoes of a similar strategy that was particularly prevalent in 1936 – that of boycotting particular businesses. Boycotts were a form of economic ostracism as public collective punishment through the deliberate, collective cessation of normal patterns of consumption, with women heavily involved. Boycotts were not new in 1936, but they reached a scale and organization hitherto unseen.[51] Boycotts were organized for political reasons, which usually centred on an individual's role in the repression, or the way they voted or campaigned for opponents during the election campaign. Women

[48] *La Tarde*, 3 Feb., 6 May 1936.

[49] *La Tarde*, 27 March 1936.

[50] P. Swett, *Neighbors and Enemies: the Culture of Radicalism in Berlin, 1929–1933* (Cambridge, 2004), pp. 216, 221, 294.

[51] Particularly after the 1933 elections (*Avance*, 7 Dec. 1933, 16 Jan. 1934). For Gijón in 1931, see P. Radcliff, *From Mobilization to Civil War: the Politics of Polarization in the Spanish City of Gijón, 1900–1937* (Cambridge, 1996), p. 285.

in La Felguera tried to prevent female market-sellers from the neighbouring municipality of Siero from hawking their produce in La Felguera for allegedly having voted for the right.[52] The JS in Bimenes called for the boycott of two business owners, one of whom was accused of doing 'what he could to condemn us so that we rotted in prison' in 1935.[53] As a strategy, boycotts were not limited to the left: a female baker in Oviedo suffered a boycott for having spoken in support of the Popular Front. A committee of socialist women retaliated by calling on couriers to stop delivering bread to the women who objected to the baker.[54] The latter did not constitute a boycott in the strict sense of the word; rather the term had developed into a byword for ostracism or a collective economic sanction.

The distinctiveness of boycotts in 1936 lay not just in their number, but their high degree of organization and the fact that they functioned, like the purges, as a form of popular justice. Far from ad hoc measures, left-wing boycotts were formalized and rationalized. The Socialist and Communist Youths in Langreo issued 'certificates' for market-sellers so that 'every good citizen, left-wing man or woman' could ensure they bought from a 'reputable' supplier.[55] There were boycott commissions, meetings, and justifications of boycotts printed in the press.[56] Boycotts tended to be local affairs, but there were some limited attempts to organize them on a wider basis. Socialists from Langreo appealed to all Asturian working-class political and union organizations to send them information on which businesses they should boycott.[57]

The boycott commissions developed elaborate procedures which mimicked aspects of a trial. In June, the Sotrondio boycott commission organized an assembly attended by delegates from thirty-four organizations to discuss the cases of Manuel Ordiz and Manuel Álvarez. Those present agreed to uphold the boycott against Ordiz, who was accused of reporting individuals to the authorities and blackmailing others with the threat of denunciation, and decreed a boycott against Álvarez for collaborating with

[52] *El Noroeste*, 21 Feb. 1936; *La Tarde*, 23 March 1936.

[53] *La Tarde*, 18 March 1936.

[54] *La Tarde*, 8 Apr. 1936. For a similar case in Sanlúcar de Barrameda (Cádiz), see J. A. Viejo Fernández, *La Segunda República en Sanlúcar de Barrameda (1931–36)* (Sanlúcar de Barrameda, 2011), p. 316. For right-wing boycotts, see also *La Tarde*, 23 March 1936.

[55] *La Tarde*, 2 March 1936.

[56] For example, three cases in San Martín del Rey Aurelio (*La Tarde*, 15 May 1936).

[57] *La Tarde*, 16 March 1936. See also *Avance*, 7 July 1936; J. Uría, 'Asturias 1920–1937, el espacio cultural comunista y la cultura de la izquierda: historia de un diálogo entre dos décadas', in *Los comunistas en Asturias (1920–1982)*, ed. F. Erice (Gijón, 1996), p. 275.

the authorities by identifying revolutionaries. Attendees heard pre-trial reports, evidence was presented and heard from both sides, there was a face-to-face confrontation (*careo*), and the accused was allowed to defend himself. The case ended with a sentence, which could later be revised.[58] This formal mechanism of community justice identified local citizens, as represented by delegates from local organizations, as sovereign in these matters.

Imitating legal procedure attempted to show fairness and logic – at least in the eyes of the organizers. Boycotts were punitive and divided communities but, like the investigations into militants' conduct, they did allow redemption and re-integration into the community. Boycotts were an orderly, non-violent and circumscribed strategy. Once a sentence had been served, a boycott could be lifted.[59] They channelled desires for revenge and served as an attempt to remake communities in spring 1936 after their fracturing in the insurrection and repression. A boycott was a strategy for defending the working class and asserting leftist power, yet the militancy was undercut by fragility. Boycotts meant a retrenchment to combatting divisions in their own communities. This was an inward-facing radicalism.

It is difficult to see how the targets of boycotts, whose livelihoods were under threat, could consider a time-limited sentence as just or magnanimous, or the rhetoric as anything less than threatening given its militant edge. Socialist trade unions in Langreo declared their intention 'to boycott and sink all businessmen and professionals who during the period of persecution and ignominy suffered by the Spanish people served as snitches and stalwarts of reaction'.[60] The Antifascist Popular Front in Trubia instructed that the working class must not 'contribute with your money to enrich the murderers of the working class. All-out war on those who betray our class aspirations'.[61] Boycotts bred greater animosity towards the left and were symptoms of the chaos and *desgobierno* of the Popular Front. The quasi-judicial role adopted by boycott commissions seemed to show left-wing organizations' usurpation of the state, or the latter's abdication, in its role as arbiter in questions of justice.

Fears that the state's authority was under threat were fed by a further development: left-wing activists were assuming the task of stopping and searching individuals for arms in public spaces across the country in spring 1936. As *Región* astutely observed, the searches meant that 'the security

58 *Avance*, 7 July 1936.

59 E.g. see the case of Figaredo in *La Tarde*, 11 May 1936.

60 *La Tarde*, 16 March 1936.

61 *La Tarde*, 2 March 1936.

and safety of each individual depends on the sympathy or antipathy held towards us by those of the "Popular Front"'.[62] Yet the situation was not one of revolutionary violence or of widespread extra-judicial murder. It is impossible to measure the effects of these frequent, intimate encounters between left and right, but the removal of weapons by local political opponents could only have increased anger and resentment among rightists.

This improvised policing had begun in Asturias in January, when the government reinstated constitutional guarantees and left-wing political activities were normalized in public life. It became more prevalent across the country in late March after rumours that an order by the ministry of the interior authorized governors to appoint them to the role.[63] These '*guardias de vista*' worked alongside municipal police to search rightists, as occurred in El Entrego (San Martín del Rey Aurelio), although there were also reports that such guards had been arrested by the Civil Guard for carrying firearms.[64] The emergence of the patrols was part of the wider growth of left-wing militias. By May, the antifascist militias of the Communist MAOC, which had only established itself after the elections, were carrying out drills on Mount Naranco, overlooking Oviedo.[65]

Whereas in 1932 groups of JS members had pressured the municipal council for the Republican project to be implemented, the policing of the Republic in 1936 was different. The patrols confidently took the security of the Republic into their own hands. The groups moved between acting autonomously and requesting authorization to function as a para-state body. In early April, the PCE cell in Sama requested that the governor appoint them 'guarantors of order' so that they could prevent 'false rumours' or 'any surprises' from the armed forces. They also asked the mayor to ban rightists from leaving the municipality at 'certain times' to prevent alarm.[66] The militias saw themselves as upholding the values and authority of the Republican government – and their vision of the Republic more broadly – but in doing so, they undermined state power. At the beginning of

[62] *Región*, 30 Apr. 1936.

[63] The 'red police' in Malaga even received a daily wage. González Calleja, *En nombre*, p. 280. For restrictions on the right in La Mancha, Rey, *Paisanos*, pp. 522–31.

[64] *Región*, 1, 4 Apr. 1936.

[65] *La Tarde*, 6 May 1936; J. A. Blasco Rodríguez, 'Las MAOC y la tesis insurreccional del PCE', *Historia contemporánea*, xi (1994), 129–51, at pp. 140–2, 145; J. C. Gibaja Velázquez, 'La tradición improvisada: el socialismo y la milicia', *Historia contemporánea*, xi (1994), 107–27, at p. 123.

[66] Letter to Comarcal de Langreo from Célula de Calle de Sama, 3 Apr. 1936, CDMH, PS Gijón, H Series, box 15, file 18; letter from Frente Popular de Langreo to Comarcal de Langreo, 2 June 1936, CDMH, PS Gijón, H Series, box 15, file 18.

April, there were attempts to curb the activities of the non-official police, including a circular issued by the ministry of the interior ordering an end to the initiatives across the country, although this had little effect.[67]

The patrols derived from suspicions regarding right-wing activities and an intense distrust of the security forces bred by the repression. The memory of torture and beatings weighed heavily. The fixation with the security forces was not solely an Asturian phenomenon; newspapers like Madrid-based *Ayuda*, the newspaper of the SRI, also published long lists of the names of 'hangmen' from the repression.[68] Asturian newspapers printed not only testimonies of the repression and denunciations of officials for their roles, but also continued to report on the movements and transfers of civil and assault guards.[69] This was not *Avance*'s broad-brush 1934 narrative of a state 'at war' with the working class, but a much more personalized and intimate expression of a fissure between the state security forces and the left. Guards had names and faces rather than simply constituting the anonymous expression of state power.

Scrutiny of the security forces drew not only on the repression but also on concerns of collusion between the police and the right. The left had long been distrustful of the politics of the security forces, but in 1936, these fears became more acute. The Civil Guard in Aller were reported to be 'cohabiting' with the SCOM prior to the elections and the council investigated reports that a municipal employee had been training 'fascist militias' and disseminating propaganda 'against the republican regime'.[70] Accusations of double standards fed this criticism, according to which the Civil and Assault Guard frisked or beat Popular Front supporters, but ignored those performing fascist salutes and shouting death to the Republic.[71] The veracity of such claims in the polarized climate of 1936 is difficult to assess, but the wider European context, in which the police was more vigorous in clamping down on the left than the right, shows that it would not have been unusual.[72]

The vigilance of state power was also an important component in the construction of an antifascist identity that connected Asturias with the circumstances facing left-wing activists across the world. Focusing on the

[67] González Calleja, *En nombre*, pp. 284–5.

[68] *Ayuda*, 18 May 1936.

[69] E.g. *La Tarde*, 8 Apr. 1936.

[70] *La Tarde*, 7 Feb. 1936; AA, Actas, 5 Dec. 1935 to 23 Apr. 1937, f. 58.

[71] *La Tarde*, 27 March, 4 May 1936.

[72] E.g. for Germany, see D. Schumann, *Political Violence in the Weimar Republic, 1918–1933: Fight for the Streets and Fear of Civil War* (New York, 2012), p. 252.

plight of prisoners and alleging the arbitrary, excessive and politicized use of state power linked Asturias – and Spain – to the conditions under right-wing dictatorships in particular. A rally in Oviedo and a petition raised awareness and protested against the incarceration of Brazilian Communists, while the left-wing press, like the SRI's *Ayuda*, regularly called attention to the plight of imprisoned leftists across the world.[73] Such cases functioned as a mirror in which Spanish leftists could recognize their own plight and integrate themselves into a wider imagined community of antifascist struggle.

The militancy in the streets was in stark contrast to the situation at the workplace. The mining industry continued to struggle with a low demand for coal, yet labour conflict was practically absent until late May. Even then, the wave of strikes was 'channelled through institutional mechanisms'.[74] Short-time working and unpaid wages eventually led to a general mining strike called by the SOMA for 3 June.[75] The eighteen-day strike was remarkably peaceful, given the tense political situation. The SOMA presented a list of demands, most of which were unremarkable, such as the disbursement of unpaid wages and pensions. The final two, however, were more radical: the state seizure of mines abandoned or closed for unjustified reasons and the appointment of a commission to study the nationalization of the industry.[76] Yet the solution agreed to end the strike did not mention nationalization, but instead focused on pragmatic solutions to improve the workforce's living standards.[77] Soliciting nationalization was a radical rhetorical façade that veiled a more pragmatic interior.

The rhetoric embraced by the SOMA leadership and the newly re-launched *Avance* during the strike was radical. Graciano Antuña, the SOMA secretary, told the rank and file it was impossible to achieve all of their strike objectives within a bourgeois regime and invoked the revolutionary insurrection, in what had become an obligatory gesture.[78] For *Avance*, a revolutionary horizon was beginning to clear; the masses were no longer 'toys', but rather 'capable of guiding the tiller of the country on their own'.[79] But there was no real attempt to promote a revolutionary project behind the radical rhetoric. Instead, the words asserted a muscular role for the socialist

[73] *La Tarde*, 29 May 1936; *Avance*, 2 July 1936; e.g., *Ayuda*, 1 June 1936

[74] Castejón Rodríguez, 'La patronal', p. 433.

[75] *El Carbayón*, 4 June 1936; Castejón Rodríguez, 'La patronal', p. 436.

[76] *La Tarde*, 1 June 1936.

[77] Castejón Rodríguez, 'La patronal', p. 436. Details of the solution in *Avance*, 27 June 1936.

[78] *La Tarde*, 22 June 1936.

[79] *Avance*, 2 July 1936.

rank and file in defending the Republic. In contrast to 1934, the left seemed to be reassuringly in control.

The relative calm in the Asturian mines was not reflected in other parts of Spain. Official statistics for Zaragoza reported seventy strikes during the first half of 1936, 'as many … as had ever before been recorded in a single year'. This was due to a range of factors, including the resurgence of the CNT and a contraction in the sugar beet industry.[80] Unrest deepened in the south of the country in particular. Unemployment had grown thanks to the prolongation of the winter rain – 'the heaviest of the century' – which reduced the demand for labour, and strikes erupted once the harvest started.[81] At the same time, there was a much more muscular assertion of power by rural workers that undermined rural bosses' control of the labour process, such as unions dictating the length of the working day or deciding on the number of workers required for a task without regard for the employer's own needs. Such moves struck 'deeply at the autonomy of property owners'.[82]

Parts of Andalusia, Madrid, Toledo, Salamanca and Extremadura also saw land invasions, in which peasants entered and occupied land. Only in Extremadura did these take place on a mass scale: 81,000 *yunteros* occupied 270,000 hectares in late March.[83] The *yunteros* were hired hands with a head of oxen and, although a heterogeneous group, they tended to be peasants who had fallen on hard times. During the Republic, *yunteros* had invaded estates in 1932 and 1933 and 1,400 were settled in 1934 thanks to the 1932 agrarian reform law. But many were later evicted and sought to return to the land in 1936. The government began to circulate proposals in March to settle thousands of rural labourers and the FNTT, which experienced an influx of new members, stepped up its rhetoric. The promise of land reform precipitated the invasions of estates, which the government was powerless

[80] G. Kelsey, *Anarchosyndicalism, Libertarian Communism and the State: the CNT in Zaragoza and Aragon, 1930–37* (Amsterdam, 1991), pp. 136–7.

[81] E. Malefakis in *Agrarian Reform and Peasant Revolution in Spain: Origins of the Spanish Civil War* (New Haven, Conn., 1970), p. 367; F. Cobo Romero, *De campesinos a electores: modernización agraria en Andalucía, politización campesina y derechización de los pequeños propietarios y arrendatarios: el caso de la provincia de Jaén, 1931–1936* (Madrid, 2003), pp. 322, 324.

[82] Cobo Romero, *De campesinos*, p. 321; F. Espinosa Maestre, *La primavera del Frente Popular: los campesinos de Badajoz y el origen de la Guerra Civil (marzo–julio de 1936)* (Barcelona, 2007), p. 112; Collier, *Socialists*, pp. 140–1, the quotation at p. 141.

[83] J. Carmona and J. Simpson, 'Campesinos unidos o divididos? La acción colectiva y la revolución social de los *yunteros* durante la Segunda República en España (1931–1936)', *Historia Social*, lxxxv (2016), 123–44, at p. 130.

to stop.[84] Faced with the mass wave of direct action, the authorities legalized the occupations, with the result that many more peasants obtained land in 1936 than after the 1932 agrarian reform law. Over the following months, the government worked hard to reorganize the Land Reform Institute and prepare a bill for a more vigorous, wide-ranging land reform than the toothless 'reform of the land reform' of 1935. But, in the eyes of those opposed to the Popular Front, retroactive legalization only confirmed a vision of a lawless rural society which the government was unable and unwilling to resist.

The layers of the Republican state – municipal, provincial and national – thus faced a number of challenges in spring 1936. The resolution of these problems was not aided by the instability of the parliament, despite the Popular Front majority in the Cortes. The parliament did not meet until mid March and investigations into electoral fraud meant the make-up of the Cortes was not agreed until April (and elections were rerun in Cuenca and Granada in early May). Almost as soon as the Cortes sessions began, President Alcalá Zamora was impeached on a procedural technicality. On 10 May, Manuel Azaña replaced him as president of the Republic. The elevation of the icon of left Republicanism to presidential office removed an able politician from the nitty gritty of everyday governmental politics. Azaña had hoped that Prieto would follow him as prime minister, but Prieto was hamstrung by his own party. The socialist left refused to countenance a revival of a Republican-socialist coalition government as the socialist internal struggle between the Caballeristas and Prietistas continued.[85] Instead, the premiership fell to the Galician IR politician, Santiago Casares Quiroga, who formed a Republican administration. Due to obstructions in parliament, the government tended to rule through decrees that were later transformed into laws and continued to extend the state of alarm until the Civil War.[86]

The weak government and the challenges facing the country led to some brief negotiations aimed at forming a national unity government, although the talks and the plan were doomed to fail. CEDA moderates Luis Lucía and Manuel Giménez Fernández entered discussions with socialists to

[84] This account is based on S. Riesco Roche, *La reforma agraria y los orígenes de la Guerra Civil: cuestión yuntera y radicalización patronal en la provincia de Cáceres (1931–1940)* (Madrid, 2006); Espinosa, *La primavera*; Malefakis, *Agrarian reform*, pp. 36–71.

[85] For socialist politics, see Graham, *Socialism*, ch. 2. For an overview of Republican politics, see Preston, *Coming of the Spanish Civil War*, pp. 183–5.

[86] M. Bizcarrondo, *Historia de la UGT*, iii: *Entre la democracia y la revolución, 1931–1936* (6 vols, Madrid, 2008), pp. 186–7; González Calleja, *Contrarrevolucionarios*, p. 243.

form an administration to stabilize social conflict.[87] Talks had little chance of success even before they began. The socialist movement was divided and there was no sign of support from the wider CEDA, in which anti-Republican sentiment was fiercer than ever. Gil Robles, who had not taken the negotiations seriously, terminated them on 2 June.[88]

Rather than seeking solutions to the problems facing the Republic, Gil Robles was more interested in attacking the regime. Together with Renovación Española leader José Calvo Sotelo, he used the platform afforded by the Cortes to accuse the government of promoting chaos and disorder across the country. In his speeches to parliament, Calvo Sotelo combined denunciations of violence, strikes and alleged chaos across the country to criticize the left and the impotency of the government. He announced that if a state without strikes and disorder was a 'fascist state', he 'share[d] the idea of that [kind of] state, I believe in it [and] I declare myself a fascist'.[89] An editorial in *Región* at the end of May expressed a similar sentiment: the alleged crisis of authority was more pressing than upholding the tenets of democratic rule. Other countries had shown that a move away from democracy was 'not a catastrophe'.[90]

Both Gil Robles and Calvo Sotelo were cognizant of plans to destroy Republican democracy. By spring 1936 there were multiple conspiracies against the regime, which eventually coalesced around the project designed by General Emilio Mola, who was stationed in the Carlist heartland of Navarra (although Mola struggled to sign up the Carlists to his project). In late May, Mola, the 'director', began dictating the instructions which would provide the foundation for the July rebellion. Through June and July, Gil Robles instructed CEDA cadres to support the coup when it occurred and transferred CEDA funds to the conspirators.[91] Gil Robles's actions were largely symbolic, for the CEDA's star had been eclipsed. In the wake of the elections, its youth organization, the JAP, had all but collapsed as many members switched to the FE-JONS – as many as 15,000 overall, including half of the membership of the JAP in Gijón.[92] The growth in membership and activity of the FE-JONS came despite the jailing of its leader, José Antonio Primo de Rivera, and the party having to operate underground, as the Republican authorities grappled with

87 Montero, *La CEDA*, ii. 178–201, 206–7.

88 J. Tusell, *Historia de la democracia cristiana en España* (2 vols, Madrid, 1974), i. 358.

89 González Calleja, *Contrarrevolucionarios*, p. 334.

90 *Región*, 28 May 1936.

91 González Calleja, *Contrarrevolucionarios*, pp. 340–88.

92 González Calleja, *Contrarrevolucionarios*, p. 358; Suárez Cortina, *El fascismo*, p. 187.

its anti-left and anti-Republican agitation, particularly the problem of violence.

Violence

Late on 14 March, Manuel José G. Q. sat drinking cider in a bar called 'La Polesa' in Sama. Three individuals entered the bar and started an argument with him about politics, accusing Manuel José of being a plain-clothes civil guard and a fascist. When he pulled out his work permit and military papers as evidence of proletarian identity, they claimed them to be false and threw them on the floor. A brawl ensued. Manuel José drew a knife and stabbed his three assailants, one of whom died instantly from a wound to the heart.[93] Two days previously and in very different circumstances, the leading socialist jurist Luis Jiménez de Asúa was fired upon as he left his home on Goya Street in Madrid. Jiménez de Asúa, who had presided over the commission which had drafted the 1931 Constitution, survived, but his bodyguard died from his injuries.[94]

These two incidents capture some of the principal characteristics of violence in spring 1936. Both were brief, small-scale encounters resulting in one fatality.[95] Manuel José's reaction was founded on defending his honour as a working-class male. Policing a particular space was also central to the incident in La Polesa. Manuel José's opponents aggressively policed the local tavern as their social space: what right did a plain-clothes civil guard have to be in a working-class bar in Sama in March 1936? The violent policing of working-class spaces was also evident in other targeted attacks at the level of local politics or the community, from two brothers killing a teacher for denouncing them after the insurrection to cars being stopped and fired at in Moreda and Laviana, the former belonging to the parish priest.[96] These attacks were often part of a of tit-for-tat chain of escalating encounters between left and right at the local level.

The murder of Jiménez de Asúa was the result of FE-JONS switching to a new a strategy of targeted assassinations, the aim of which was to incite a climate of violence and chaos. The strategy of targeted killings was also employed in Asturias. In Asturias, unidentified assailants killed

[93] AHPA, AP, box 78441, file 62 (1936).

[94] Details taken from *El Sol*, 13 March 1936.

[95] In 77% of incidents of political violence involving fatalities only one person died (González Calleja, 'La necro-lógica').

[96] L. Borque López, *El magisterio primario en Asturias (1923–1937): sociedad y educación* (Oviedo, 1991), pp. 210–11; *Región*, 1, 23 May 1936. For similar 'ambushes' towards the end of the Weimar Republic, see Schumann, *Political Violence*, pp. 253–64.

Alfredo Martínez, ex-minister and PRLD leader, at his home, and there was an attempt on the life of the civil governor in May.[97] In Sotrondio, an individual reported that six men had threatened to kill him for political reasons and in Siero hired hit men attempted to murder a teacher who led the Socialist Group.[98] The motives included revenge and intimidation. The two were linked: while murders could be an attempt to frighten opponents into submission, the far right also intended to spark an escalating dynamic of attack and counter-attack in order to spread a sense of chaos and undermine Republican authority.[99] The rightist press amplified these incidents by grouping them together on newspaper pages.

The spectacle of political violence in public space did not disappear. Violence clustered around demonstrations as opponents attempted to disrupt collective expressions of strength or project an image of disorder on a public stage. In early April, an impromptu celebratory march in Oviedo to welcome the return of those exiled in the USSR after the insurrection led to a brawl when a passer-by shouted '*arriba España*!' The Assault Guard beat several of the marchers and a fascist was arrested.[100] On the anniversary of the proclamation of the Republic, a similar scene occurred in Ourense while in Madrid a civil guard in civilian clothes and a student were killed when shots and small explosions interrupted the military procession. The funeral for the civil guard turned into a right-wing anti-Republican demonstration, at which five died and 170 were arrested.[101]

Iconoclastic and anticlerical violence also returned across Spain. The attacks included arson attacks on churches and shrines and the destruction of stone crosses in public spaces. A recent calculation estimates there were thirty-five such attacks in Asturias in spring 1936.[102] In a return to the early years of the Republic – and in contrast to October 1934 – the targets were

[97] *Región*, 24 March 1936; *La Tarde*, 27 March, 4 May 1936.

[98] *Región*, 29 Feb. 1936; *Avance*, 4 July 1936. Preston noted the hiring of hit men in *Coming of the Spanish Civil War*, p. 187.

[99] For this dynamic in action in the Aragonese town of Calatayud, see N. Moreno Medina, *La ciudad silenciada: Segunda República y represión fascista en Calatayud, 1931–1939* (Calatayud, 2008), pp. 84–6.

[100] *La Tarde*, 3 Apr. 1936.

[101] J. Prada Rodríguez, *De la agitación republicana a la represión franquista (Ourense 1934–1939)* (Barcelona, 2006), p. 91; Cruz, *En el nombre*, pp. 134–7; A. Barea's recollections in *The Forging of a Rebel* (London, 2018 [1946]), pp. 474–6.

[102] M. Álvarez Tardío and R. Villa García, 'El impacto de la violencia anticlerical en la primavera de 1936 y la respuesta de las autoridades', *Hispania sacra*, lxv (2013), 693–764, at p. 705. See also M. Thomas, *The Faith and the Fury: Popular Anticlerical Violence and Iconoclasm in Spain, 1931–1936* (Eastbourne, 2013), pp. 69–70, 72.

overwhelmingly buildings and objects as opposed to the bodies of priests or religious brothers. The attacks tended not to occur in large urban centres in the coalfields, but in more remote and rural areas, where the political right and Catholic observance were stronger, and grouped in waves such as around Holy Week.[103] This renewed anticlericalism did not prevent the public celebration of Corpus Christi. The election results had revealed the village of Boo to be polarized politically, yet the Corpus procession took place in the streets without a problem.[104]

Despite a dominant image of state helplessness and left-wing proto-revolutionary violence, the state security forces caused most fatalities as the authorities attempted to respond to left- and right-wing militancy.[105] The state also used arrests in order to curb violence and reassert its authority. The attempted assassination of Jiménez de Asúa in March shocked the country and prompted a crackdown on FE-JONS, which was forced to operate underground. FE-JONS leaders were arrested across the country. Primo de Rivera was detained two days after the attack, and tried and re-arrested on different charges in March and April.[106] Thirty-seven were jailed in the first wave of arrests in Asturias. Further waves of arrests of rightists – Falangists and CEDA members – and fines followed in April and May.[107]

Supporters of FE-JONS challenged the arrests, which created a further problem for the authorities. The right, including *Región*, bemoaned the alleged chaos and lack of authority even as the state asserted its power by arresting right-wing leaders. The detentions only confirmed the narrative that the right was being persecuted by a state controlled by the left. Deserted by state power, citizens now had to assume the 'terrible' responsibility to take 'justice into their own hands'.[108] When arrests were made in Aller, which was developing into a centre of the radical right, sympathizers came out to support them en masse, performing the fascist salute and crying 'viva Catholic Spain!'. *Región* revelled in the defiance shown towards the Republican authorities:

[103] Álvarez Tardío and Villa García, 'El impacto', pp. 750–2. See *Región* for Valdecuna and Villoria (*Región*, 17 March, 11 Apr., 20 May 1936). See also AHPA, AP, box 79465, files 9, 96, 133 (1936).

[104] *Región*, 2 July 1936.

[105] As shown by Cruz and González Calleja. See the latter's 'La necro-lógica' and Cruz, *En el nombre*, p. 179.

[106] S. Payne, *Fascism in Spain, 1923–1977* (Madison, Wis., 1999), pp. 190–3.

[107] *Region*, 15 March, 21, 24 Apr. 1936; J. M. García de Tuñón Aza, *Apuntes para una historia de la Falange asturiana* (Oviedo, 2001), p. 85; *La Tarde*, 11 May 1936.

[108] *Región*, 24 March 1936.

> Not in Bello, nor in Casomera, nor in Collanzo, nor in Felechosa, nor in other areas does the oppressive politics practised by the municipal authorities [in Aller] … receive adulation or sympathy. The fascist militias are enjoying greater influence and growth in all of Aller ever since their persecution and despite having been dissolved.[109]

Arrests legitimized their anti-Republican position. In Aller, conflict over religion was an exacerbating factor in the arrest of right-wing leaders. The protests were energized by heightened tensions locally over the removal of religious education, which had long been a vexing and divisive issue in the municipality.[110]

Left-wing activists did not conceal their antipathy towards the security forces, but in contrast, aligned themselves with the Republic – or a particular idea of the Republic. The socialists strongly identified with Bosque, the IR civil governor, for he embodied the more assertive and uncompromising left-oriented view of the Republic that matched their own.[111] They exhibited willingness to police their towns and villages as they considered the Republic increasingly incapable of defending itself. The militant attitude was aligned with the Republican project as the regime was still identified as supporting their interests. The Communist newspaper *Mundo Obrero* declared in mid June that the government could 'rely on the militias for whatever it takes to maintain and develop the policies undertaken under the banner of the Popular Front'.[112] They saw their own militias policing the streets as unproblematic insofar as they were working to uphold the Republic.

An incident in late May underlined leftist distrust of the security forces and the difficulties faced by the civil governor. On the evening of 23 May, shots were fired in the midst of a crowd enjoying a two-night open-air public party in central Oviedo. JS and JC members disarmed the individual responsible. Plain-clothes assault guards intervened, but were also disarmed, beaten and insulted by the youths, who handed the weapons to the authorities. The following evening, the Assault Guard attempted to heal its wounded pride by reasserting its authority. A 'tall, young, blond individual' fired into the air 'as though it were a signal', and assault guards fired into the crowd. The lights went out and panic ensued. The governor, who had forbidden the presence of the Assault Guard after the previous evening,

[109] *Región*, 6 May 1936; *La Tarde*, 6 Apr. 1936.

[110] *Región*, 12, 15, 17, 21 March 1936.

[111] When Bosque was forced to resign, telegrams of support and protest were sent by political parties, trade unions and municipal councils, and a strike was called in Mieres (*Avance*, 7 July 1936).

[112] Cited in Blasco Rodríguez, 'Las MAOC', p. 138.

ordered the guards return to their barracks. They disobeyed. Two trucks of guards attended the scene and opened fire. The mayor, public prosecutor and other political leaders rushed to the scene and managed to diffuse the incident. More than 100 shots had been fired, leaving twenty-one injured. *La Tarde* claimed that the attack had been orchestrated.[113]

The Assault Guard's aggressive reaction to being disarmed by citizens supports arguments that emphasize the importance of honour in how the security forces understood their collective identity and policing role.[114] It is not clear if the attack was premeditated, but it is difficult to imagine it was not connected to the brawl the previous evening. A signal from a youth with a Teutonic appearance verges on the cliché, but does match the model of a Falangist strategy of tension in which there were attempts to spark an escalating spiral of violence and in so doing, spread a sense of chaos. *Región* was unusually subdued in its depiction of the incident and minimized the importance of the injuries.[115] This contrasted starkly with its habitual amplification of conflict and violence.

The reaction of the left to the incident was an exhibition of collective power and a willingness to take responsibility for policing the local population. The morning after the incident, the unions shut down Oviedo with a general strike, which continued until midday the following day. Using a general strike to close down a locality as a gesture of protest and to demonstrate peaceful left-wing control had occurred on previous occasions, as in Sama in September 1934. But this time it affected the provincial capital, and left-wing authority was more organized and assertive. Rather than simply closing shops and factories or providing an escort for a funeral procession, activists' roles extended further. Circulation was controlled through safe-conducts, a 'red guard' kept order and traffic access into the city was restricted. Even the national cycle race, the *Vuelta a España*, was turned away from the city.[116] *Región* accused the left of holding the city to ransom in a much more vocal criticism of the strike than of the Assault Guard violence which had precipitated it.[117]

The incident was not the only occasion in which the security forces were absent as the left controlled the streets. López Mulero, the socialist mayor

[113] *La Tarde*, 27 May 1936; *Región*, 27 May 1936.

[114] F. Chamberlin, 'Honor-bound: the military culture of the Civil Guard and the political violence of the Spanish Second Republic, 1931–1936' (unpublished UCSD PhD thesis, 2017).

[115] *Región*, 27 May 1936.

[116] *La Tarde*, 27 May 1936; *Región*, 27 May 1936.

[117] *Región*, 27 May 1936.

of Oviedo, requested that the security forces not be present at a Popular Front rally in March. The civil governor agreed.[118] The 1 May celebrations took place in similar circumstances and *La Tarde* proudly highlighted the lack of 'a single incident ... which demonstrates that we do not need foreign bodies to maintain order'.[119] Such sentiments recalled declarations prior to the revolutionary insurrection, but much more sharply defined than in 1934 was the contrast between the security force's policing methods and the order, discipline and serenity that were the watchwords of leftist militancy and antifascist identity in 1936. In his speech on 1 May, Mulero eulogized the 'discipline' of the 'red militias' and their massed ranks as 'the firmest bulwark of the security of the Republic'. They were not simply political activists but a disciplined 'proletarian Army', and the crowd's applause allegedly even sounded like a 'machine gun'.[120] At least this was the idealized image that socialist ranks had of themselves as antifascist militants.

The rallies, strikes and demonstrations in spring 1936 were an exhibition of left-wing strength. Organizations had recovered after operating underground during the long 1935. There had been a rapid growth in Socialist Youth, the reorganization of women's groups and an intensification of political activities involving men and women. Julia Morán, who had criticized the political and social pressures in Laviana in 1934, declared her satisfaction at returning to the struggle after 'seventeen months of forced silence'. She felt 'more revolutionary' and ready to prepare for the 'definitive battle'.[121] In contrast to other areas of Spain, where the Popular Front 'never extended beyond the election committee', in Asturias it became a 'vehicle for working-class demands and action' thanks to local traditions of organization and political activity, although these activities were not always sustained and there were complaints that not all members were engaged.[122] For *Avance*, Popular Front committees were 'organisms of combat then and should

[118] On these themes, see also Cruz, *En el nombre*, pp. 146–7.

[119] *La Tarde*, 4, 6 May 1936.

[120] *La Tarde*, 4 May 1936.

[121] See the list of JS sections prepared for the JS congress in Apr., CDMH, PS Gijón, F Series, box 92, file 3. For female activism, see M. A. Mateos, *¡Salud, compañeras! Mujeres socialistas en Asturias (1900–1937)* (Oviedo, 2007), pp. 190–5 and for a personal testimony, see Á. Flórez Peón, *Memorias de Ángeles Flórez Peón "Maricuela"* (Oviedo, 2009), pp. 65–70. For Morán, see *La Tarde*, 18 March 1936.

[122] A. Shubert, 'A reinterpretation of the Spanish Popular Front: the case of Asturias', in *The French and Spanish Popular Fronts: Comparative Perspectives*, ed. M. Alexander and H. Graham (Cambridge, 1989), pp. 223–4. For warnings about the lack of political engagement, see the letter from Purificación Tomás to Lola Rivas, 29 May 1936, CDMH, PS Gijón, H series, box 15, file 16.

continue to be so now'.[123] Unity again became an important watchword. By mid July, the Popular Front and re-launched Workers' Alliances appear to have combined into an entangled and indistinguishable whole, with an increasing prominence accorded to the language of antifascism and the need for unity of action to forestall an attack from the right.[124]

In other areas of Spain, the left flexed its muscles in the spring of 1936, from unions pushing closed-shop practices to municipal councils introducing new taxes on the Church or wresting back control of hiring processes.[125] This assertion of left-wing power meant a destabilization of the traditional social order and economic practices, which was experienced as an encroachment and a threat by certain groups. In areas like Jaén, smallholding peasants who periodically relied on wage labourers turned to the radical right to defend their interests. In the Asturian coalfields, the situation was different. Rather than the left encroaching on terrain traditionally the preserve of local elites, such as management of the labour process, there was a recovery and reassertion of left-wing power at the local level. A greater sense of change was palpable in Oviedo, which had its first socialist mayor, and where left-wing demonstrations were more common than in previous years. For rightist inhabitants of Oviedo, the sound of dynamite to signal the 1 May parade can only have revived memories of October 1934 and stoked fears of a revolutionary threat.

Some prefer to see this encroachment, whether the growth in left-wing organizations or the more radical assertion of power by new municipal authorities, as a 'revolution' or 'dictatorship' from below.[126] There was an assertive, radical left attempting to shift the dynamics of power at the local level, but no clear revolutionary project. Largo Caballero had returned to his revolutionary posturing, but there was no revolutionary plan to back his rhetoric. For the socialist left, the 'erosion' the government was suffering was a problem for the Republican parties rather than affecting the Popular Front or indeed the Republic itself.[127] Nor was the PCE conspiring to bring down the Republic, for the Comintern policy of Popular Frontism required the Communists support Republican democracy. The CNT, which did not form part of the Popular Front, repudiated the insurrectionary path at its congress in Zaragoza in May.

[123] *Avance*, 28 June 1936.

[124] E.g., the creation of an 'Antifascist Popular Front' in Oñón (Mieres) (*Avance*, 11 July 1936).

[125] Prada Rodríguez, *De la agitación*, pp. 102–3; Cobo Romero, *De campesinos*, pp. 328–9.

[126] E.g. Macarro Vera, *Socialismo*, p. 428.

[127] Juliá, *La izquierda*, pp. 30–3.

Different visions of the Republic continued to compete in 1936, as they had done since the beginning of the Republic. In 1936, the Republic demanded on the streets of Asturias – and more widely – was an uncompromisingly militant social Republic, the Popular Front's prize for having won the elections. In some ways, the militancy was similar to the socialist rhetoric prior to the 1933 elections, but rather than focusing on the socialists gaining power, the rhetoric in 1936 was a broader principle of a leftist, worker-led Republic, which would impose itself on those who would not accept reform. This vision of the Republic would provide a foundation for the antifascist reconstruction of the Republican ideal during the Civil War.

There was a new wave of violence in Asturias at the end of June and rumours spread of a possible uprising. A bombing campaign by the far right targeted the Asturian leftist publications *La Tarde* and *Combate*, a Communist newspaper kiosk, the PCE headquarters in Oviedo, and the town hall and a bank in Sama.[128] Patrols by left-wing militants increased at the end of June as rumours spread of a possible uprising, and there were reports of right-wing 'subversive elements' sleeping at the Civil Guard post in Aller.[129] Socialists in Siero reported suspicious movements to the Civil Guard who then searched the homes of 'fascists'.[130]

The socialist press swung between frustration and bullishness. *Avance* was exasperated that the state refused to protect left-wing activists who were the first line of defence for the Republic. Not only were individuals 'at the service' of the Republic on trial for seizing weapons from their opponents and handing them to the authorities, but they also received longer prison sentences than the owners of the firearms.[131] At the same time, self-assured militias in Sama claimed to be disappointed when a rumoured uprising did not materialize.[132] *Avance* piled pressure on rank-and-file militants. The security of the Republic was a personal responsibility; they had to be vigilant and embody the necessary militant attitude at all times:

> All citizens have to be faithful guardians of the basic freedoms that we enjoy. The defence of the Popular Front entails the persecution of open or hidden enemies. Going out onto the streets on a given night is not enough to defend the security of the regime. The security of the regime relies on making it invincible to any attack, whatever its level of importance.[133]

[128] *Avance*, 7, 8 July 1936.

[129] *Avance*, 30 June, 1, 2 July 1936.

[130] *Avance*, 4 July 1936.

[131] *Avance*, 1, 11, 14 July 1936.

[132] *Avance*, 4 July 1936.

[133] *Avance*, 2 July 1936.

Yet beneath this radical, bellicose posturing, internal purges and boycotts continued as the left continued to attempt to police its own internal ranks and reaffirm its hegemony over the local community.[134] The radicalism was fragile and defensive.

For *Avance*, the situation was 'like in 1933, but worse'. No longer were the forces of 'reaction' content with gaining control of the Republic, they were now intent on destroying it.[135] Yet there was no suggestion of a creeping, conspiratorial threat of fascism installing itself from government, as in 1934. The fascist threat was in the street. *Avance* demanded that the authorities deal with fascist '*pistolerismo*' or else the 'working class' would.[136] In fact, it would be an escalating case of *pistolerismo* in Madrid that hastened the coming of war. On the evening of 12 July, José Castillo, a socialist Assault Guard lieutenant, was shot dead by rightist gunmen.[137] Hours later assault guards retaliated by murdering Renovación Española leader Calvo Sotelo. His death convinced the conspirators to bring forward the planned coup.[138]

On Friday 17 July, news filtered through to the peninsula of an uprising in the Spanish Protectorate in Morocco. The following day crowds gathered in the streets of Madrid outside union buildings and cafes to share news, rumours and to listen to the radio.[139] In Asturias, most of *Avance*'s front page was blanked out by order of the censor, leaving only a snippet of a report on workers' patrols and a cartoon showing muscular workers of the Workers' Alliance standing in the way of a train whistling monarchist conspiracies that was driven by Azaña.[140] The civil governor, political leaders and union officials gathered in the civil government building in central Oviedo to monitor developments. They were joined by the military commander of the province, Colonel Aranda, who enjoyed the confidence of both Republican loyalists and the rebels. Aranda readily agreed to a request from Indalecio Prieto, socialist leader and a personal friend, to send a column of mineworkers to defend Madrid. Three thousand volunteers departed Asturias for the capital that same 18 July. The following day, a Sunday,

[134] E.g. *Avance*, 26 June 1936.

[135] *Avance*, 26 June 1936.

[136] *Avance*, 9 July 1936.

[137] Cruz attributes the death to Falangists (*En el nombre*, pp. 138, 198). Ian Gibson's research led him to identify Carlists as responsible, as cited in J. Casanova and C. Gil Andrés, *Twentieth-Century Spain: a History* (Cambridge, 2014), p. 156.

[138] Details in González Calleja, *Contrarrevolucionarios*, pp. 327–9.

[139] Barea, *Forging*, pp. 528–9; R. Fraser, *Blood of Spain: an Oral History of the Spanish Civil War* (New York, 1979), p. 54.

[140] *Avance*, 18 July 1936.

the streets of Oviedo were quiet and cafes deserted. Having conveniently reduced the threat posed by left-wing activists, Aranda slowly concentrated the province's security forces in the capital. That evening, as a light drizzle started to fall, Aranda intercepted an order sent from Madrid for his own arrest and finally made his move by declaring himself for the rebellion.[141]

[141] For first-hand accounts of the coup in Oviedo, see J. A. Cabezas, *Asturias: catorce meses de guerra civil* (Madrid, 1975), pp. 14–21; C. Martínez, *Al final del sendero* (Gijón, 1990), pp. 223–4; J. Ambou, *Los comunistas en la resistencia nacional republicana: la guerra en Asturias, el País Vasco y Santander* (Madrid, 1978), pp. 13–19.

Conclusion

The military coup of July 1936 divided the country. It was successful in an arc of north-central Spain, from Navarra in the north-east through Castile to Galicia in the north-west, and also gained a foothold in the south in Cádiz and Seville. The coup failed in much of the south, east and centre of the country, as well as a strip along the northern coast consisting of the Basque Country, the province of Santander, and Asturias, which remained in the hands of the Republic. Aranda's rising meant that Oviedo, however, lay in rebel hands and the city was surrounded until Francoist forces carved a corridor to relieve it in October 1936. The final offensive to end the war in the north began in spring 1937 when Francoist forces pushed through the Basque Country, moving westwards. Bilbao fell in June, Santander followed in August and the Francoist army entered Asturias in late summer. Resistance in the mountainous east of the province, particularly at the battle of El Mazucu, only served to delay the inevitable. On 21 October 1937, almost exactly three years after the defeat of the revolutionary insurrection, the last ships transporting Republican commanders, troops and citizens departed Gijón. The Spanish Civil War lasted another eighteen months, but military hostilities in the north had come to an end.

The military rebellion of July 1936 failed as a coup, but paralysed the Republican state, 'shattering both army and police command structures'.[1] The centrifugal forces unleashed by the coup radically shifted the locus of political power to the locality or the neighbourhood. Republican and left-wing parties and unions formed local committees to control their town or village, which often entailed pursuing revolutionary policies, as they had done in Asturias in October 1934. Over the following months, the Republican state was slowly rebuilt and drew competing sources of authority under its control. Reconstruction in a civil war during the 1930s also entailed a sharper antifascist re-drawing of the Republic.

This recasting of the Republic along antifascist lines owed much to the radicalism of the pre-war years described in this book. This current of radicalism also explains why many activists took up arms to resist the

[1] H. Graham, *The Spanish Republic at War, 1936–1939* (Cambridge, 2002), p. 79. To what extent the state collapsed is still debated. For a critical meditation, see R. Cruz, *En el nombre del pueblo: república, rebelión y guerra en la España de 1936* (Madrid, 2006), pp. 247–8.

rebellion. The number of volunteers who seized arms or wielded those provided by the reluctant Republican authorities to resist the rebellion should not be exaggerated, for the image of a spontaneous 'people at arms' was romanticized and a product of Republican war culture.[2] Yet the energetic initial response to the coup observable in Asturias is inexplicable without pre-war radicalism, which was central to the emergence of antifascism and to the defence of the Republic during the Civil War. Historians have emphasized that antifascism was a transnational movement and a 'culture of exile' during the 1930s, yet this book underlines that it also emerged from the political culture and social circumstances of small communities.[3]

These communities were not just the location of radicalism. This book has argued that 'community' is central to understanding the dynamics of radicalism. The lines of fracture at the local level and the politicized context of the Second Republic led to a fierce contest to capture the nature of the community and imbue it with a particular political character. Articles in the press, demonstrations and even episodes of violence were all ways of delineating the boundaries of the community. This process of policing was central to how politics was understood and, by extension, how the process of radicalization unfolded. Importantly, while the left was hegemonic in the Asturian coalfields during the 1930s, it did not monopolize politics and culture. Catholicism continued to play a role in coalfield communities, whether in the company schools, annual fiestas or the presence of churches and shrines, and the political right existed in the coalfields, even if it was much less organized and visible than the left. Moreover, even as the socialist SOMA was the dominant union, anarchism had thousands of followers and Communist influence outweighed its very small size. Common reference points and a shared political idiom provided the foundations for mutual understanding but also bitter antagonism.

The local community, whether imagined as left-wing, anticlerical or Catholic, was a vital reference point for the understanding of politics at the local level and this was related to the wider national and international context.[4] Factors like anticlericalism, policing and fascism became drivers

[2] The volunteers were a minority and over the course of the war, the Republic would have to rely on conscription. See M. Alpert, *The Republican Army in the Spanish Civil War, 1936–1939* (Cambridge, 2013) and J. Matthews, *Reluctant Warriors: Republican Popular Army and Nationalist Army Conscripts in the Spanish Civil War, 1936–1939* (Oxford, 2012).

[3] E. Traverso, *Fire and Blood: the European Civil War, 1914–1945* (London, 2016), p. 262.

[4] In a similar vein, see J. Häberlen's emphasis on how German leftists understood the political options available to them in the early 1930s in 'Scope for agency and political options: the German working-class movement and the rise of Nazism', *Politics, Religion and Ideology*, xiv (2013), 377–94.

of radicalism because they were interpreted according to a combination of local, national and international frames of reference. The bonds between the local left-wing community and the wider state soured in the spring of 1934 and were embittered by the experience of the repression after the insurrection. These affective relationships shaped political understanding and were central to the emergence of radicalism. Terms like 'alienation' and 'disaffection' are common in interpretations of the crisis of liberal democracy in interwar Europe, but often limited to the realm of metaphor rather than embedded in the mechanics of political processes. This book has shown how the decisions of actors in the coalfields were shaped by how local political experience was perceived to align or diverge from the wider state. This underscores the importance of collective mental frameworks, fears and experiences of frustration and humiliation in the context of the Second Republic as interpreted through actions and language.

A variety of factors contributed to the radicalizing dynamic in Asturias. Radicalism first emerged in 1932 against the backdrop of a desire to see the local fruition of Republican secularizing policies, the re-emergence of the political right, the declining fortunes of the mining industry and intra-left rivalry. Importantly, the context of the Republic changed what it meant to be radical for the activists in the coalfields. In a democratic, secularizing regime buttressed by socialist support, the political playing field had shifted. Whereas socialists had been content to proclaim their moderation and sensibleness in 1931, the following year they attempted to wrest back the self-descriptor 'radical' from their political rivals and combine it with moderate political practice. Radicalism was therefore contingent and could be inflected with different qualities, even if the socialists were unsuccessful on this occasion. The socialist leadership also faced a challenging situation in the lines. Far from radicalizing into line with the rank and file as is frequently described, the SOMA only succeeded in alienating sections of the mining workforce, particularly younger workers as the economic situation in the coalfields deteriorated. The relationship between the union leadership and the membership continued to be fractious through 1933 and 1934.

These factors combined with other developments, including tenant activism and political tensions at the local level and anger at the attempted Sanjurjo coup, to create a wave of frustration. But this led to the crystallization of a socialist demand for a particular kind of Republic – a *social* Republic – as opposed to disaffection with the regime. The 'social Republic' that the socialists defined in 1932 and 1933 served to distinguish socialists from the Republicans and pointed to a reformist programme of government which would be much more uncompromising in its application. As this book has demonstrated, static notions of democracy and the Republic are unhelpful for understanding the period between 1931 and 1936.[5] Sensitivity to the contested, shifting ideas of the Republic is essential to understanding the dynamics of political evolution during the Republic, including radicalism.

The factors outlined shaped the initial radical impulse in the coalfields, but do not explain how the revolutionary insurrection occurred in October 1934. Two further factors were crucial. The first was fascism. Nazism's ascension to power in early 1933 sparked the emergence of fascism as a common frame for understanding the political right in the Asturian coalfields in 1933, yet the meaning of fascism and how it could manifest were unclear. Fascism was paradoxically believed to represent the traditional political right and a new, existential, hidden threat, especially in the coalfields, where fascists were difficult to locate. Nevertheless, the November 1933 election results appeared to prove that fascism *did* exist in the coalfields and heightened fears about the nature of the coalfield communities. Again, the elusive nature of fascism exacerbated anxieties further through 1934. While it is a commonplace to dismiss the role of fascism by pointing out the lack of actual fascists in 1933, this reasoning is insufficient for understanding political practice and neglects the interplay of local, national and international politics. The dark future augured by the perceived fascist threat conditioned politics in the coalfields in 1933 and 1934.

This threat appeared to become more real in the distinctive shift caused by the elections that delivered a conservative majority in the Cortes. Specifically, a more assertive policing strategy in 1934 brought home, quite literally, the change in the nature of the Republic to the residents of the coalfields. The frisking of workers and the searching of political and union centres stoked an escalating dynamic of protest and anxieties over the trajectory of the Spanish state: could authoritarianism or fascism be installed from above, as in other European countries? *Avance* was adept at capturing and driving the sense of humiliation among militants in the coalfields and the growing fissure between local left-wing communities and the wider state apparatus. The newspaper increasingly depicted the state – in terms of the government and the security forces – as belligerent, persecutory and, importantly, as a foreign force. Civil and assault guards invaded the coalfields, rendering resistance a legitimate form of community defence, which drew on existing ideas of the 'self-policing' *pueblo*. Even as this array of factors explains how men and women in the coalfields were motivated to participate in the insurrection, they do not explain its timing

[5] For a more nuanced and richer approach, see T. Buchanan, 'Anti-fascism and democracy in the 1930s', *European History Quarterly*, xxxii (2002), 39–57.

or the preparations for the movement, responsibility for which lies in the upper echelons in the socialist movement.

Like any revolution, the October 1934 revolutionary insurrection was paradoxical, multifaceted and contested. It was a reassertion and a recuperation of power and the radical left-wing self-image of the coal valleys after the humiliation and frustration of the previous months. But it was also a sincere attempt at revolution that should be understood as a process rather than simply as an event. Committees introduced measures that sought to recast social, economic and political relationships in the valleys. Together with the militias, they also attempted to define the nature of the revolution through policing its boundaries, including the role violence would play in shaping the new order. Through the proclamations they produced, the committees staked a claim to participating in a longer, wider tradition of revolution, stretching beyond the 1930s. It is this revolutionary impulse that sets the Asturian October apart from other episodes of left-wing protest and collective action in 1934.

The revolutionary insurrection and the harsh repression that followed were critical moments in the polarization of Spanish society. Much has been written on the importance of amnesty to the victory of the Popular Front, but little on the effects of the repression on the coalfields themselves. The long 1935 saw the inability of the right to take advantage of the opportunity to re-channel the Republic at the local level, due to a lack of interest, resistance from the underground left and a reliance on the threat of revolution combined with a dependence on the armed forces. For the left, the combination of torture, imprisonment, cancelling of work contracts and the removal of pillars of social and political life, such as union centres, had a profound and traumatic effect on coalfield society. Individuals tried to navigate the radically changed context of the long 1935 in different ways. Some concealed their beliefs, while others became informers or joined right-wing trade unions, whether due to opportunism, economic or social pressures, or a sincere damascene conversion.

The bitterness engendered by the repression and the different strategies employed to survive the long 1935 provided the fuel for a renewed wave of radicalism in 1936. The victory of the Popular Front shifted the political context locally and nationally and sparked a range of initiatives, including purges and boycotts, as left-wing militants grappled with the legacy of the revolution and the repression. This revealed a crisis of the community as the struggle to reassert radical left-wing hegemony retrenched to the communities themselves. The radicalism that these mechanisms generated had a harder, brittle edge. This radicalism combined with bellicose rhetoric and a profound distrust of the state police, which challenged the state's monopoly on coercive power. Faced by right-wing violence in the streets, leftists, desperate for the regime to protect itself, saw no problem in assuming the role of policing the Republic in the streets, for they saw themselves as aligned with a militant, antifascist Republic – an understanding far removed from April 1931. Leftists had kept order on previous occasions, such as during funerals, and had contested the role of the state when demanding the release of detained comrades from jail. The willingness to undertake this task was due to the crisis of community in 1936, which saw the 'balance of initiative' shift to the level of the town, as Collier argued for Andalusia, but also drew on traditions of the 'self-policing *pueblo*'.[6] The demand for the community to police itself was not a question of the lack of state penetration or the weakness of state construction, but about how the social order was understood in moral and political terms.

Radicalization remains a touchstone in histories of the Republic and an important prism through which to understand the evolution of the Republic. This book has argued that radicalism requires redefining and relocating to capture fully the richness and dynamics of 1930s Spanish politics, and to understand the revolutionary insurrection of October 1934. Radicalism was a confrontational, militant style of politics shaped by the historical context of the 1930s and a combination of local, national and international political dynamics. Radicalism was not intrinsically linked to revolutionary politics, nor was it necessarily anti-Republican. Radicalism was located not only in press discourse, union instructions or Largo Caballero's speeches, but also in everyday experiences on a personal and collective level. It manifested itself in an assertive, even aggressive, policing of political and geographical communities. Radical politics was entwined with the personal and private, from stabbings in and outside bars, to the effects of rumours and social pressures on individual reputations. Homing in on this micro-level of radicalism illuminates its gendered facet, including the mocking of the *beatas* and conflicts over religious marriages. Individuals were not the passive receptors of a radicalization process from above but active agents in pressuring their fellow citizens as activists, neighbours and colleagues at the workplace to conform to certain beliefs and behaviour.

The front page of *Avance* on 18 July was heavily censored to remove reports of the coup d'état underway in Spanish Morocco. The blanked-out headline should have read '*Cojones* and dynamite'.[7] Bellicose, macho and assertive, it

[6] G. Collier, *Socialists of Rural Andalusia: Unacknowledged Revolutionaries of the Second Republic* (Stanford, Calif., 1987), p. 142. For a similar argument regarding the Weimar Republic, see P. Swett, *Neighbors and Enemies: the Culture of Radicalism in Berlin, 1929–1933* (Cambridge, 2004).

[7] J. A. de Blas et al., *Historia general de Asturias: la guerra civil, primera parte*, ix (Gijón, 1978), 18.

underscored key characteristics of radicalism as a political style during the Second Republic. The figure of the radical, antifascist miner brandishing dynamite resonates with a mythical image of proletarian males fashioned by struggles in the depths of the mines and has proven to be an enduring mythical symbol of 'red Asturias'. But radicalism was a more complex force, produced by a variety of conflicts and cleavages in the Asturian coalfields both in and beyond the mines, as men and women – citizens, neighbours and political activists – attempted to navigate the challenges facing them in the context of the Spanish Republic, the European 1930s and their own communities.

Bibliography

Press

ABC (1931, 1934, 1936)

Acción (1932, 1935)

Ahora (1934)

Asturias (1935)

La Aurora Social (1929, 1931)

Avance (1931–4, 1936)

Ayuda (1936)

Boletín Oficial de la Provincia de Oviedo (1934, 1936)

Boletín de la Unión General de Trabajadores de España (1933)

El Carbayón (1936)

Cruz y raya: revista de afirmación y negación (1934)

Gaceta de Madrid (1931, 1932, 1934, 1936)

Heraldo de Madrid (1933, 1934)

Hoja parroquial de Santa María la Real de la Corte (1932)

La Libertad (1930, 1936)

Mundo Gráfico (1934, 1937)

Noticiero de Soria (1932)

El Noroeste (1931–6)

Le Populaire (1935)

Región (1931–6)

Renovación (1934)

Revista Industrial Minera Asturiana (1933)

El Socialista (1934)

El Sol (1934, 1936)

Solidaridad (1931)

La Tarde (1935–6)

La Veu de Catalunya (1934)
La Voz de Asturias (1931, 1934, 1936)

Unpublished primary sources

Archivo de Aller
Actas municipales (1931–4, 1935–6)
Fondos Municipales

Archivo de Langreo
Actas municipales (1931–5)

Archivo de Mieres
Actas municipales (1931–6)

Archivo Histórico Provincial de Asturias
Actas de la comisión de la Diputación Provincial (1931–6)
Audiencia Provincial
Sección de la Guerra Civil

Archivo de Oviedo
Actas municipales (1931–6)

Centro Documental de la Memoria Histórica
Político-Social Gijón
Político-Social Madrid

Archivo Histórico Nacional
Gobernación

Memoirs, official publications and historical and contemporary accounts

Ambou, J., *Los comunistas en la resistencia nacional republicana: la guerra en Asturias, el País Vasco y Santander* (Madrid, 1978).

Álvarez Suárez, M., *Sangre de octubre: U.H.P. Episodios de la revolución en Asturias* (Madrid, 1936).

Araquistáin, L., 'The October Revolution in Spain', *Foreign Affairs*, xiii (1935), 247–61.

Arlt, R., *Aguafuertes (andaluzas, marroquíes, gallegas asturianas, vascas y madrileñas)* (Paracuellos de Jarama, 2015).

Asociación Católica Nacional de Propagandistas de Oviedo, *Asturias roja (octubre de 1934): sacerdotes y religiosos perseguidos y martirizados* (Oviedo, n.d. [1935]).

Baráibar, C. de, *Las falsas 'posiciones socialistas' de Indalecio Prieto* (Madrid, 1935)

Barea, A., *The Forging of a Rebel* (London, 2018 [1946]).

Benavides, M., *La revolución fue así (octubre rojo y negro)* (Barcelona, 1935).

Bolín, L., *Spain: the Vital Years* (London, 1967).

Brenan, G., *The Spanish Labyrinth: an Account of the Social and Political Background of the Civil War* (London, 1966 [1943]).

Cabezas, J. A., *Asturias: catorce meses de guerra civil* (Madrid, 1975).

— *Morir en Oviedo: historia en directo (vivencias de un periodista)* (Madrid, 1984).

Canel, J. [J. Díaz Fernández], *Octubre rojo en Asturias* (Barcelona, 1984 [1935]).

Camín, A., *El valle negro* (México, 1938).

Coca, G. M. de, *Anti-Caballero: crítica marxista de la bolchevización del partido socialista (1930–1936)* (Madrid, 1975 [1936]).

Corman, M., *Incendiarios de ídolos: un viaje por la revolución de Asturias* (Oviedo, 2009 [1935]).

Episodios de la revolución en Asturias: los pasionistas de Mieres (Asturias) y la revolución de octubre de 1934. Episodios narrados por los mismos protagonistas (Santander, 1935).

Estadística Minera y Metalúrgica de España [1931] (2 vols, Madrid, 1931).

Estadística Minera y Metalúrgica de España [1934] (Madrid, 1934).

Flórez Peón, A., *Memorias de Ángeles Flórez Peón 'Maricuela'* (Oviedo, 2009).

Fontalbat, C. and C. Álvarez, *Ceferino Álvarez Rey: historia de un minero de Asturias (1907–2009)* (Oviedo, 2010).

Ford, R., *A Handbook for Travellers in Spain* (2 vols, Cambridge, 2011 [1845]).

García Montes, R., *Ángeles rojos sin alas para volar* (Siero, 2009).

Grossi, M., *La insurrección de Asturias* (Madrid, 1978 [1935]).

Ibárruri, D., *Memorias de Dolores Ibárruri, Pasionaria: la lucha y la vida* (Barcelona, 1985).

Ignotus [M. Villar], *La represión de octubre* (Barcelona, 1936).

Jove y Canella, J. M., *Topografía médica del concejo de San Martín del Rey Aurelio* (Madrid, 1923).

— *Topografía médica del concejo de Langreo* (Madrid, 1925).

— *Topografía médica del concejo de Laviana* (Madrid, 1927).

Langdon-Davies, J., *Behind the Spanish Barricades* (New York, 1936).

Largo Caballero, F., *Escritos sobre la República: notas históricas de la guerra en España (1917–1940)* (Madrid, 1985).

Lavilla, I., *Los hombres de octubre* (Gijón, 2004).

Llano Roza de Ampudia, A. de, *Pequeños anales de quince días: revolución en Asturias octubre de 1934* (Oviedo, 1935).

López Ochoa, E., *Campaña militar de Asturias en octubre de 1934 (narración táctica-episódica)* (Madrid, 1936).

Los mártires de Turón: notas biográficas y reseña del martirio de los religiosos bárbaramente asesinados por los revolucionarios en Turón (Asturias) el 9 de octubre de 1934 (Madrid/Barcelona, 1934).

Los presos de Asturias ¡Acusamos! ... (n.p., 1935).

Manning, L., *What I Saw in Spain* (London, 1935).

Martínez, C., *Al final del sendero* (Gijón, 1990).

Martínez, F., *Dos jesuitas mártires en Asturias* (Burgos, 1936).

Ministerio del Trabajo, *Censo de la población de España* [1930] ... *regiones de Asturias y León. Cuadernos III y X* (Madrid, 1942).

Molins i Fábrega, N., *UHP: la insurrección proletaria en Asturias* (Gijón, 1977 [1935]).

Nelken, M., *Por qué hicimos la revolución* (Barcelona, 1936).

Neuberg, A., *Armed Insurrection* (London, 1970 [1928]).

Nevares, S., *El patrono ejemplar: una obra maestra de Acción Social* (Madrid, 1936).

Noval Suárez, S., *Langreo Rojo: historia del martirio y persecución de los sacerdotes en el Arciprestazgo de Langreo durante los sucesos revolucionarios del año 1934* (La Felguera, 1935).

Prieto, I. (ed.), *Documentos socialistas: escritos de Indalecio Prieto, Ramón González Peña, Toribio Echevarría, Amador Fernández, Antonio Llaneza, Alejandro Jaume, Francisco Torquemada, jóvenes presos de Asturias y de Madrid, etc., etc.* (Madrid, n.d.).

Rosal, A. del, *1934: el movimiento revolucionario de octubre* (Madrid, 1984).

Salazar Alonso, R., *Bajo el signo de la revolución* (Madrid, 1935).

Solano Palacio, F., *La revolución de octubre: quince días de comunismo libertario* (Madrid, 1994 [1936]).

Spain, October 1934 (Paris, 1935).

Tagüeña Lacorte, M., *Testimonio de dos guerras* (Barcelona, 1978).

Vidarte, J. S., *El bienio negro y la insurrección de Asturias* (Barcelona, 1978).

Villar, M., *El anarquismo en la insurrección de Asturias: la CNT y la FAI en octubre de 1934* (Madrid, 1994 [1935]).

XXX, *Lo que yo he visto: La Felguera en la revolución asturiana* (New York, 1935).

Books and articles

Aguado Sánchez, F., *La revolución de octubre de 1934* (Madrid, 1972).

Aguiar García, C. D. and Y. Hermida Martín, 'Techo y dignidad. La lucha del Sindicato de Inquilinos de Tenerife durante la Segunda República', in *Culturas políticas en la contemporaneidad: discursos y prácticas políticas desde los márgenes a las élites. Culturas políticas y acción colectiva desde la izquierda durante el S. XX*, ed. J. A. Caballero Machí, R. Mínguez Blasco and V. Rodríguez-Flores Parra (Valencia, 2015), pp. 115–18.

Alba, V., *La Alianza Obrera: historia y análisis de una táctica de unidad en España* (Madrid, 1978).

Alimi, E. Y., L. Bosi and C. Demetriou, *The Dynamics of Radicalization: a Relational and Comparative Perspective* (Oxford, 2015).

Alpert, M., *The Republican Army in the Spanish Civil War, 1936–1939* (Cambridge, 2013).

Álvarez Chillida, G., '*Negras tormentas* sobre la República. La intransigencia libertaria', in *Palabras como puños: la intransigencia política en la Segunda República española*, ed. F. del Rey (Madrid, 2011), pp. 45–110.

Álvarez Fernández, M. V., *La escuela del paternalismo industrial asturiano (1880–1937)* (Gijón, 2006).

Álvarez Tardío, M. and R. Villa García, 'El impacto de la violencia anticlerical en la primavera de 1936 y la respuesta de las autoridades', *Hispania sacra*, lxv (2013), 693–764.

— 'The impact of political violence during the Spanish general election of 1936', *Journal of Contemporary History*, xlviii (2013), 463–85.

Álvarez, C., *El Sindicato Único de Mineros de Asturias* (Oviedo, 2004).

Álvarez, J. E., 'The Spanish Foreign Legion during the Asturian uprising of October 1934', *War in History*, xviii (2011), 200–24.

Anderson, P., 'Singling out victims: denunciation and collusion in the post-Civil War Francoist repression in Spain, 1939–1945', *European History Quarterly*, xxxix (2009), 7–26.

— *The Francoist Military Trials: Terror and Complicity, 1939–1945* (New York, 2010).

Arbeloa, V. M., *La semana trágica de la Iglesia en España (8–14 octubre de 1931)* (Madrid, 2006).

Arendt, H., *On Revolution* (Harmondsworth, 1973 [1963]).

Aresti, N., 'El crimen de Trubia: género, discursos y ciudadanía republicana', *Ayer*, lxi (2006), 261–85.

Arias González, L. and F. de Luis Martín, 'Las Casas del Pueblo y sus implicaciones geograficas', *Biblio 3W: Revista bibliográfica de geografía y ciencias sociales*, xv (2010), available at <http://www.ub.edu/geocrit/b3w-884.htm> [accessed 12 Sept. 2018].

Arias González, L. and M. J. Álvarez García, *Los palacios obreros: Casas del Pueblo socialistas en Asturias, 1902–1937* (Oviedo, 2010).

Aróstegui, J., *Largo Caballero: el tesón y la quimera* (Barcelona, 2013).

Avilés Farré, J., *La izquierda burguesa y la tragedia de la Segunda República* (Madrid, 2006).

— 'Los socialistas y la insurrección de octubre de 1934', *Espacio, tiempo y forma, serie v, Historia contemporánea*, xx (2008), 129–57.

Baker, K. M. and D. Edelstein (eds), *Scripting Revolution: a Historical Approach to the Comparative Study of Revolutions* (Stanford, Calif., 2015).

Balduz, J., *Segunda República y Guerra Civil en Villava (1931–1939)* (Villava, 2006).

Balfour, S., *Deadly Embrace: Morocco and the Road to the Spanish Civil War* (Oxford, 2002).

Barrio Alonso, Á., *Anarquismo y anarcosindicalismo en Asturias (1890–1936)* (Madrid, 1988).

Barron, H., *The 1926 Miners' Lockout: Meanings of Community in the Durham Coalfield* (Oxford, 2009).

Baumeister, M., 'Castilblanco or the limits of democracy – rural protest in Spain from Restoration Monarchy to the early Second Republic', *Contemporary European History*, vii (1998), 1–19.

Bell, D. H., *Sesto San Giovanni: Workers, Culture and Politics in an Italian Town, 1880–1922* (New Brunswick, N.J., 1986).

Ben-Ami, S., *The Origins of the Second Republic in Spain* (Oxford, 1978).

— *Fascism From Above: the Dictatorship of Primo de Rivera in Spain, 1923–30* (Oxford, 1983).

Benavides, D., 'Arboleya y su interpretación de la revolución de octubre', in *Octubre 1934: cincuenta años para la reflexión*, ed. G. Jackson et al. (Madrid, 1985), pp. 253–67.

— *El fracaso social del catolicismo español: Arboleya Martínez, 1870–1951* (Barcelona, 1973).

Benito del Pozo, C., *El ayuntamiento republicano de Oviedo, 1931–1936* (Oviedo, 1989).

Berger, S., 'Difficult (re-)alignments – comparative perspectives on social democracy and religion from late-nineteenth-century to interwar Germany and Britain', *Journal of Contemporary History*, liii (2018), 574–96.

Berlière, J. M., 'The difficult construction of a "Republican" police', in *Policing Interwar Europe: Continuity, Change and Crisis, 1918–1940*, ed. G. Blaney (Basingstoke, 2007), pp. 14–30.

Berman, S., *The Social Democratic Moment: Ideas and Politics and the Making of Interwar Europe* (Cambridge, Mass., 1998).

Bessel, R., *Political Violence and the Rise of Nazism: the Storm Troopers in Eastern Germany, 1925–1934* (New Haven, Conn., 1984).

— 'Revolution', in *The Cambridge History of the First World War*, ed. J. Winter (3 vols, Cambridge, 2014), pp. 126–44.

Bizcarrondo, M., *Octubre del 1934: reflexiones sobre una revolución* (Madrid, 1977).

— 'Democracia y revolución en la estrategia socialista de la Segunda República', *Estudios de Historia Social*, xvi–xvii (1981), 227–459.

— *Historia de la UGT*, iii: *Entre la democracia y la revolución, 1931–1936* (6 vols, Madrid, 2008).

Blas Guerrero, A. de, *El socialismo radical en la II República* (Madrid, 1978).

Blas, J. A. de et al., *Historia general de Asturias*: *La guerra civil, primera parte, ix* (12 vols, Gijón, 1978).

Blasco Herranz, I., '"Tenemos las armas de nuestra fe y de nuestro amor y patriotismo; pero nos falta algo": la Acción Católica de la Mujer y la participación política en la España del primer tercio del siglo XX', *Historia social*, xliv (2002), 3–20.

— *Paradojas de la ortodoxia: política de masas y militancia católica femenina en España (1919–1939)* (Zaragoza, 2003).

Blasco Rodríguez, J. A., 'Las MAOC y la tesis insurreccional del PCE', *Historia contemporánea*, xi (1994), 129–51.

Blinkhorn, M., *Carlism and Crisis in Spain 1931–1939* (Cambridge, 1975).

Blom, J. C. H., 'Pillarisation in perspective', *West European Politics*, xxiii (2000), 153–64.

Borque López, L., *El magisterio primario en Asturias (1923–1937): sociedad y educación* (Oviedo, 1991).

Boswell, L., *Rural Communism in France 1920–1939* (Ithaca, N.Y., 1998).

— 'Rural society in crisis', in *The Oxford Handbook of European History, 1914–1945*, ed. N. Doumanis (Oxford, 2016), pp. 243–60.

Boyd, C., 'The second battle of Covadonga: the politics of commemoration in modern Spain', *History and Memory*, xiv (2002), 37–64.

Branciforte, L., 'Legitimando la solidaridad femenina internacional: el Socorro Rojo', *Arenal*, xvi (2009), 27–52.

— *El Socorro Rojo Internacional en España (1923–1939): relatos de la solidaridad antifascista* (Madrid, 2009).

Brown, T. S., *Weimar Radicals: Nazis and Communists Between Authenticity and Performance* (New York, 2009).

Buchanan, T., 'Anti-fascism and democracy in the 1930s', *European History Quarterly*, xxxii (2002), 39–57.

— 'Beyond Cable Street: new approaches to the historiography of antifascism in Britain in the 1930s', in *Rethinking Antifascism: History, Memory and Politics, 1922 to the Present*, ed. H. García, M. Yusta, X. Tabet and C. Clímaco (New York, 2016), pp. 61–75.

Bunk, B. D., 'Revolutionary warrior and gendered icon: Aida Lafuente and the Spanish Revolution of 1934', *Journal of Women's History*, xv (2003), 99–122.

— *Ghosts of Passion: Martyrdom, Gender, and the Origins of the Spanish Civil War* (Durham, N.C., 2007).

Calhoun, C., *The Roots of Radicalism: Tradition, the Public Sphere and Early Nineteenth-Century Social Movements* (Chicago, Ill., 2012).

Callahan, W. J., *The Catholic Church in Spain, 1875–1998* (Washington, D.C., 2000).

Canal, J., *El carlismo: dos siglos de contrarrevolución en España* (Madrid, 2000).

Cañete Marfil, R. and F. Martínez Mejías, *La Segunda República en Bujalance (1931–1936)* (Córdoba, 2010).

Carmona, J. and J. Simpson, 'Campesinos unidos o divididos? La acción colectiva y la revolución social de los *yunteros* durante la Segunda República en España (1931–1936)', *Historia Social*, lxxxv (2016), 123–44.

Carmona, J., J. R. Rosés and J. Simpson, 'The question of land access and the Spanish land reform of 1932', *Economic History Review*, lxxii (2019), 669–90.

Carsten, F. L., *Revolution in Eastern Europe* (London, 1972).

Casanova, J., *Anarchism, the Republic and Civil War in Spain (1931–1939)* (Abingdon, 2004).

— 'Republic, civil war and dictatorship: the peculiarities of Spanish history', *Journal of Contemporary History*, lii (2017), 148–56.

Casanova, J. and C. Gil Andrés, *Twentieth-Century Spain: a History* (Cambridge, 2014).

Christian, W. A., *Person and God in a Spanish Valley* (Princeton, N.J., 1972).

Church, R. and Q. Outram, *Strikes and Solidarity: Coalfield Conflict in Britain, 1889–1966* (Cambridge, 1998).

Claeys, G. and C. Lattek, 'Radicalism, republicanism and revolutionism: from the principles of '89 to the origins of modern terrorism', in *The Cambridge History of Nineteenth-Century Political Thought*, ed. G Claeys and G. Stedman Jones (Cambridge, 2011), pp. 200–54.

Cobo Romero, F., *De campesinos a electores: modernización agraria en Andalucía, politización campesina y derechización de los pequeños propietarios y arrendatarios: el caso de la provincia de Jaén, 1931–1936* (Madrid, 2003).

— *Revolución campesina y contrarrevolución franquista en Andalucía: conflictividad social, violencia política y represión franquista en el mundo rural andaluz, 1931–1950* (Granada, 2004).

Cohen, A., *The Symbolic Construction of Community* (London, 1985).

Collier, G., *Socialists of Rural Andalusia: Unacknowledged Revolutionaries of the Second Republic* (Stanford, Calif., 1987).

Cruz, R., *El Partido Comunista de España en la Segunda República* (Madrid, 1987).

— *En el nombre del pueblo: república, rebelión y guerra en la España de 1936* (Madrid, 2006).

— *Una revolución elegante: España 1931* (Madrid, 2014).

— *Protestar en España* (Madrid, 2015).

Delanty, G., *Community* (London, 2003).

Delgado Ruiz, M., 'Anticlericalismo, espacio y poder: la destrucción de los rituales católicos, 1931–1939', *Ayer*, xxvii (1997), 149–80.

Díaz Freire, J. J., *Expectativas y frustaciones en la Segunda República (Vizcaya 1931–1933)* (Bilbao, 1990).

Díaz Nosty, B., *La comuna asturiana: revolución de octubre de 1934* (Bilbao, 1974).

Doumanis, N. (ed.), *The Oxford Handbook of European History, 1914–1945* (Oxford, 2016).

Durgan, A., *BOC 1930–1936: el Bloque Obrero y Campesino* (Barcelona, 1996).

Ealham, C., *Class, Culture and Conflict in Barcelona, 1898–1937* (Abingdon, 2005).

Eley, G., *Forging Democracy: the History of the Left in Europe, 1850–2000* (Oxford, 2002).

Elorza, A. and M. Bizcarrondo, *Queridos camaradas: la Internacional Comunista y España, 1919–1939* (Barcelona, 1999).

Erice, F. (ed.), *Los comunistas en Asturias (1920–1982)* (Gijón, 1996).

— 'El PCE en Asturias, de los orígenes a la guerra civil', in *Los comunistas en Asturias (1920–1982)*, ed. F. Erice (Gijón, 1996), pp. 41–84.

— 'Mujeres comunistas: la militancia femenina en el comunismo asturiano, de los orígenes al final del franquismo', in *Los comunistas en Asturias (1920–1982)*, ed. F. Erice (Gijón, 1996), pp. 313–44.

— 'El octubre asturiano: entre el mito y la interpretación histórica', in *De un octubre a otro: revolución y fascismo en el periodo de entreguerras, 1919–1934*, ed. A. Andreassi and J. L. Martín Ramos (Madrid, 2010), pp. 199–250.

Espinosa Maestre, F., *La primavera del Frente Popular: los campesinos de Badajoz y el orígen de la Guerra Civil (marzo – julio de 1936)* (Barcelona, 2007).

Felgueroso Durán, A. R. and A. Fernández García, 'La gestión de los socialistas en el Ayuntamiento de Langreo entre 1909 y 1936', in *Historia del socialismo en Langreo 1897–1997*, ed. A. Fernández García and J. Girón (Gijón, 1997), pp. 145–95.

Fernández García, A., *Langreo: industria, población y desarrollo urbano* (Gijón, 1980).

Fernández Pérez, A., *Tiempos heroicos: diccionario biográfico del socialismo asturiano* (Oviedo, 2013).

Fitzpatrick, S. and R. Gellately (eds), *Accusatory Practices: Denunciation in Modern European History, 1789–1989* (Chicago, Ill., 1997).

Fraser, R., *Blood of Spain: an Oral History of the Spanish Civil War* (New York, 1979).

Fritzsche, P., 'Did Weimar fail?', *Journal of Modern History*, lxviii (1996), 629–56.

Fusi, J. P., *Política obrera en el País Vasco, 1880–1923* (Madrid, 1975).

— *El País Vasco: autonomía, revolución, guerra civil* (Madrid, 2002).

Gallego, F., *Barcelona, mayo de Barcelona: la crisis del antifascismo en Cataluña* (Barcelona, 2007).

Garai, J. R., J. Gutiérrez and J. Chueca, *Octubre de 1934 en Euskal Herria* (Oñati, 2014).

García de Tuñón Aza, J. M., *Apuntes para una historia de la Falange asturiana* (Oviedo, 2001).

García, H., *The Truth About Spain! Mobilizing British Public Opinion, 1936–1939* (Brighton, 2010).

— 'De los soviets a las Cortes: los comunistas ante la República', in *Palabras como puños: la intransigencia política en la Segunda República española*, ed. F. del Rey (Madrid, 2011), pp. 111–57.

— 'Was there an antifascist culture in 1930s Spain?', in *Rethinking Antifascism: History, Memory and Politics, 1922 to the Present*, ed. H. García, M. Yusta, X. Tabet and C. Clímaco (New York, 2016), pp. 92–113.

García, H., M. Yusta, X. Tabet and C. Clímaco (eds), *Rethinking Antifascism: History, Memory and Politics, 1922 to the Present* (New York, 2016).

Garralda García, Á., *La persecución religiosa del clero en Asturias 1934, 1936 y 1937: martirios y odiseas* (Avilés, 2009 [1977]).

Geary, D., 'The myth of the radical miner', in *Towards a Comparative History of Coalfield Societies*, ed. S. Berger, A. Croll and N. LaPorte (Aldershot, 2005), pp. 43–64.

Gerwarth, R., 'The central European counter-revolution: paramilitary violence in Germany, Austria and Hungary after the Great War', *Past & Present*, cc (2008), 175–209.

— *The Vanquished: Why the First World War Failed to End* (London, 2016).

Gerwarth, R. and M. Conway, 'Revolution and counterrevolution', in *Political Violence in Twentieth-Century Europe*, ed. D. Bloxham and R. Gerwarth (Cambridge, 2011), pp. 140–75.

Gerwarth, R. and J. Horne (eds), *War in Peace: Paramilitary Violence after the Great War* (Oxford, 2012).

Gibaja Velázquez, J. C., 'La tradición improvisada: el socialismo y la milicia', *Historia contemporánea*, xi (1994), 107–27.

Giddens, A., *Beyond Left and Right: the Future of Radical Politics* (Stanford,Calif., 1994).

Gil Andrés, C., *Echarse a la calle: amotinados, huelguistas y revolucionarios (La Rioja, 1890–1936)* (Zaragoza, 2000).

— *La República en la plaza: los sucesos de Arnedo de 1932* (Logroño, 2002).

Gillingham, J., *Industry and Politics in the Third Reich: Ruhr Coal, Hitler and Europe* (London, 1985).

Girón, J., 'Asturias, Octubre de 1934: el fracaso de un intento de alianza electoral entre socialistas y comunistas', in *Octubre 1934: cincuenta años para la reflexión*, ed. G. Jackson et al. (Madrid, 1985), pp. 197–205.

González Calleja, E., 'La violencia y sus discursos: los límites de la "fascistización" de la derecha española durante el régimen de la Segunda República', *Ayer*, lxxi (2008), 85–116.

— 'La necro-lógica de la violencia sociopolítica en la primavera de 1936', *Mélanges de la Casa de Velázquez*, xli (2011) <http://journals.openedition.org/mcv/3825> [accessed 13 Jan. 2019].

— *Contrarrevolucionarios: radicalización violenta de las derechas durante la Segunda República, 1931–1936* (Madrid, 2011).

— 'La historiografía sobre la violencia política en la Segunda República española', *Hispania: revista de historia contemporánea*, xi (2013), 403–36.

— *En nombre de la autoridad: la defensa del orden público durante la Segunda República Española (1931–1936)* (Granada, 2014).

— *Cifras cruentas: las víctimas mortales de la violencia sociopolítica en la Segunda República española (1931–1936)* (Granada, 2015).

Gonzàlez i Vilalta, A., M. López Esteve and E. Ucelay-Da Cal (eds), *6 d'octubre: la desfeta de la revolució catalanista de 1934* (Barcelona, 2014).

González Probados, M., *O socialismo na Segunda República (1931–1936)* (Sada, 1992).

Goodwin, J., J. M. Jasper and F. Polletta (eds), *Passionate Politics: Emotions and Social Movements* (Chicago, Ill., 2001).

Graham, H., *Socialism and War: the Spanish Socialist Party in Power and Crisis, 1936–1939* (Cambridge, 1991).

— *The Spanish Republic at War, 1936–1939* (Cambridge, 2002).

Grandío Seoane, E., *Los orígenes de la derecha gallega: la CEDA en Galicia (1931–1936)* (Sada, 1998).

Gross, J., *Revolution from Abroad: the Soviet Conquest of Poland's Western Ukraine and Western Belorussia* (Princeton, N.J., 2002).

Gruber, H., *Red Vienna: Experiment in Working Class Culture, 1919–1934* (New York, 1991).

Guereña, J-L., 'El burdel como espacio de sociabilidad', *Hispania*, lxiii (2003), 551–69.

Häberlen, J., 'Scope for agency and political options: the German working-class movement and the rise of Nazism', *Politics, Religion and Ideology*, iv (2013), 377–94.

— *The Emotional Politics of the Alternative Left: West Germany, 1968–1984* (Cambridge, 2018).

Harsch, D., *German Social Democracy and the Rise of Nazism* (Chapel Hill, N.C., 1993).

Heywood, P., *Marxism and the Failure of Organised Socialism in Spain, 1879–1936* (Cambridge, 1990).

Hickey, S. H. F., *Workers in Imperial Germany: the Miners of the Ruhr* (Oxford, 1985).

Hodgson, K., *Fighting Fascists: the British Left and the Rise of Fascism, 1919–1939* (Manchester, 2010).

Horn, G.-R., *European Socialists Respond to Fascism: Ideology, Activism and Contingency in the 1930s* (New York, 1996).

Izquierdo, E., 'Hacia la unidad sindical, 1933–1934', *Estudios de Historia Social*, xxxi (1984), 113–22.

Jackson, G. et al., *Octubre 1934: cincuenta años para la reflexión* (Madrid, 1985).

Jackson, J., *The Politics of Depression in France, 1932–1936* (Cambridge, 1985).

— *The Popular Front in France: Defending Democracy, 1934–38* (Cambridge, 1988).

James, L., *The Politics of Identity and Civil Society in Britain and Germany: the Miners in the Ruhr and South Wales, 1890–1926* (Manchester, 2008).

Jasper, J. M. and J. W. Duyvendak (eds), *Breaking Down the State: Protestors Engaged* (Amsterdam, 2015).

Jeffery, C., *Social Democracy in the Austrian Provinces, 1918–1934: Beyond Red Vienna* (London, 1995).

Jenkins, B. and C. Millington, *France and Fascism: February 1934 and the Dynamics of Political Crisis* (Abingdon, 2015).

Jiménez Campo, J., *El fascismo en la crisis de la Segunda República española* (Madrid, 1979).

Jiménez Lozano, J., *Los cementerios civiles y la heterodoxia española* (Barcelona, 2008 [1978]).

Jones, M., *Founding Weimar: Violence and the German Revolution, 1918–19* (Cambridge, 2016).

Juliá, S., *La izquierda del PSOE (1935–1936)* (Madrid, 1977).

— *Orígenes del frente popular en España* (Madrid, 1979).

— *Madrid, 1931–1934: de la fiesta popular a la lucha de clases* (Madrid, 1984).

— 'Los socialistas y el escenario de la futura revolución', in *Octubre 1934: cincuenta años para la reflexión*, ed. G. Jackson et al. (Madrid, 1985), pp. 103–30.

— 'República, revolución y luchas internas', in *El socialismo en España: desde la fundación del PSOE hasta 1975*, ed. S. Juliá (Madrid, 1986), pp. 231–54.

— '"Preparados para cuando la ocasión se presente": los socialistas y la revolución', in *Violencia política en la España del siglo XX*, ed. S. Juliá (Madrid, 2000), pp. 145–90.

Kalyvas, S., 'The ontology of "political violence": action and identity in civil wars', *Perspectives on Politics*, i (2003), 475–94.

Kaplan, T., *Red City, Blue Period: Social Movements in Picasso's Barcelona* (Berkeley, Calif., 1992).

— 'Female consciousness and collective action: the case of Barcelona, 1910–1918', *Signs*, vii (1982), 545–66.

Kelsey, G., *Anarchosyndicalism, Libertarian Communism and the State: the CNT in Zaragoza and Aragon, 1930–37* (Amsterdam, 1991).

Kerr, C. and A. Siegel, 'The interindustry propensity to strike – an international comparison', in *Industrial Conflict*, ed. A. Kornhauser, R. Kubin and A. Ross (New York, 1954), pp. 189–212.

Kerry, M., 'Painted tonsures and potato-sellers: priests, passing and survival in the Asturian Revolution', *Cultural & Social History*, xiv (2017), 237–55.

— 'The bones of contention: culture wars and the secularisation of cemeteries and death practices in the Spanish Second Republic', *European History Quarterly*, xlix (2019), 73–95.

Kirk, T., *Nazism and the Working Class in Austria: Industrial Unrest and Political Dissent in the 'National Community'* (Cambridge, 1996).

Knotter, A., '"Little Moscows" in Western Europe: the ecology of small-place communism', *International Review of Social History*, lvi (2011), 475–510.

Kohn, M., *Radical Space: Building the House of the People* (Ithaca, N.Y., 2003).

Lannon, F., *Privilege, Persecution and Prophecy: the Catholic Church in Spain, 1875–1975* (Oxford, 1987).

Lawson, G., 'Within and beyond the "Fourth Generation" of revolutionary theory', *Sociological Theory*, xxxiv (2016), 106–27.

Lisón Tolosana, C., *Belmonte de los Caballeros: Anthropology and History in an Aragonese Community* (Princeton, N.J., 1983).

López Villaverde, A. L., *El gorro frigio y la mitra frente a frente: construcción y diversidad territorial del conflicto político-religioso en la España republicana* (n.p., 2008).

Lowe, S., *Catholicism, War and the Foundation of Francoism* (Eastbourne, 2010).

Macarro Vera, J. M., 'Causas de la radicalización socialista en la II República', *Revista de historia contemporánea*, i (1982), 178–226.

— *Socialismo, República y revolución en Andalucía (1931–1936)* (Seville, 2000).

Macintyre, S., *Little Moscows: Communism and Working Class Militancy in Interwar Britain* (London, 1980).

Madariaga, M. R. de, *Los moros que trajo Franco* (Barcelona, 2006).

Majuelo Gil, E., *Luchas de clases en Navarra (1931–1936)* (Pamplona, 1989).

Malefakis, E., *Agrarian Reform and Peasant Revolution in Spain: Origins of the Spanish Civil War* (New Haven, Conn., 1970).

Mann, M., 'The autonomous power of the state: its origins, mechanisms and results', *European Journal of Sociology*, xxv (1984), 185–213.

Martín Ramos, J. L., *Historia de la UGT*, ii: *Entre la revolución y el reformismo, 1914–1931* (Madrid, 2008).

Martorell Linares, M., '"The cruellest of all forms of coercion": the Catholic Church and conflicts around death and burial in Spain during the Restoration (1874–1923)', *European History Quarterly*, xlvii (2017), 657–78.

Mateos, M. A., ¡Salud, compañeras! Mujeres *socialistas en Asturias (1900–1937)* (Oviedo, 2007).

Mato Díaz, A., *La escuela primaria en Asturias (1923–1937): los procesos de alfabetización y escolarización* (Oviedo, 1992).

— *La Atenas del norte: ateneos, sociedades culturales y bibliotecas populares en Asturias (1876–1937)* (Oviedo, 2008).

Matthews, J., *Reluctant Warriors: Republican Popular Army and Nationalist Army Conscripts in the Spanish Civil War, 1936–1939* (Oxford, 2012).

Mayer, A. J., *The Furies: Violence and Terror in the French and Russian Revolutions* (Princeton, N.J., 2000).

Mazower, M., *Dark Continent: Europe's Twentieth Century* (London, 1998).

McLaughlin, P., *Radicalism: a Philosophical Study* (Basingstoke, 2012).

McMeekin, S., *The Red Millionaire: a Political Biography of Willy Munzenberg, Moscow's Secret Propaganda Tsar in the West* (New Haven, Conn., 2003).

Mennen, K., 'Necessary evil, last resort or totally unacceptable? Social democratic discussions on political violence in Germany and the Netherlands', in *Political Violence and Democracy in Western Europe, 1918–1940*, ed. C. Millington and K. Passmore (London, 2015), pp. 97–111.

Merriman, J., *The Red City: Limoges and the French Nineteenth Century* (New York, 1985).

Miller, P., 'Un movimiento de oposición radical: el PCE en Asturias, 1931–1934', *Estudios de Historia Social*, xxxi (1984), 131–7.

Millington, C., 'Street-fighting men: political violence in interwar France', *English Historical Review*, cxxix (2014), 606–38.

Mintz, J., *The Anarchists of Casas Viejas* (Bloomington, Ind., 1994 [1982]).

Miralles, R., *El socialismo vasco durante la II República: organización, ideología, política y elecciones, 1931–1936* (Bilbao, 1988).

Montero, J. R., *La CEDA: el catolicismo social y político en la II República* (2 vols, Madrid, 1977).

Moradiellos, E., *El Sindicato de los Obreros Mineros de Asturias, 1910–1930* (Oviedo, 1986).

Moral Roncal, A. M., *La cuestión religiosa en la Segunda República española: iglesia y carlismo* (Madrid, 2009).

Moreno Medina, N., *La ciudad silenciada: Segunda República y represión fascista en Calatayud, 1931–1939* (Calatayud, 2008).

Muñiz Sánchez, J., *Del pozo a casa: genealogías del paternalismo minero contemporáneo en Asturias* (Gijón, 2007).

— 'Encontrando el norte: Manuel Llaneza y la influencia francesa en el sindicalismo español de principios del siglo XX', *Hispania: Revista española de historia*, lxix (2009), 793–820.

Nagy, Z., 'Budapest and the revolutions of 1918–19', in *Challenges of Labour: Central and Western Europe, 1917–1920*, ed. C. Wrigley (London, 1993), pp. 72–86.

Nash, M., *Defying Male Civilization: Women in the Spanish Civil War* (Denver, Colo., 1995).

Navarro Comas, R., 'El Frente Único, las Alianzas Obreras y el Frente Popular: la evolución teórica de los anarquistas ante la colaboración obrera', *Mélanges de la Casa de Velázquez*, xli (2011), 103–20.

Núñez Seixas, X. M., *¡Fuera el invasor! nacionalismos y movilización bélica durante la guerra civil española (1936–1939)* (Madrid, 2006).

Ojeda, G., *Asturias en la industrialización española, 1833–1907* (Madrid, 1985).

Passmore, K., *From Liberalism to Fascism: the Right in a French Province* (Cambridge, 1997).

Payne, S., 'Political violence during the Spanish Second Republic', *Journal of Contemporary History*, xxv (1990), 269–88.

— *Fascism in Spain, 1923–1977* (Madison, Wis., 1999).

— *The Collapse of the Spanish Republic, 1933–1936: the Origins of the Civil War* (New Haven, Conn., 2006).

Pérez-Fuentes Hernández, P., *'Ganadores de Pan' y 'amas de casa': otras miradas sobre la industrialización vasca* (Bilbao, 2003).

Perry, M., *Prisoners of Want: the Experience and Protest of the Unemployed in France, 1921–1945* (Aldershot, 2007).

— *'Red Ellen' Wilkinson: Her Ideas, Movements and World* (Manchester, 2015).

Piqueras, J. A. and V. Sanz Rozalén (eds), *A Social History of Spanish Labour: New Perspectives on Class, Politics and Gender* (New York, 2007).

Pitt-Rivers, J., *The People of the Sierra* (London, 1954).

Plamper, J., *The History of Emotions: an Introduction* (Oxford, 2015).

Polletta, F. and B. G. Gardner, 'Narrative and social movements', in *The Oxford Handbook of Social Movements*, ed. D. Della Porta and M. Diani (Oxford, 2015), pp. 534–48.

Pozo Andrés, M. del M. and B. Hortañón González, 'El laicismo en la escuela pública', in *Laicismo y catolicismo: el conflicto político-religioso en la Segunda República*, ed. J. de la Cueva Merino and F. Montero García (Alcalá de Henares, 2009), pp. 295–319.

Prada Rodríguez, Julio, *De la agitación republicana a la represión franquista (Ourense 1934–1939)* (Barcelona, 2006).

Preston, P., *The Coming of the Spanish Civil War: Reform, Reaction and Revolution in the Second Republic* (London, 1978).

— *The Spanish Holocaust: Inquisition and Extermination in Twentieth-Century Spain* (London, 2012).

Priestland, D., 'The left and the revolutions', in *The Oxford Handbook of European history, 1914–1945*, ed. N. Doumanis (Oxford, 2016), pp. 77–96.

Purkiss, R., *Democracy, Trade Unions and Political Violence in Spain: the Valencian Anarchist Movement, 1918–1936* (Brighton, 2011).

Quiroga, A., *Making Spaniards: Primo de Rivera and the Nationalization of the Masses, 1923–30* (Basingstoke, 2007).

Rabinbach, A., 'Freedom for Thälmann: the Comintern and the orchestration of the campaign to free Ernst Thälmann, 1933–39', in *Rethinking Antifascism: History, Memory and Politics, 1922 to the Present*, ed. H. García, M. Yusta, X. Tabet and C. Clímaco (New York, 2016), pp. 23–42.

— *The Crisis of Austrian Socialism: from Red Vienna to Civil War, 1927–1934* (Chicago, Ill., 1983).

Radcliff, P., *From Mobilization to Civil War: the Politics of Polarization in the Spanish City of Gijón, 1900–1937* (Cambridge, 1996).

— 'Women's politics: consumer riots in twentieth-century Spain', in *Constructing Spanish Womanhood: Female Identity in Modern Spain*, ed. V. Lorée Enders and P. Radcliff (New York, 1999), pp. 301–23.

— 'The political "left" in the interwar period, 1924–1939', in *The Oxford Handbook of European History, 1914–1945*, ed. N. Doumanis (Oxford, 2016), pp. 282–98.

Ramírez, C., *Balance de una ruptura: los socialistas en el gobierno, en la guerra y en la revolución* (Madrid, 2012).

Ranzato, G., 'El peso de la violencia en los orígenes de la guerra civil de 1936–1939', *Espacio, tiempo y forma, serie v, Historia contemporánea*, xx (2008), 159–82.

— 'The Spanish Civil War in the context of total war', in *'If You Tolerate This...': the Spanish Civil War in the Age of Total War*, ed. M. Baumeister and S. Schüler-Springorum (Frankfurt, 2008), pp. 234–43.

Rees, T., 'Deviation and discipline: anti-Trotskyism, Bolshevization and the Spanish Communist Party, 1924–34', *Historical Research*, lxxxii (2009), 131–56.

— 'Living up to Lenin: leadership culture and the Spanish Communist Party, 1920–1939', *History*, 97 (2012), 230–55.

Reichardt, S., 'Violence and community: a micro-study on Nazi Storm Troopers', *Central European History*, xlvi (2013), 275–97.

Reiss, M. and M. Perry (eds), *Unemployment and Protest: New Perspectives on Two Centuries of Contention* (Oxford, 2011).

Rey, F. del (ed.), *Palabras como puños: la intransigencia política en la Segunda República española* (Madrid, 2011).

— *Paisanos en lucha: exclusión política y violencia en la Segunda República española* (Madrid, 2008).

Rider, N., 'The practice of direct action: the Barcelona rent strike of 1931', in *For Anarchism: History, Theory, and Practice*, ed. D. Goodway (London, 1989), pp. 79–105.

Riesco Roche, S., *La reforma agraria y los orígenes de la Guerra Civil: cuestión yuntera y radicalización patronal en la provincia de Cáceres (1931–1940)* (Madrid, 2006).

Rodríguez Infiesta, V., 'Asturias en los siglos xx y xxi', in *Historia de Asturias*, ed. A. Fernández Pérez and F. Friera Suárez (Oviedo, 2005), pp. 697–881.

Rodríguez Muñoz, J., *La revolución de octubre de 1934 en Asturias: orígenes, desarrollo y consecuencias* (Oviedo, 2010).

Roman, C. F., 'Liminality, the execution of Louis XVI and the rise of terror during the French Revolution', in *Breaking Boundaries: Varieties of Liminality*, ed. A. Horvath, B. Thomassen and H. Wydra (New York, 2015), pp. 141–63.

Romero Salvadó, F. J. and A. Smith (eds), *The Agony of Spanish Liberalism: from Revolution to Dictatorship 1913–23* (Basingstoke, 2010).

Rosenhaft, E., *Beating the Fascists? The German Communist Party and Political Violence, 1929–1933* (Cambridge, 1983).

Rossol, N., *Performing the Nation: Sort, Spectacle and Political Symbolism, 1926–1936* (Basingstoke, 2010).

Ruiz, D., *Insurrección defensiva y revolución obrera: el octubre español de 1934* (Barcelona, 1988).

— *Octubre de 1934: revolución en la República española* (Madrid, 2008).

Ruiz, D. et al., *Asturias contemporánea, 1808–1975: síntesis histórica. Textos y documentos* (Madrid, 1981).

Salomón Chéliz, M. P., *Anticlericalismo en Aragón: protesta popular y movilización cívica (1900–1939)* (Zaragoza, 2002).

— 'Beatas sojuzgadas por el clero: la imagen de las mujeres en el discurso anticlerical en la España del primer tercio del siglo XX', *Feminismo/s*, ii (2003), 41–58.

Sánchez Marroyo, F., *La España del siglo xx: economía, demografía y sociedad* (Madrid, 2003).

Sassoon, D., *One Hundred Years of Socialism: the Western European Left in the Twentieth Century* (London, 1996).

Saz, I., *Fascismo y franquismo* (Valencia, 2004).

Schumann, D., *Political Violence in the Weimar Republic, 1918–1933: Fight for the Streets and Fear of Civil War* (New York, 2012).

Scott, J. C., 'Foreword', in *Everyday Forms of State Formation: Revolution and the Negotiation of Rule in Modern Mexico*, ed. G. M. Joseph and D. Nugent (Durham, N.C., 1994), pp. vii–xii.

Seidman, M., *The Victorious Counterrevolution: the Nationalist Effort in the Spanish Civil War* (Madison, Wis., 2011).

Selbin, E., *Revolution, Rebellion, Resistance: the Power of Story* (London, 2010).

Shearer, J. R., 'Shelter from the storm: politics, production and the housing crisis in the Ruhr coal fields, 1918–24', *Journal of Contemporary History*, xxxiv (1999), 19–47.

Shubert, A., 'Entre Arboleya y Comillas: el fracaso del sindicalismo católico en Asturias', in *Octubre 1934: cincuenta años para la reflexión*, ed. G. Jackson et al. (Madrid, 1985), pp. 243–52.

— *The Road to Revolution in Spain: the Coal Miners of Asturias, 1860–1934* (Urbana, Ill., 1987).

— 'A reinterpretation of the Spanish Popular Front: the case of Asturias', in *The French and Spanish Popular Fronts: Comparative Perspectives*, ed. M. Alexander and H. Graham (Cambridge, 1989), pp. 213–25.

— *A Social History of Modern Spain* (London, 1990).

Siemens, D., *Stormtroopers: a New History of Hitler's Brownshirts* (New Haven, Conn., 2017).

Sierra Álvarez, J., 'Política de vivienda y políticas industriales paternalistas', *Ería*, viii (1985), 61–71.

— *El obrero soñado: ensayo sobre el paternalismo industrial (Asturias, 1860–1917)* (Madrid, 1990).

— '"Rough characters": miners, alcohol and violence in Linares at the end of the nineteenth century', in *A Social History of Spanish Labour: New Perspectives on Class, Politics and Gender*, ed. J. A. Piqueras and V. Sanz Rozalén (New York, 2007), pp. 176–96.

Simpson, J., *Spanish Agriculture: the Long Siesta, 1765–1965* (Cambridge, 1995).

Smith, A. (ed.), *Red Barcelona: Social Protest and Labour Mobilization in the Twentieth Century* (London, 2002).

Somers, M. R., 'Narrativity, narrative identity, and social action: rethinking English working-class formation', *Social Science History*, xvi (1992), 591–629.

Souto Kustrín, S., 'De la paramilitación al fracaso: las insurrecciones socialistas de 1934 en Viena y Madrid', *Pasado y memoria*, ii (2003), 193–220.

— 'Taking the street: workers' youth organizations and political conflict in the Spanish Second Republic', *European History Quarterly*, xxxiv (2004), 131–56.

— *'Y ¿Madrid? ¿Qué hace Madrid?': movimento revolucionario y acción colectiva (1933–1936)* (Madrid, 2004).

— 'Octubre de 1934: historia, mito y memoria', *Hispania Nova: revista de historia contemporánea*, xi (2013), 473–506.

— *Paso a la juventud: movilización democrática, estalinismo y revolución en la república española* (Valencia, 2013).

Stone, D., *Responses to Nazism in Britain: Before War and Holocaust* (Basingstoke, 2003).

Stovall, T., *The Rise of the Parisian Red Belt* (Berkeley, Calif., 1990).

— *Paris and the Spirit of 1919: Consumer Struggles, Transnationalism and Revolution* (Cambridge, 2012).

Suárez Cortina, M., *El fascismo en Asturias* (Gijón, 1981).

Swett, P., *Neighbors and Enemies: the Culture of Radicalism in Berlin, 1929–1933* (Cambridge, 2004).

Taibo II, P. I., *Asturias, octubre 1934* (Barcelona, 2013).

Thomas, M., *The Faith and the Fury: Popular Anticlerical Violence and Iconoclasm in Spain, 1931–1936* (Eastbourne, 2013).

Thompson, E. P., 'The moral economy of the English crowd in the eighteenth century', *Past & Present*, l (1971), 76–136.

— 'Rough music reconsidered', *Folklore*, ciii (1991), 3–26.

Tortella, G., *The Development of Modern Spain: an Economic History of the Nineteenth and Twentieth Centuries* (Cambridge, Mass., 2000).

Townson, N., *The Crisis of Democracy in Spain: Centrist Politics Under the Spanish Second Republic* (Brighton, 2000).

Traverso, E., *Fire and Blood: the European Civil War, 1914–1945* (London, 2016).

Trullén Floría, R., 'Castilblanco como sinécdoque: el discurso contrarrevolucionario de interpretación de la Segunda República', *Historia social*, lxxxiii (2015), 55–71.

Tumblety, J., 'Rethinking the fascist aesthetic: mass gymnastics, political spectacle and the stadium in 1930s France', *European History Quarterly*, xliii (2013), 707–30.

Tusell, J., *Las elecciones del Frente Popular* (Madrid, 1971).

— *Historia de la democracia cristiana en España* (2 vols, Madrid, 1974).

Ullman, J. C., *Tragic Week: a Study of Anticlericalism in Spain* (Cambridge, Mass., 1968).

Uría, J., 'Cultura y comunicación de masas en Asturias (1931–1934): aproximación a su estudio', *Estudios de Historia Social*, xxxi (1984), 145–60.

— 'La taberna en Asturias a principios del siglo XX: notas para su estudio', *Historia contemporánea*, v (1991), 53–72.

— 'Asturias 1920–1937, el espacio cultural comunista y la cultura de la izquierda: historia de un diálogo entre dos décadas', in *Los comunistas en Asturias (1920–1982)*, ed. F. Erice (Gijón, 1996), pp. 249–308.

— 'Asturias, 1898–1914: el fin de un campesinado amable', *Hispania*, lxii (2002), 1059–98.

— 'Traditional popular culture and industrial work discipline', in *A Social History of Spanish Labour: New Perspectives on Class, Politics and Gender*, ed. J. A. Piqueras and V. Sanz Rozalén (New York, 2007), pp. 153–75.

Valero, S., *Republicanos con la monarquía, socialistas con la República: la Federación Socialista Valenciana durante la II República y la Guerra Civil (1931–1939)* (Valencia, 2015).

Viejo Fernández, J. A., *La Segunda República en Sanlúcar de Barrameda (1931–36)* (Sanlúcar de Barrameda, 2011).

Vincent, M., 'The politicization of Catholic women in Salamanca, 1931–1936', in *Elites and Power in Twentieth Century Spain: Essays in Honour of Sir Raymond Carr*, ed. F. Lannon and P. Preston (Oxford, 1990), pp. 107–26.

— *Catholicism in the Second Spanish Republic: Religion and Politics in Salamanca, 1930–1936* (Oxford, 1996).

— '"The keys of the kingdom": religious violence in the Spanish civil war, July–August 1936', in *The Splintering of Spain: Cultural History and the Spanish Civil War, 1936–1939*, ed. C. Ealham and M. Richards (Cambridge, 2005), pp. 68–90.

— 'Spain', in *The Oxford Handbook of Fascism*, ed. R. J. B. Bosworth (Oxford, 2009), pp. 362–79.

— 'Political violence and mass society: a European civil war?', *The Oxford Handbook of European History, 1914–1945*, ed. N. Doumanis (Oxford, 2016), pp. 388–403.

Viñas, R., *La formación de las Juventudes Socialistas Unificadas (1934–1936)* (Madrid, 1978).

Ward, S., 'The Means Test and the unemployed in South Wales and the north-east of England, 1931–1939', *Labour History Review*, lxxiii (2008), 113–32.

— *Unemployment and the State in Britain: the Means Test and Protest in 1930s South Wales and North-East England* (Manchester, 2013).

Wardhaugh, J., *In Pursuit of the People: Political Culture in France, 1934–1939* (Basingstoke, 2009).

Wasserman, J., *Black Vienna: the Radical Right in the Red City, 1918–1938* (Ithaca, N.Y., 2014).

Weinhauer, K., A. McElligott and K. Heinsohn (eds), *Germany 1916–23: a Revolution in Context* (Bielefeld, 2015).

Weir, T., 'The Christian front against godlessness: anti-secularism and the demise of the Weimar Republic, 1928–1933', *Past & Present*, ccxxix (2015), 201–38.

Whitney, S., *Mobilizing Youth: Communists and Catholics in Interwar France* (Durham, N.C., 2009).

Williams, C., *Capitalism, Community, and Conflict: the South Wales Coalfield, 1898–1947* (Cardiff, 1998).

Wrigley, C. (ed.), *Challenges of Labour: Central and Western Europe, 1917–1920* (London, 1993).

Zemon Davis, N., 'The reasons of misrule: youth groups and charivaris in sixteenth-century France', *Past & Present*, l (1971), 41–75.

Zukas, A., 'Explaining unemployed protest in the Ruhr at the end of the Weimar Republic', in *Unemployment and Protest: New Perspectives on Two Centuries of Contention*, ed. M. Reiss and M. Perry (Oxford, 2011), pp. 137–74.

— 'Inscribing class struggle in space: unemployed protest in the Ruhr in late Weimar Germany', *Labour History Review*, lxxx (2015), 31–62.

Unpublished texts

Blaney, G., 'The Civil Guard and the Spanish Second Republic (1931–1936)' (unpublished London School of Economics PhD thesis, 2007).

Castejón Rodríguez, M., 'La patronal hullera asturiana en la Segunda República' (unpublished UNED PhD thesis, 2009).

Chamberlin, F., 'Honor-bound: the military culture of the Civil Guard and the political violence of the Spanish Second Republic, 1931–1936' (unpublished UCSD PhD thesis, 2017).

Corkett, T., 'Interactions between the Confederación Nacional del Trabajo and the Unión General de Trabajadores in Spain and Catalonia, 1931–1936' (unpublished University of Glasgow PhD thesis, 2011).

Online resources

'Alteraciones de los municipios en los censos de población desde 1842' <http://www.ine.es/intercensal/>

'Diccionario biográfico del socialismo español' <http://www.fpabloiglesias.es/archivo-y-biblioteca/diccionario-biografico>

'Crítica republicana a la Segunda República' <http://www.asturiasrepublicana.com/crirep.asp>

Magnum Photograph Agency <https://pro.magnumphotos.com>

Index

RHS New Historical PERSPECTIVES

Recent and forthcoming titles

The Family Firm: Monarchy, Mass Media and the British Public, 1932–53 (2019)
Edward Owens

Cinemas and Cinema-Going in the United Kingdom: Decades of Decline, 1945–65 (2020)
Sam Manning

Civilian Specialists at War: Britain's Transport Experts and the First World War (2020)
Christopher Phillips

Individuals and Institutions in Medieval Scholasticism (2020)
edited by Antonia Fitzpatrick and John Sabapathy

Unite, Proletarian Brothers! Radicalism and Revolution in the Spanish Second Republic (2020)
Matthew Kerry

Masculinity and Danger on the Eighteenth-Century Grand Tour (2020)
Sarah Goldsmith

Coal Country: The Meaning and Memory of Deindustrialization in Postwar Scotland (2021)
Ewan Gibbs

CPSIA information can be obtained
at www.ICGtesting.com
Printed in the USA
BVHW090856221120
593558BV00001B/1

9 781912 702503